BUILDING

MUSCLE
How to Make a Good Engine Great

The Complete Street Machine Library™

BUILDING
Muscle
How to Make a
Good Engine Great

Printed in 2006.

Published by National Street Machine Club
under license from MBI Publishing Company.

Tom Carpenter
Creative Director

Heather Koshiol
Managing Editor

Julie Cisler
Book Design and Production

Jen Weaverling
Senior Book Development Coordinator

3 4 5 6 7 / 10 09 08 07 06

ISBN 1-58159-239-6

©Colin Date and Mitch Burns, 2005; Jim
Richardson, 2002, 2005; Jeff Hartman, 2003, 2005;
Richard Newton, 2003, 2005; Huw Evans, 2004,
2005.

National Street Machine Club
12301 Whitewater Drive
Minnetonka, MN 55343
www.streetmachineclub.com

Contents

Introduction

How To Hot Rod Your Carbureted Small-Block Chevy, page 172.

Every engine is a good engine. Whether you just pulled it out of a car in the far corner of the scrapyard, inherited it from a friend, bought it on a whim or just like to look at it under the hood of your own car ... the potential for more horsepower is right there.

You just have to know what to do with all that potential.

It's not an easy job. Yes, you could pay somebody to do the work and find all that potential. But you don't get any fun out of that. Neither does your pocket-book. So how do you make that engine everything it can be ... *and much more?*

A little hard work never hurts. None of us are afraid of that. A willingness to get a little greasy and dirty helps. For most of us this is actually more of a "need." And some time is essential. So carve a little chunk of that into your schedule every week.

But you also need ideas and instructions — simple, straightforward projects that will really make a difference in your engine's horsepower production and

Carburetors: High Aspirations, page 134.

overall performance. You don't need theories or fluff from armchair "experts." You need real how-to from people who really do the work.

And that's just what you'll find in the pages of *Building Muscle: How to Make a Good Engine Great.* We've pulled together the projects you need, from some of the best hands-on guys in the world of engines, and gathered them all together

History: Who Started It All? on page 8.

in a package of simple words and detailed pictures that will show you how to make any engine faster and more powerful.

You really can build muscle into any engine. You'll see exactly how on the pages that follow.

First, walk step-by-step through a *complete* engine rebuild. Then discover chassis and driveline improvements that will help you get all that newfound power off the ground. See how to improve brakes and suspension, because sooner or later you have to safely slow down and stop all that speed. And discover a wide selection of engine upgrade projects.

It's time to start building extra speed, power and performance into your engine ... and make it truly great. *Building Muscle* shows you how.

Chapter 1

ENGINE REBUILD

The engine is the heart of any street machine. In this chapter you get a top-to-bottom look at how to rebuild your car's engine and increase its performance at the same time. Although it focuses on the most popular engine—the small-block Chevy—the principles described here can be applied to any engine you choose.

History: Who Started It All?

Jim Richardson

If one four-barrel is good on a street rod, two are better, or so the thinking went until recently.

Chevrolet was losing ground in the early 1950s. Any old-time hot rodder can tell you why. It wasn't because the Bow Tie offerings of the era were bad cars—indeed, they were good looking, dependable, and long lasting. However, largely because of Chevy's obsolescent inline six-cylinder motors, Chevys were regarded as "old people's cars."

The earlier stovebolt-six with its cast-iron pistons and poured babbitt rod bearings was slow off the line and couldn't take much revving, though it was a smooth, long-lived engine when operated within its design envelope. Of course, by the early 1950s Chevy's new Blue Flame 235 six-cylinder engine was thoroughly modern, with insert bearings, aluminum pistons, and pressure lubrication to its connecting rods. But it was too little too late. By that time the company's reputation was established and it needed something dramatic to make a change.

Ford began winning over the younger crowd way back in the 1930s with its inexpensive new flathead V-8s. Then

Early 1955 motors didn't have a cast-in oil filter boss, so an external bypass-type filter was a must.

Power steering, power brakes, air conditioning, Powerglide, Turboglide, and other accessories were popular on tri-five Chevys, and the small block had the muscle to handle them.

share rapidly. General Motors appointed engineer Ed Cole—World War II production wonder boy and designer of the new Cadillac V-8—to the task of turning Chevy's image around.

General Motors gave him just two years, instead of the usual four, to do it.

Styling for the 1955 models was already in the works by the time Cole came aboard, but previous efforts to come up with a new engine had fallen flat. A V-6 the company developed in the late 1940s didn't produce enough power, so that project was scrapped. Then Chevrolet's chief engineer and designer of the inline six-cylinder engine (I-6), Edward H. "Crankshaft" Kelly, came up with a smaller (230 ci) knock-off of the Cadillac V-8. However, Kelly's model was too expensive to produce.

Oldsmobile heated up the horsepower race by introducing its overhead valve, high-compression V-8 in 1948. Cadillac followed in 1949 with its own modern V-8. But Chevy and Plymouth still remained slow, solid, six-cylinder alternatives to the peppy new Fords.

By 1952 the brass at General Motors—the automobile colossus that produced nearly half of all the cars sold in the 1950s—knew they had to do something quickly about the division's image, because it accounted for 25 percent of profits and they were losing market

When Cole took over the division, he doubled the size of the engineering staff and began working on an entirely new engine. What they came up with in just 14 months was probably the best American production engine ever. Fifty years later it is still being built, though in a very updated form. Chevy's new V-8 for 1955 was smaller, lighter (50 pounds lighter than the Ford V-8), and more powerful than anything the other low-priced car makers had to offer.

Much of the weight savings was achieved by developing thin-wall casting techniques, and by ending the crankcase at the centerline of the crankshaft rather than continuing it on down below the main bearings. As a result, Chevrolet's small-block crankshaft hangs out into the pan, unlike Ford's heavier Y-block V-8 of the time period.

Stamped-steel rocker arms that pivoted on studs (rather than the standard heavier, cast rockers that rotated on shafts) and light, hollow pushrods were also added. Cole's division borrowed these innovations from the new 1955 Pontiac engine: they made the Bow Tie engine cheaper to

produce, while the lower reciprocating mass allowed higher rpm.

The new V-8's crankshaft was short and sturdy and made of forged, pressed steel rather than nodular iron (although many later crankshafts were made of nodular iron). In addition, all of the rotating assembly components were balanced independently so that they could be used interchangeably. (The later 400-ci engines are externally balanced, so if you use a 400 crank in a 350, you will need a 400 flywheel and vibration damper to make it properly balanced. Otherwise, it will vibrate.)

The intake manifold was designed to be efficient. Indeed, Chevy small blocks have never had problems breathing well on the intake side, though the exhaust valves and manifolds are somewhat limited for high-performance purposes. The intake manifold also acts as the lifter valley cover, saving weight and simplifying the engine further.

The exhaust port runners on the heads were short, and they went up and out through Chevy's trademark ram's horn cast-iron manifolds for better breathing efficiency and more effective cooling. Also, the new heads were cast to be interchangeable left-to-right, with the intake manifold providing a common water outlet for

each of them, making production much simpler.

Chevrolet dubbed the new V-8 the Turbofire. Equipped with a two-barrel carburetor, it produced 162 horsepower on regular gasoline with a fairly low 8:1 compression ratio. This was a big leap over the traditional six's 136 horsepower, and the V-8 was 40 pounds lighter to boot.

At midyear in 1955, a Super Turbofire option was offered that included a Rochester four-barrel carburetor and dual exhausts to boost the engine to 180 horsepower. Hot on its heels came the Special Power Pack kit, intended primarily for racing, which pumped the ponies up to 195.

The 283 for 1957 was a hot performer, but it didn't prevent Ford from outselling Chevrolet that year.

Small-block Chevys are still hair-raising performers, especially when built to the hilt, blown, and injected.

Stock car racers soon took advantage of the newfound horsepower and torque. Chevy racers won at Darlington and 13 other races that year as well. The little V-8 became known among racers as the

"Mighty Mouse," named for a popular cartoon character of the time. The small block's racing career was truly launched and it is still going strong today. Chevy mouse motors have been put in almost

Rochester fuel injection, first available in 1957, made an impressive 283 horsepower from 283 ci.

everything that moves, from handmade Italian Bizzarrini sports cars to Indy cars to 1941 Willys coupes.

In 1957, the renowned engineer Arkus Duntov—designer of the Ardun over-head-valve conversion for the Ford flat-head V-8—was hired by Chevrolet to make its engines even hotter because Ford and Chrysler were mounting stout competition of their own. His innovations made it possible for a small-block Chevy engine to run up Pike's Peak in a record-breaking 17 minutes—2 minutes faster than the Ford of that year.

The new V-8 wasn't an unalloyed success at first. Early 1955 engines burned a quart of oil every 200 miles, apparently because the rings would not seat against the cylinder bores. Legend has it that some mechanics of the era even resorted to putting a little Bon Ami cleanser down the carb to help scuff the cylinder walls and make the rings seat. Also, the early 265-ci engines had no cast-in oil filter boss.

Because the engine came with hydraulic lifters, fitting an accessory bypass oil filter became a must to prevent lifter wear and eventual collapse from oil contamination. This problem was soon rectified with a cast-in oil filter boss at the rear of the engine for a full-flow filter. As a result of these initial shortcomings, in models as late as 1956,

The Chevy V-8 was pure magic in the Corvette, making it America's first real sports car.

The 283 engine with two four-barrels pumped out 270 horsepower at 6,000 rpm.

almost half of the Chevys sold had the old six-cylinder engine in them.

The car that gained the most from the new engine was the Corvette. Equipped with an inline six and a two-speed Powerglide transmission upon its introduction in 1953, the car enjoyed only limited success. When the 265-ci V-8 and manual transmission were added in 1955, Chevrolet's sports car became a real contender to the European Ferraris, Jaguars, and Alfa Romeos on the road racing tracks of the United States.

Birth Of The 283

Ford and Chrysler were mounting their own performance efforts by the mid-1950s, so Chevrolet could not rest on its laurels for long. The 283 made its debut in 1957—the most sought-after year of the classic tri-five Chevys—even though Ford outsold Chevrolet that year. What cost Chevy its sales was not horsepower, but warmed-over styling compared with Ford and Plymouth's fresh new appearances. In fact, in 1957 Chevy was the first of the low-priced three to be able to boast one horsepower per cubic inch out of its new fuel injection–equipped engine.

The 283 was a 265 bored out to 3.88 inches. Its stroke remained at 3.00. The Turbofire single four-barrel version made 185 horsepower and had a compression ratio of 8.5:1. The Super Turbofire came with a 9.5:1 compression ratio and, equipped with a single four-barrel, it made 220 horsepower at 4,800 rpm. With two four-barrels, the 283 pumped out 245 horsepower at 5,000 rpm.

A high-lift cam version of the twin four-barrel 283, which was available only with a three-speed, close-ratio manual transmission, yielded 270 horsepower at 6,000 rpm. The injection-equipped engines with a 10.5:1 compression ratio made an honest 283 horsepower at 6,200 rpm. The 283 was such a success that it was built essentially unaltered for the next 10 years. It, along with the later 327, 302, 350, and 400 engines, made the Chevrolet small-block V-8 the most popular performance engine of all time.

Finding An Engine: The Search Is On

Jim Richardson

There are many reasons why you may have to hunt down a new engine. It could be that the one in your classic is too far gone to rebuild, or possibly you just want to swap out a smaller engine for a 350 or 400. Whatever the case may be, you will need to make sure you are getting what you bargained for.

The biggest problem with finding exactly what you want is that Chevy small-block engines almost all look alike. The newest Generation III computerized, injected engines certainly have a distinctive look, but the earlier blocks from the 1980s back to the 1950s are so similar in appearance that it is hard to tell whether you are looking at a 400, 350, 327, 307, 305, or 283 block, unless you know them well or have access to the casting numbers.

With the possible exception of the 262, which was an ill-fated attempt to meet the smog laws and fuel restrictions of the 1970s, they are all great engines. (Even the 262 was dependable enough, but it lacked power and provided only marginal fuel economy.) Almost any small-block Chevy engine can be made to perform well, but if you are looking for a 350-ci engine, you won't want to

Chevy small blocks have been put into everything from Italian sports cars to modified Model Ts because they are the best American production engines ever.

A later, super-tuned small block will drop right in a mid-1950s Chevy pickup.

You don't want the engine out of this car. The driveline is bent and bashed, and who knows what happened to the rapidly spinning crankshaft.

These early engines are also easy to identify because the oil vent tube is cast-in, and the early 265s made in 1954 and 1955 have no cast-in boss for an oil filter. An accessory bypass filter can be added to such motors and it's a good idea to do so, because these engines came with hydraulic lifters that need a steady supply of clean oil to operate properly.

A 265 can withstand being bored a maximum of .125," which essentially makes them into a 302. The crankshaft journals in this engine are 2.30" and the crankshafts are forged. They were good motors and can be made to perform. However, unless you are restoring an original Chevy and want to keep it stock, you'd be better off with one of the later engines with the bigger bores and crankshaft journals.

283
(Bore: 3.875" Stroke: 3")

This was Chevy's mainstay for years and was a superb engine. Because they were produced for a long time, they are not nearly as rare as 265 motors. Those made in 1957 can be safely bored .125" over, but blocks from 1958 to 1962 can only be over bored .060" at a maximum. General Motors went back to thinner cylinder walls again from 1963 to 1967, so motors from these years can only safely stand a .060" overbore. Crank journals are small, at 2.30", and crankshafts are cast.

The 283 can be super-tuned to give good performance, though it is limited somewhat by its displacement. However, unless you are going to get into serious bracket racing, a 283 is a great street mill. It is rugged, dependable, and made of good stuff. Parts are also plentiful to rebuild and performance-tune this engine.

327
(Bore: 4" Stroke: 3.25")

This engine debuted in 1962 in the Corvette and served as Chevy's performance engine for years. Both the bore and stroke were increased for this engine, and that necessitated a redesigned bottom end to allow for larger counterweights on the crank. By the mid-1960s, these engines were producing 375 horsepower with fuel injection, and 365 horsepower normally carbureted. The 327

buy a 283 or 305 by mistake. Here's how you can tell them apart:

265
(Bore: 3.770" Stroke: 3")

This was Chevrolet's first modern V-8. (Chevy's first V-8 came out much earlier, but it was not successful.) The new engine made its debut in the 1955 model year and was produced until 1957, when the 283 replaced it. This early engine is fairly uncommon these days, except in original cars from the era. However, the 265 was still available in 1957 and was common in trucks. You can spot a 1957 model year 265 by its distinctive yellow color.

powered the mighty Corvettes of the 1960s and achieved glory for the Chaparral team in 1966.

The 327 is valued for its comparative rarity these days and because it can really pump out the power at higher rpms. These engines have no real shortcomings, and they can be made to perform with a little work. The 327 blocks were all equipped with two-bolt main bearing caps. Earlier engines had 2.30″ small-crank journals, but in 1968, Chevy went to midsize 2.45″ journals. These engines will easily handle a .040″ rebore, but .060″ is risky.

302

(Bore: 4″ Stroke: 3″)

These engines were designed for racing in the Trans-Am series, and they are real screamers, literally. When the prototypes were dynoed at 8,000 rpm by its designers, the exhaust—which was piped directly out of the lab—made people nearby think they were hearing an air raid siren. It was the short stroke and big bore that made these engines such capable revvers. What they lacked in torque at the bottom end, they more than made up for in horsepower at the top end.

In 1967 these engines came with small (2.30″) crank journals and two-bolt mains, but in 1968 and 1969 they sported 2.45″ crank journals and four-bolt mains, making them extremely rugged. If you find a rebuildable 302 of either configuration, grab it. They are very sought-after today. They go like stink right out of the box, and with a little massaging they can be awesome performers.

307

(Bore: 3.875″ Stroke: 3.25″)

At the time, the 327 was blowing the doors off of everything and it was considered Chevy's high-performance engine. The company decided it also needed a V-8 for Joe Station Wagon, hence the 307. It only came with a two-barrel and no high-performance goodies, but it can be made to run like a scared cat with a few performance add-ons. The

heads and other castings are thick and the metallurgy is good.

Most 307 blocks can be easily opened up .060″ over. All of these engines had two-bolt mains and used the same stroke as the 327, which is 3.25″. The 307 was used from 1968 through 1973 in a number of applications. It had a stroke of 3.25″. If you find one of these at a cheap price and in good condition, you might want to give it some thought.

350

(Bore: 4″ Stroke: 3.48″)

It's been put into every kind of race car, hot rod, dragster, and speedboat imaginable. Everything is available for the 350 at competitive prices, making it the most popular engine of all time to build up for the street. Millions of 350s have been produced, and they're still making them in one form or another today.

The 350 was first offered in the 1967 Camaro. The earlier engines can easily be bored .040″ over and will often go to .060″, though I wouldn't recommend it. All Generation I and II motors came

The painted numbers at the upper left indicate the block has been bored .030″ over. The 010 below tells you that the block is 10 percent nickel, making it stronger.

Even essentially stock small blocks can kick up dust with a little tweaking.

Casting Number	Displacement	Years	Installed In:
3703524	265	1955	Cars (No oil filter)
3720991	265	1956–1957	Cars, trucks
3731548	283	1957	Cars (No side motor mounts)
3556519, 3737739, 3837739, 3756519, 3794226	283	1958–1963	Cars, trucks
3789935, 3849852, 3864812, 3790721, 3792582, 3834812	283	1962–1965	Cars, trucks
3782870, 3789817, 3852174, 3858180, 3959512	327	1962–1964	Cars, trucks
3834810	283	1964–1966	Cars, trucks
3849852, 3849935, 3896944, 393288, 3862194, 3849935, 3896944	283	1965–1967	Cars, trucks
3782870, 3789817, 3792563, 3794460, 3814660, 3830944, 3852174, 3858174, 3858180, 3892657, 3903352, 3914660, 3970041	327	1964–1967	Cars, trucks
3892657, 3914678, 3932386, 3956618, 3970010	302	1967–1969	Z-28 Camaro
3814660, 3914678, 3932386, 3955618	327	1968–1969	Corvette, Camaro, High-performance applications
376450, 3855961, 3914678, 3932386, 3932388, 3958618, 6259425	350	1967–1976	Cars (Two-bolt 3858618, 3892657 mains)
3956618, 3970010, 3932386	350	1968–1973	High-performance, trucks (Four-bolt mains)
3970014	350	1972	Two- and four-bolt mains
362245, 366287, 460703	350	1978–1979	
366299	350	1978–1979	Aluminum. Four-bolt mains
3914636, 3914653, 3932371, 3932373, 3956632, 3970020	307	1968–1973	Cars, trucks
3951511	400	1970–1973	Cars, trucks (Four-bolt mains)
330817	400	1972–1980	(Two-bolt mains)
3951509, 3030817	400	1974–1978	Cars, trucks (Two-bolt mains)
355909, 360851	262	1975–1976	Nova, Monza
361979, 460776, 460777, 460778, 4715111	305	1978–1980	Cars, trucks

Look for the engine-casting number on the back of the engine, behind the head on the driver's side. The arrow and dots on the right indicate on which shift the block was cast.

with medium-sized crank journals of 2.45" and 3.48" strokes. These engines were also available with two- or four-bolt main bearing caps. Since 1986, these engines were designed to take one-piece rear main bearing seals, and since 1987 they were also available with roller cams.

Generation III 350s came out in the 1997 Corvettes. They have aluminum blocks and six-bolt main bearing caps, making them very light and strong powerplants. These engines use iron cylinder sleeves bored to 3.90," and have 3.62" strokes, to provide an actual displacement of 346-ci. Over-boring is limited to cleaning up the cylinder walls because of their thin iron cylinder liners.

267

(Bore: 3.50" Stroke: 3.48")

Produced between 1979 and 1982, these engines were designed to meet the smog and fuel economy restrictions of the era. A 267 can only be safely bored .030" over, due to its thin-wall block casting. All of them had two-bolt mains. These are good motors, with no special problems, but they are not good candidates for street rod use because of their small displacement and low-compression heads.

400

(Bore: 4.125" Stroke: 3.76")

This was the biggest small-block of them all. To make this displacement happen within the confines of the original external configuration, the cylinders had to be siamesed together, allowing no water to circulate between them. These blocks can be bored .040" over and can occasionally go to .060." Yet, if their water jackets are badly corroded, heating problems may develop, even if the block cleans up at .060. The 400-ci blocks were available with either two- or four-bolt mains from 1970 through 1980. The 400 was also the only configuration available with 2.65" crank journals and 3.76" strokes.

The 400 small block was externally balanced, meaning that the rotating assembly was balanced as a whole, so you can't just switch flywheels without rebalancing the rest of the engine. The same applies if you make your 350 into a stroker 383. You will need to provide your engine balancer with a 400 flywheel or flexplate.

305

(Bore: 3.75" Stroke 3.48")

The 305s—especially the later, Vortec 5000 models—are gaining in popularity among street rodders. With the stroke of a 350 and the bore of a 283, these engines are torquey, and you can use many of the same go-fast goodies on them as the other engines. Blocks manufactured since 1986 have a one-piece rear main seal. Also, many later blocks have been cast for use with roller cams.

When Originality Counts

If you are doing a meticulous restoration and need to have all the numbers match, or if you are driving a rare car such as a 1955 Chevy equipped with one of those early 265 engines that has no cast-in oil filter boss, you may want to have your old block fixed. In many cases fractures can be welded, but the process is expensive.

To weld up a cast-iron engine block requires a specialist, and the block must be heated in an oven to cherry-red first. This can cause warping, stresses, and other problems, so the block must then be remachined and align-bored. If you decide to go this route, Excelsweld U.S.A. in Oakland, California (510-534-3303), can help you.

If a broken rod damaged a cylinder bore, you could be in trouble. Deep damage to cylinder walls can only be fixed

Check any prospective purchase for cracks using a Magnaflux Spotcheck Jr. kit.

After some tests, it was discovered that this old Chevy still had a good block in it, although the engine was tired.

Judging from the odometer and the old Chevy's condition, we would assume that the reading is in fact more like 132,456.

by boring them away completely and wet sleeving the block. Just keep in mind that the most common reason an old engine self-destructs is overheating caused by a corroded cooling system. Cylinder walls on the water-jacket side rust away and become too thin to dissipate heat properly, which causes the engine to fail. Having a machinist install wet sleeves in all the cylinders is one answer to this prob-

lem if you must stick with an original block.

Cracked heads can be fixed, too, but if the cracks are between valve seats, the repairs may not last because of the fragile castings in those areas. It is better to look for a replacement head in sound condition, rather than attempting to fix an old one. You'll most likely be money ahead, and you won't have to worry about problems later.

The alternative to fixing a bad engine is to look for another with the same numbers. If your car came from the local area, there is a good chance that a bunch of cars, equipped the same way and made around the same time, were sent to the same place. Check local salvage yards and swap meets; also join the Chevy club in your area to find another block with the same numbers and casting date.

The Short And Long Of It

You will hear the terms "short" and "long" block when checking around for engines. A short block only includes the bottom end of an engine, or the block, crank, and pistons, but it does not include the heads, manifolds, or accessories. If all you did was damage the block in an otherwise decent engine, the short block may be just what you need. A long block is a complete engine, including heads and valvetrain, but you still need to use your old manifolds and accessories with them.

Salvage Yard Treasures

Whoever said one man's junk is another man's treasure knew what they were talking about. But just to make sure you don't buy a pig in a poke, take the time to carefully examine your prospective purchase. Here are a few tips on what to look for and what to avoid:

Don't accept a junk engine that has been hit in its vibration damper or timing gear housing. Such an engine could easily have a damaged crankshaft or camshaft. You don't want an engine and transmission combination that has been hit hard from the rear, either, because the entire driveline could have been knocked out of alignment. Also, inspect the donor car, if possible. If it appears to have been well maintained until an accident, its engine is probably sound. But if the car was sadly neglected or is worn out, the engine will be too. It's not out of the question to buy a non-running engine, but be sure to remove the heads and inspect it before making a purchase.

Most junkyards will start an engine for you if you ask, whether it is in a car or not. But hearing it run won't tell you much more than whether there are major problems. Look for blue smoke, which is an indication of worn rings or leaking valve guides, causing oil consumption problems. Listen for rhythmic clunks, clanks, and bonks that would indicate rod or main bearing wear.

To really determine your prospective engine's condition, warm it up for 15 to 20 minutes, then shut it off, block its

choke and throttle open, and run a compression check. To do that, you need to remove all of the spark plugs, and ground the coil high-tension lead to prevent a fire from starting. Of course, you will also need to know the correct compression spec for that particular engine, which can be found in a shop manual.

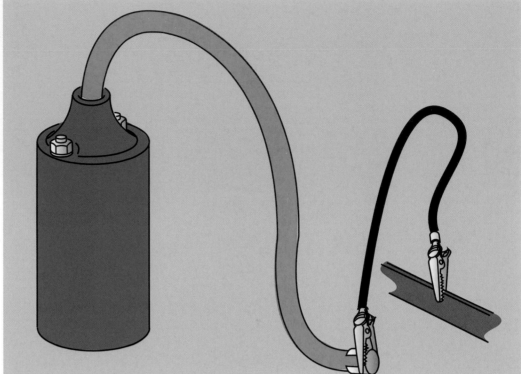

Ground the coil high-tension wire to the block using a couple of alligator clips and a piece of 10–inch-gauge wire.

If you can't hear a prospective purchase run, take a head off and look inside it before making a purchase.

This isn't such a bad deal because you can check everything out before you make the purchase. And I'll bet that price becomes more flexible as the afternoon wears on.

If you've got the money, you can buy all the go-fast parts with one check and easily bolt together a pretty hot street machine.

Look the plugs over too. If they are wet with oil or rusty, avoid that engine. Oil on the plugs indicates ring or valve guide problems, and water in the combustion chambers means a leaky head gasket or a cracked block or head.

Finally, look inside the cooling system and around the freeze plugs for signs of corrosion. An engine that is extremely rusty inside will need cleaning out at the very least, and it could have major problems.

Another thing to keep in mind while engine hunting is that you want the entire engine, including brackets, manifolds, valve covers, carb, and so on, if it is coming from a car that is not the exact year and model of yours. Some items can be very similar and yet not fit from engine to engine. It is a good idea to also get the throttle linkage because bending new linkage to fit is no easy task.

Your donor engine's cylinders should be within six pounds of the specification. If the compression is 10 pounds or lower all across, the engine is in need of an overhaul. If the compression is down in two adjacent cylinders, it probably has a leaking head gasket or a cracked head or block. If the compression is down in just one cylinder, it could be rings, valves, a holed piston, or a bad head gasket. If you shoot a little oil down the cylinder, re-test it, and the compression comes up, the problem is rings. If the compression stays down, it is probably valves. If it only comes up a little, both the rings and the valves need work.

Hot Swaps

There is nothing more appealing at a show than a correct, original, restored car, but some such cars just don't make very good drivers. There are cases where the engine for your particular year wasn't as good as the one in next year's model, or perhaps your car is equipped with a six and you'd like to put in a V-8. Well, you can do it, but it might be more complicated than you think.

Plan ahead, talk to people who have made the swap you intend to make, and be sure to get all of the accessories and the throttle linkage when you find your replacement engine. Just remember, the bigger and more powerful the new engine is, the more stress you will be placing on a classic's stock driveline. Another problem is that some smaller unit-bodied cars have actually been known to crack, due to metal fatigue at their door frames from being twisted by the torque of a big mill, which makes them very dangerous vehicles to drive.

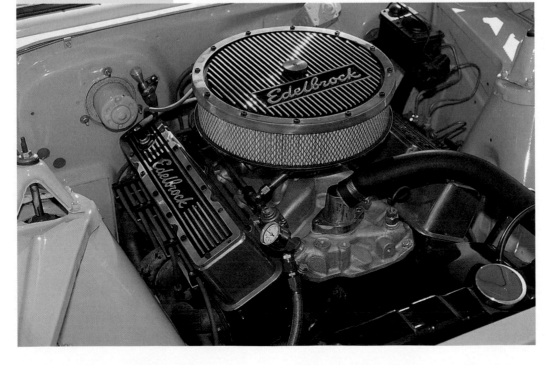

Removal: A Complicated Divorce

Jim Richardson

Is it really necessary to extricate your engine?

Car magazines are full of ads selling "Bolt-on horsepower" components that work well. If your engine is fresh with little mileage on it, there is probably no need to jerk it out of the chassis and go through it. It's pretty easy just to bolt on manifolds, carbs, and heads. You can install headers and even racing cams in most cars without pulling the motor. Unless you are a contortionist with very small hands, however, it's quite difficult to do much to the rotating assembly (pistons, rods, crankshaft, and flywheel or flexplate) without pulling the engine.

TIME
4 Hours

SKILL LEVEL
★★☆☆

COST
Less than $200

APPLICABLE MODELS/YEARS
All

YOU'LL NEED

- Cherry picker hoist
- Transmission jack (automatic transmissions only)
- Propane or acetylene torch
- Sturdy jack stands
- Inexpensive digital or film camera
- Hand tools
- Hand cleaner
- Rags
- Drip pan
- Containers for old oil and coolant
- Plastic plug for transmission output shaft hole
- Corrugated cardboard
- Ziploc plastic bags or plastic containers for parts
- Felt marker pen or china marker
- Masking and duct tape
- Coat hanger wire
- Engine stand
- Sharp knife
- Golf tee
- 3 feet of chain with welded links
- Plug wrench
- Compression gauge
- Vacuum gauge
- Squirt can with motor oil
- Shop manual
- Tachometer (optional)
- Funnel and rubber tube (optional for leak-down testing)
- Leak-down tester (optional)

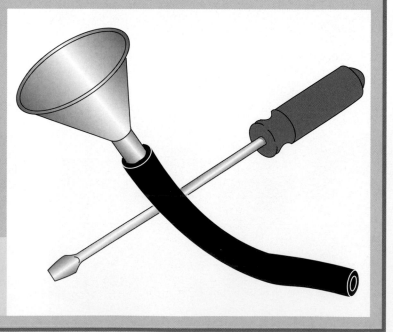

A long screwdriver and a funnel with a bit of rubber tubing can be used to pinpoint ominous engine noises.

Left: A compression test will tell you most of what you need to know about your engine's health. One end of the tester is pushed or screwed into the spark plug hole and then the engine is cranked to test the pressure.

Right: Be sure to take note of your results, then set the tester back to zero before testing the next cylinder.

Left: Block the throttle and choke wide open before testing your engine's compression.

Right: A long screwdriver can be used to check the strength of valve springs. Simply insert it and twist it. If the idle smooths out, the valve spring is weak.

Checking Compression

The most common procedure for determining an engine's condition is the compression test. It has been around since the horseless carriage, it is simple to do, and it is accurate enough to tell you almost everything you need to know about your engine's top end. But before attempting it, make sure your engine is in proper tune, with its valves correctly adjusted if they use solid lifters, and its battery fully charged. Otherwise, your readings will be faulty.

Compression should always be checked with the engine at full operating temperature. Take your car out for at least a 20-minute drive on a nice warm day so all of its metal parts can warm up and expand to their correct clearances. Don't go by the temperature gauge. That only tells you localized temperature. Next, check a shop manual to verify what the compression should be for your engine.

Shut the engine off, block the choke and throttle wide open, and remove the spark plugs. Ground the coil wire to prevent sparks. Have a friend crank the engine while you check the compression.

Push the nipple of the gauge into each spark plug hole while the engine turns over several times. Note each cylinder's reading, and return the gauge to zero before testing the next cylinder.

As a general rule, a difference of up to 6 psi is acceptable from one cylinder to another for normal use. If your engine is consistently a few pounds lower than the specified compression in your shop manual, it just means it has aged due to use. But, if any of the cylinders are more than 10 pounds low, your engine needs work. If the cylinders are all 10 pounds low or lower, you're in for an overhaul if you intend to push the engine at all.

If your compression checks out low in any cylinder, the problem could be rings or valves, or a combination of the two. To determine if you have worn rings, squirt a little oil in the spark plug hole for that cylinder, and then test it again. If the compression test comes up to normal, rings are your trouble and an overhaul is in order.

If the compression does not come up on re-testing, a burned valve or a blown head gasket is the likely problem. If the compression comes up a little upon oiling and re-testing, but not enough, the problem may be rings and valves.

If the compression is down in two adjacent cylinders, the problem is likely to be a blown head gasket. Sometimes, re-torqueing the head will solve the problem, but most likely you will need to remove the head and replace the gasket.

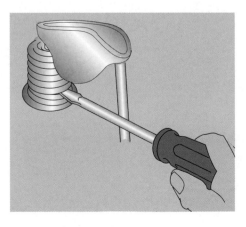

Using A Vacuum Gauge

Because an internal combustion engine is essentially a big air pump, much can be learned about its condition by monitoring the flow of air being sucked into it during operation. For that you need a vacuum gauge. A vacuum gauge will indicate the difference between the air pressure inside the intake manifold and the atmospheric pressure outside the manifold.

If you know how to use one, a vacuum gauge can tell you a number of things about your engine. Not only can it tell you about manifold leaks and burned valves, but it can also tell you about late ignition timing, poor carburetor adjustment, and exhaust back pressure problems. For our purposes, we'll be using a vacuum gauge to determine your small block's overall condition, but it would pay to learn how to use one for other things too.

Because a vacuum gauge measures the difference between atmospheric pressure and the pressure in your intake manifold (rather than measuring from some fixed benchmark), if you live above sea level you need to take into account the lower atmospheric pressure when using your gauge. The following table lists what can be expected at various altitudes. The readings are measured in inches of mercury, which refers to the number of inches the pressure would cause mercury to move up a glass tube in an old-fashioned barometric gauge.

The following figures are normal for a well-tuned engine at idle:

Sea level to 1,000 feet	18 to 22 inches
1,000 to 2,000 feet	17 to 21 inches
2,000 to 3,000 feet	16 to 20 inches
3,000 to 4,000 feet	15 to 19 inches
4,000 to 5,000 feet	14 to 18 inches
5,000 to 6,000 feet	13 to 17 inches

Use a vacuum gauge to check your engine's health. Maybe you don't need to pull it from the car.

To use a vacuum gauge, you will need to remove a plug on the intake manifold or carb, and install a fitting that will let you hook up the rubber tubing from your vacuum gauge. Set the idle, then warm the engine thoroughly before beginning the test. Use a tachometer, if you have one, to make sure your engine is idling at the correct speed while testing. A shop manual will give you the exact figure to expect.

On cars not equipped with a tach, you can simply adjust the throttle so the car will roll along at about 7 to 10 miles an hour in low gear with your foot off of the gas. Assuming the test is being done at sea level, if your engine is in good condition your vacuum gauge should show a steady reading between 18 and 22 inches at idle (figure 1).

Open and close the throttle quickly and observe the results on your gauge. The reading should drop down to 2 inches when the throttle is all the way open, but should bounce up to 25 momentarily as soon as you let up.

If the needle fluctuates below normal with the engine idling (figure 2), it could indicate an air leak at the intake manifold, its gasket, or at the carburetor gasket. It could also indicate a leaking head gasket.

Another valuable diagnostic tool for old car engines is a vacuum gauge. It's good for diagnosing manifold leaks, valve problems, carb malfunctions, and a number of other things.

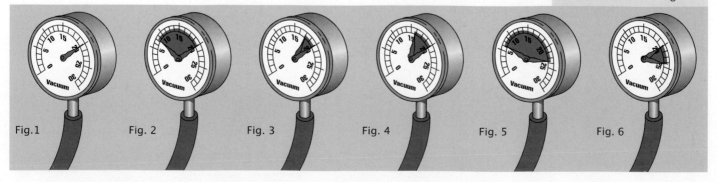

Fig.1   Fig. 2   Fig. 3   Fig. 4   Fig. 5   Fig. 6

A regular, intermittent drop below normal (figure 3) indicates a leaking valve. Most likely it will be an exhaust valve that is adjusted too tight, in the case of solid lifters, or perhaps burned. Readjust the valves and check the vacuum again.

A rapid intermittent dropping from normal reading (figure 4) indicates sticking valves or dirty hydraulic lifters. Next, try vacuum readings with open and closed throttle. If you see fluctuations increasing with engine speed (figure 5), the problem is weak valve springs.

If, with the engine idling, fast vibrations of normal vacuum are evident (figure 6) it is an indication of ignition trouble. On the other hand, slow movement at normal vacuum indicates incorrect carburetor adjustment.

A more sophisticated way of checking for upper cylinder problems is the leak-down test. Air is pumped into the cylinder and then checked to see how fast it leaks down past rings and valves.

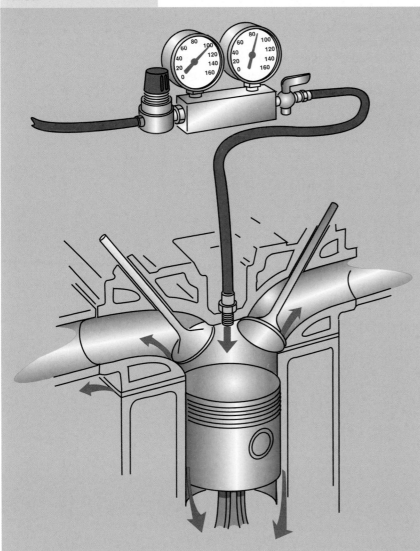

Leak-Down Test

This is a technique used by aircraft engine mechanics that has become popular with street rodders recently. It is probably the most accurate type of test for determining the sealing abilities of an engine's valves and piston rings. Leak-down testing involves pumping compressed air into a cylinder through a spark plug hole and verifying how long it takes for the air to leak down past the rings and valves.

Each cylinder must be brought up to Top Dead Center (TDC) on the compression stroke, so that both valves are closed before the test can be performed. Of course, you can do a simple leak-down test just by pumping compressed air into the cylinder and then listening using a funnel and rubber tube. You can hear the air leaking out, just as it would from a bad tire if the rings or valves were not up to par.

In addition to the leak-down tester, you will need a source of compressed air capable of at least 80 pounds of pressure. The tester costs about $100 and can be a little hard to find. Try professional tool sources. If you are going to race seriously, you'll want to have one.

Extricating Your Engine

Getting the engine out of the car is the dirtiest and toughest part of the whole job. It's not that it takes much skill, it's just that our classic Chevys were designed to be put together, not taken apart. At the other end of this project, you'll find that installing a clean new engine and buttoning things up isn't any big deal. You see, a great deal of engineering goes into making production cars easy to put together on a moving assembly line. But not much thought is given to the fact that 5, 10, or 20 years down the line, the engine might need to be taken apart and rebuilt.

To begin with, for safety reasons you'll need a place to work that is off-limits to little kids and inquisitive pets. Chevy small-block V-8s are heavy and full of old oil and toxic coolant. You'll need to keep your wits about you while you work to prevent making a poisonous mess. You will want a friend who doesn't mind getting dirty to help you. You will also need a camera nearby.

The Most Important Tool

By far the most important tool you have is your brain. If you use it correctly, everything will fall into place. But if you allow your emotions to take over, you can easily ruin expensive parts. Be patient and analytical. If a part doesn't fit, find out why. Never try to force-fit anything on an engine. You'll just damage parts if you do. If a fastener won't come loose, don't get a three-feet-long extension and try to muscle it. That's a great way to run headlong into a wall and break off a fastener.

Instead, shoot on a little penetrating oil and let the item sit overnight. If that doesn't help, get a brass hammer and tap on the fastener rapidly and repeatedly. Hitting it hard will just swage the bolt into place and damage things, but a rapid tapping can break the molecular bond. If that doesn't work, try heating the head of the fastener with a propane torch and then letting it cool down. This helps break the corrosion loose. Never heat the surrounding metal, though, because you can do serious damage that way.

Cast iron crumbles when overheated, and aluminum will suddenly melt without even glowing red when the temperature gets too high. Steel will lose its strength, and many parts will warp and distort under high heat. Be patient, and if none of your approaches does the job, try combinations, such as heating, then tapping. If you do break off a bolt head, find a professional who can weld on a lever to turn the fastener, or have the item drilled out on a drill press.

When loosening a tight bolt, never push the wrench away from you. Always arrange yourself so you pull the wrench toward you. That way if you slip, you won't bang your knuckles on nearby structures. Also, if a stubborn bolt or nut won't turn, and you can't pull it toward you, slap the wrench with your hand or a rubber mallet, but don't just throw all your weight into it. If you do, you could easily wind up with a broken-off stub instead of a freed fastener.

Take Pictures

Unless you've taken apart a lot of Chevys, you won't remember how that throttle linkage was set up, how that alternator was wired, or how that air conditioning bracket was attached several weeks from now when you are ready to put your engine back in. Take pictures of each assembly before you take it apart, and label each item with a felt pen or china marker before storing it. Use bits of masking tape to label small items.

If your engine is extremely filthy, you may want to take your car to one of those do-it-yourself car washes. Before you start blasting, though, make sure you cover all the electrics—such as the distributor, coil, alternator, voltage regulator, and starter—with plastic to keep them from getting wet and ruined. Wet down the engine, shake a little trisodium phosphate or Tide laundry detergent on it, let that sit for a few minutes, then go over it with a scrub brush before blasting off the dirt with the steam wand.

Attach your engine to an engine stand at the bell housing.

If you clean your engine before removing it, you'll stay cleaner and the work will be easier.

As you take things apart, take pictures and save parts in labeled plastic bags.

When you get your car home and in a spot where it can be left until you are ready to put the engine back in, take out the battery, clean it up, and store it on a wooden shelf. Do not leave it on a concrete floor. You'll also need to remove the hood on your car. Scribe around its hinges so you can reposition the hood correctly when you put it back on, and save any accompanying shims. Get a friend to help lift the hood off so you won't damage it or scratch your paint.

Drain The fluids

Jack the car up, put it on jack stands, and drain the engine oil into a waiting receptacle. Twist off the oil filter and drain it too. You will also need to drain the radiator. There is a small petcock at the bottom of the radiator that can be opened to drain it, but a little coolant will still remain in the engine block. Keep this in mind when lifting the engine out.

If the little petcock on the radiator is stuck, don't try to force it with pliers because it is made of thin brass, and you could end up just twisting it off. Instead, cut the lower radiator hose with a sharp knife, but be ready for a torrent. Drain the coolant into a drip pan and dispose of it according to local ordinances. Coolant is deceptively dangerous stuff. Although it looks innocuous, it is highly toxic and pets like the taste of it.

While you are under the car, disconnect the exhaust system and strap it up with coat hanger wire. Also disconnect the transmission cooler if you have an automatic. A golf tee and some duct tape can be used to minimize the loss of transmission fluid through the connecting hoses. Loosen its clamp and pull the lower radiator hose free of the radiator. Finally, take the battery cable and wires loose from the starter. Be sure to label all wires, describing where they are supposed to go.

Take off the air filter, throttle linkage, and alternator or generator, making sure to label all wires. Any other accessories such as power steering, air conditioning, and so on, should be taken off the engine now as well. If possible, leave the compressor for the air conditioning system hooked up to the system and just gently lift it out of the way. Otherwise you will need to bleed off the refrigerant and have the system replenished after you reinstall the engine. In any case, keep in mind that it is illegal to dump R-12 refrigerant into the atmosphere, and it is expensive to refill the system.

Choices

At this point, there are several ways you can extricate the engine. You can support the transmission on a transmission jack, then separate the engine from the transmission, and lift it up and out; or you can remove the radiator and pull the engine and transmission, as a unit, up and out through the front of the car. If you choose the latter, plastic plugs are available that can be used to plug the output shaft hole and prevent a mess of spilled transmission fluid from the rear of the transmission (this can happen even if the transmission has been drained). Another approach I happen to like is to remove the whole front clip, consisting of the bumper, grille, radiator cradle, and front fenders, then lift the transmission and engine out of the chassis as a unit.

Taking off the front clip isn't as tough as it might sound. Comparatively few bolts hold it in place. Without the front clip, getting the engine in and out and hooking it up is easy. Just make sure you have a couple of hefty friends to help you lift the clip off and place it on some heavy moving quilts to avoid damage.

If you decide to take apart as little as possible and leave the front clip in place, be sure to put layers of corrugated cardboard on the back of the radiator to protect its core. Personally, on any Chevy I would remove the radiator. Most likely, you'll want to have it serviced at a radiator shop or replaced with a new unit if you're planning to run a small block that is modified for performance. Next, remove the fan shroud, water pump, fan,

  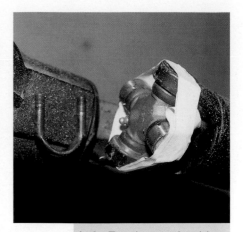

Left: To take out the drive-shaft, you must split the rear U joint. Do that by loosening and removing the yokes that hold the bearings in.

Middle: Pull the yokes out carefully and don't let the bearing caps fall off in the process.

Right: Wrap tape around the bearing caps to hold them in place, and then pull the driveshaft out. The slip joint up front can be pulled off by pulling straight back on the shaft.

and pulley before lifting the engine out. If you're removing only the engine, support the transmission using the car's chassis so that the car can be moved. If you're not going to move the car, a transmission jack provides good support, or you can build a cradle out of pieces of 2x4s. Just make sure you don't put the weight of an automatic transmission on its pan because it could crush the pan.

If you decide to take the transmission out with the engine, split the rear universal joint and tape its bearing caps in place so the needle bearings inside will not get lost or contaminated. Pull the driveshaft straight back, so that the sleeve on the transmission output shaft slides off, allowing the driveshaft to be pulled out from under the car.

Lifting The Engine

Buy, borrow, or rent a sturdy cherry picker hoist. Don't try to pull your engine out using a chainfall attached to your garage rafters. Chevy small blocks weigh approximately 500 pounds and can easily come crashing down if not properly supported. On the hoist, use at least three feet of chain with welded links that are at least 1/4 inch in diameter. If you don't need all of the chain, you can pile it on top of the engine. Never try to use a short chain because it will create dangerous side loads on its attaching bolts. Your engine can also slip in the hook because of the shallow angles created by a short chain.

If your engine uses a cast-iron intake manifold, you can remove the carburetor and attach a welded plate and hook that will allow you to lift the engine easily. Otherwise, you can lift the engine out by installing a couple of longer bolts in

place of intake manifold bolts. Use big fender washers under the bolts, backed up with other washers, and attach one end of the chain under a bolt near the front of the engine on one side, and another in the rear on the other.

Take up the slack in the chain on the hoist using the lever. Loosen the motor mounts and remove their bolts. If you are separating the engine from its bell housing and leaving the transmission in place, you may need to pry the engine loose with a big screwdriver. Inspect the engine one more time to make sure there are no fuel lines, electrical wires, ground straps, or linkages attached to it anywhere. Have a friend stand by to guide it, and then start lifting the engine slowly. Take it up a little and look things over again. The body of the car will come up with the engine because of the relieved tension on the front springs.

Take the engine up until it clears the front radiator cradle, then pull the engine clear or roll the car out from under the engine. Swing the engine around and unbolt the transmission. Pull it straight back to disengage it. Next, unbolt the bell housing and set it aside. With automatics, be careful not to let the torque converter drop out and spill fluid all over the place. For standard-shift cars, evenly loosen the bolts holding the pressure plate in place, half a turn at a time, until the tension is relieved. Otherwise, you risk warping the pressure plate. Now remove the flywheel or flexplate. Lower the engine slowly until you can slide it home in the engine stand. After a little cleanup, you will be ready for the fun of taking the engine apart and figuring out what it needs.

Systematic Disassembly: From One, Many

Jim Richardson

TIME
4–6 hours

SKILL LEVEL
★★★★

COST
Less than $200, including hoist and special tools

APPLICABLE MODELS/YEARS
All

YOU'LL NEED
- 3/8-, 1/2-inch-drive socket sets
- Combination wrenches
- Putty knife
- Engine stand
- Plastic concrete mixing tray
- Puller for vibration damper
- Pressure blaster (optional)
- Gunk or other engine degreaser
- Laundry detergent
- Small ball peen hammer and prick punch
- Camera
- Ziploc plastic bags
- Clean rags
- Paper towels, several rolls
- 2x4 or 4x4 pieces of wood
- Large plastic bag (for storage of clutch assembly)
- Duct tape
- Four long, heat-treated bolts
- Scrub brush
- Felt pen or china marker
- Wire
- Corrugated cardboard
- Rubber/plastic tubing
- Masking tape
- Propane torch
- Plastic tarp
- Rifle bore cleaning kit
- WD-40

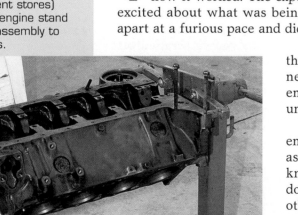

Place a concrete mixing tray (available from home improvement stores) under the engine stand during disassembly to catch drips.

The first time I tore an engine down, I was amazed at how it was designed and how it worked. The experience was a little like opening a birthday gift. I got so excited about what was being revealed at each stage that I just kept taking things apart at a furious pace and didn't organize or label anything.

I was 16 years old at the time and couldn't wait to get that engine done and back in the car. As it turned out, I never did. Instead, I ended up giving the disassembled engine to my cousin a few months after that. Later, my uncle sold it for next to nothing at a garage sale.

Back then, I didn't know that the disassembly of an engine needs to be approached with almost as much care as putting one together. In fact, there was a lot I didn't know back then. For instance, I didn't know that you don't want to mix up lifters, rods, pistons, pushrods, and other components unless you are going to replace them completely, because they have worn in together.

I also didn't realize how easy it is to forget how accessories and linkages were designed and installed. I didn't comprehend that, if you aren't careful, you could easily wind up with a big, bewildering, cast-iron jigsaw puzzle—especially if it's your first time tearing down an engine.

To ensure that won't happen to you if you're a first-timer, let's take disassembly one step at a time. It really isn't difficult or mysterious, and only a couple of special hand tools are required. We have allowed four to six hours to dismantle your engine, and that is what it will take if you are doing it for the first time and doing it right. A professional can do it in less than half that time. Here's how to do it:

Separate The Engine And Transmission

If you pulled your engine and transmission out of the car as a unit, find some short pieces of 2x4 or 4x4 to place under it at strategic points, and then let it down gently with the hoist. Never let the weight of an engine rest on its oil pan. You'll crush it if you do, or at least dent or buckle it.

Once you have the engine propped up and braced so it won't roll over onto your foot, separate the transmission from the bell housing, but don't take the engine loose from the hoist. After that, if your car is an automatic, slide the torque converter off. Be careful not to dump its fluid all over your garage floor. Finally, remove the flexplate and bell housing.

If your car has a standard transmission, remove the throwout bearing and pivot arm, then loosen the bolts, holding the clutch plate in place, half a turn at a time until the spring tension is relieved. Wear a particle mask while working on the clutch and never use compressed air to blow out the dust. Chances are it is lined with asbestos, which is a known carcinogen. Store the clutch assembly in a plastic bag so it won't get oil or dirt on its lining and pressure plate.

Check The Flywheel

Inspect the flywheel. If it is scorched and discolored, cracked, or checked, it will need to be resurfaced or even replaced if it won't clean up completely. Let your local machine shop be the judge. A defective flywheel can be extremely dangerous because it can go off like a grenade at high rpms. If there is any doubt—especially if you are building a performance engine—get a new flywheel rather than risk injury.

Put The Engine On The Stand

Jack the engine back up with the hoist and attach it to the engine stand using four long, heat-treated bolts. Place a plastic concrete-mixing tray under the engine to catch drips. (Mixing trays are available at hardware and building supply stores.) Place a plastic bag over the mouth of the carburetor and tape it in place with duct tape. Cover the hole where the distributor was inserted with duct tape too.

Attach the engine adapter (part of the engine stand) while the engine or block is still hanging from the hoist, then slip the adapter into the collar on the stand. Put the pin in the hole at the top to hold the engine in place.

Wash It Down

Now is a good time to wash the engine down again. It'll be easier to work on and you'll stay cleaner if you do. Start by digging off any caked-on filth using a putty knife and an old screwdriver. When you've scraped off all you can, shoot on a good engine degreaser, let it soak in for a few minutes, then blast the rest off using a pressure blaster or garden hose and nozzle. If you can hook up to a source of hot water, such as at your washing machine

Rust and corrosion in the water jacket may mean real problems if it is extensive.

This engine has seen a lot of miles and few oil changes. Oil has burnt under the heat riser in the intake manifold and formed a nasty sludge.

or the bottom of the water heater, so much the better.

When you've blasted all the degreaser off, shake a little powdered laundry detergent on the wet engine and let that soak in for a few minutes. Finally, using a scrub brush, give the engine a good scrubbing. Rinse and dry the engine.

Take It Apart

Remove the intake manifold and carburetor as a unit. Remove the exhaust manifolds. Take off the fuel pump. Remove any other accessories you didn't take off before pulling the engine. Store everything in an orderly fashion out of the way of your work.

Pull The Vibration Damper

Remove the accessory drive pulley by removing the three bolts holding it in place. (Early engines may only have two bolts holding the pulley on.) On some small-block Chevys there will be a large bolt and heavy washer holding the vibration damper in place. To remove it, you may need to remove the pan and wedge a piece of 2x4 between the crankshaft and the edge of the block to keep the crank from turning. If the rubber on the damper is swollen, or if its outer ring is out of alignment with the center, replace it.

You will need a special puller, available from tool stores, to remove your vibration damper. Attach the damper puller using the bolts that came with the tool. Be careful to use only bolts with the correct threads. (They can be coarse on one Chevy small block and fine on the next, so be careful.) Make sure the bolts are threaded in at least 3/8 inch so you don't end up pulling the threads out and leaving the vibration damper in place.

The damper puller should have a flat end with a small cone to center it on the nose of the crankshaft. If it doesn't, make sure you place a flat plate or other protection on the nose of the crankshaft to protect the threads in its center. Turn the puller slowly, using a large wrench, until the damper pops loose.

A special puller is needed to remove the vibration damper. Don't try to pry it off with big screwdrivers. You may damage the timing gear cover and damper if you do.

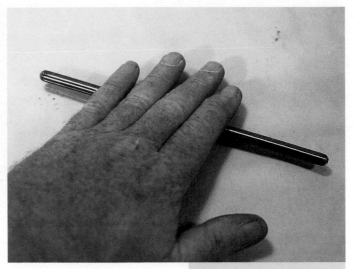

Left: Rockers that are cracked or badly worn like these should also be replaced.

Right: Roll pushrods on a piece of glass to make sure they aren't bent.

Remove The Heads

Next, remove the valve covers. Put their screws in a Ziploc bag and label it with a felt pen or china marker. Wipe any excess oil out of the valve covers and set them aside for now. Loosen and remove the rocker arms from their studs one by one, and string them on a piece of wire in order (from the front to the back of the heads). This is a critical step if you intend to reuse them.

Pull the pushrods out next, and then ease out the lifters. You may have to turn the cam to pop the lifers out if the interior of the engine is excessively dirty. Store the pushrods and lifters so they can be put back in the same location from which they were removed. I cut Xs and

slots in corrugated cardboard and slip these items into them, but any way you have for keeping these items organized is fine.

The reason for keeping things separate and organized is that these components have worn themselves into a good working relationship. If you disturb that, the engine will never be the same unless you replace all the mixed-up components with new ones. An old egg carton is good for lifters, and pushrods can be cleaned and then labeled using tape too. Or, you can drill 16 holes in a board to hold the pushrods. Just make sure you know which cylinder on which side of the engine the component fits and whether

Left: Store lifters and pushrods by slotting them into corrugated cardboard (in order) and don't mix them up.

Right: Healthy lifters should be reground like this so they are slightly domed.

This lifter is dished and worn out. It must be replaced.

Left: A thick ridge at the tops of the cylinders prevents pushing pistons out from below. It also indicates wear.

Right: Use a ridge reamer to cut out overhanging ridges so piston rings can slide up past them.

it goes with the intake or exhaust valve.

Finally, with a ½-inch-drive socket wrench and breaker bar, loosen and remove the head bolts, bag and label them, and lift the heads off. An impact wrench can be used, but don't reuse those bolts. If the heads seem to be stuck, thread two bolts back on a couple of turns, insert a pry bar or breaker bar handle in the center exhaust port, and give a quick pull up to loosen the head. You can also try using a sharp putty knife to pop the heads loose from the block. Pull the head gaskets off, label them "right" and "left" according to their orientation, then save them so you can verify that your replacements have all the right holes in the appropriate places.

Check The Bores

An engine that has seen a lot of service will have a fair amount of wear just down from the tops of the cylinder bores, where the rings ride up and down. This wear leaves a ridge at the top of the cylinder, making it impossible to get the pistons out through the top, due to ring expansion. If you find such ridges at the tops of your engine's cylinders, you will need to use a ridge reamer to remove them.

Ridge reamers are available from larger tool stores. Turn the crankshaft until each piston in turn is at or near the bottom of its stroke. Stuff oily rags in the barrels to pick up the swarf (metal shavings) from the ridge reamer so you won't damage the pistons when you remove them.

Oil the reamer's cutting blades with motor oil, then insert the reamer. Tighten it out against the ridge so it will make a slight cut, and then turn the reamer slowly with a large wrench. Keep the cylinder walls well lubricated as you rotate the cutter. Don't get too aggressive with the reamer. Just remove a little at a time, and then adjust the blades to cut a little more. Otherwise, you will damage the cutting blades and make chatter grooves and ridges in the cylinder walls.

Bottoms Up

Turn the engine over on the stand so you can get at the bottom end of the engine. Remove the screws holding the pan in place, then bag and tag them. Gently pop the pan off by tapping it at the corners with a rubber mallet or by

using a putty knife. Wipe any excess oil or sludge out of the pan with paper towels and set it aside. Remove the oil pump filter basket and then remove the oil pump and its drive.

Remove The Rods And Pistons

Next, look the connecting rods over carefully to make sure they are numbered, and that the numbers are in order. Most of the time they are labeled on the sides of the rods and caps so you can't mix them up. The engine originally came from the factory with the rods in the correct sequence from front to back, but they could easily have been mixed up during a later overhaul, so be careful. If the numbering is out of sequence, nonexistent, or for some reason unclear, use a prick punch and small ball peen hammer to number them in the correct order, away from the parting line making small marks.

Also make sure that each rod and end cap is labeled so you know which cap goes with which rod, and which way the cap faces. If bearing caps get mixed up or turned around, bearing failure could be the result. This is a critical step, so don't neglect to do it unless you will be replacing all of the rods and pistons anyway.

One at a time, remove the rod bearing caps. Slip rubber or plastic tubing on the threaded parts of the rod bolts to protect the cylinder bores and crank journals before pushing each piston out through the top of the block. Alternatively, you can wrap them with a couple of layers of masking tape, or buy special plastic protectors for this purpose.

With a prick punch, number each piston on the front quadrant of its top so you'll know which hole it goes in and which way it faces. It is possible to install pistons and rods backwards, and the result of this mistake can be disastrous. Even if you decide to install new pistons, it is nice to be able to use your old ones for reference if you are a novice.

You may have to gently tap on the pistons with the wooden handle of a hammer to get them past any slight remaining ridge, but don't use a lot of force. If you encounter resistance, make sure that the rod bolt or shoulder is not hanging up on the cylinder lip at the bottom. Novices have been known to damage pistons and rods and fracture lower cylinder walls by pounding too hard. Store the pistons and

This pan has been removed before and whoever took it off didn't take much care when doing so. A new pan is in order. Remove the old bolts evenly, and then tap the pan with a rubber mallet to pop it free.

Left: If they aren't clearly marked already, mark the rod caps and rods in order so you won't mix them up.

Right: Break loose and remove rod bolts, then push pistons out through the top of the engine.

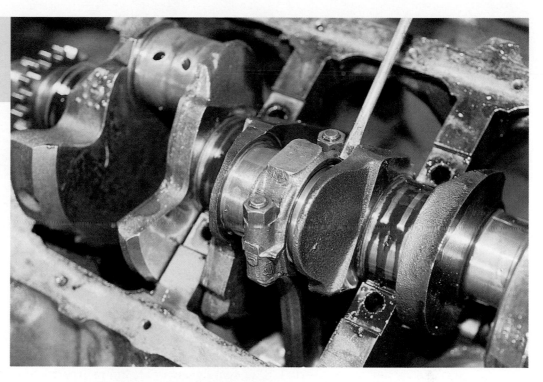

The fact that the rods can be moved around so easily in this engine means that bearings are worn and the engine probably wasn't holding proper oil pressure.

Pop off the timing cover, then remove the bolts holding the cam timing gear in place.

Inset: Timing gears that are notched and worn like this must be replaced, along with the timing chain.

rods in order in a box so they won't get mixed up.

If your engine has been sitting out and is rusty internally, spray a little penetrating oil down each cylinder barrel from both top and bottom and let the block sit overnight. You can also try heating the pistons with a propane torch, but never heat the block itself. They will expand, crushing the corrosion, then cool to pull away from it. You won't be reusing the pistons from a rusty block in any case, so if you damage them it doesn't matter; but if you heat the cylinder block too much in one place you could crack it, and besides, excessive heat can destroy cast iron.

Remove The Timing Gear

Take off the timing gear cover and set it aside. Remove the bolts holding the cam timing gear in place, and slip the gear off with the timing chain. Never reuse a timing chain, and if the timing gears are notched or worn, you will need to replace them too. In some cases, the cam timing gear is made of nylon and it will be less noisy. I always replace nylon gears with metal ones because they hold up much better. This is a must for performance engines.

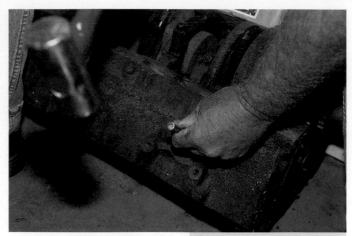

Lift Out The Crank

Number the main bearing caps down one side so you know which way they are supposed to face, then break loose their bolts and remove them. Finally, lift the crankshaft out of the block. Unless you are a rather strong sort, I recommend having a friend help with this. Crankshafts are slippery and heavier than you might think. Put the main bearing caps back in place, facing the right way, and tighten their bolts finger-tight.

Store the crankshaft standing upright. If you lay it flat, it can actually warp under its own weight. I like to put it next to a vertical timber in my garage, then loop wire around the top of the crankshaft and wrap it around a couple of nails driven into the timber to prevent the crankshaft from falling over and getting damaged, or damaging me.

Cams come out the front of the engine only. The bearings are larger in front and smaller in back, so never try to drive the cam out the back of an engine. (Some later, roller-cam engines have a thrust plate to keep the cam from walking in the block. If your engine does, you will need to remove the two locating screws and the thrust plate before extricating the cam.) Put one of the timing gear screws back

in a little bit and use it as a handle to pull the cam out. Ease the cam out carefully, using two hands, to avoid bumping its lobes or damaging its bearings.

If you wish to use your cam again, wrap it in plastic and hang it on a piece of coat hanger wire. In my experience, it is not usually worth trying to reuse a cam from a small block unless it is almost new. You run the risk of having marginal performance caused by flat or worn lobes. New cams are not expensive, especially in stock form. Also, never combine used lifters with a new cam.

Pull The Plugs

You will need to remove the freeze plugs, the plug at the rear of the cam,

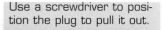

Use a screwdriver to position the plug to pull it out.

Needle-nose pliers or vise grips make popping the freeze plugs easy.

Left: Use a rifle bore cleaning kit to remove sludge from oil galleries in the block and crankshaft.

Right: Make sure you clean out the galleries adjacent to the rear cam bearing too.

help prevent your rebuilt engine from overheating. Finally, use a rifle bore cleaning kit and soft wire bottle brushes to clean out the oil galleries in the crankshaft and main bearing saddles. Also, clean out the galleries at the rear of the engine next to the cam retainer. Scrub until your brush comes out clean.

If you have a parts cleaning tub, clean all of your engine components of grease, dirt, and sludge. It is preferable to use a water-soluble, biodegradable degreaser, but you can also use a little

and the little oil gallery plugs nearby so your engine block can be hot-tanked and baked clean. Drive an old screwdriver into each one near the edge, and then use the screwdriver as a lever to pop it out. You may find a pair of vise grips necessary to help pull the plugs out.

Use a screwdriver to dig as much rust and scale out of the water jackets in the block and heads as possible. This will aid in getting the block clean and will

kerosene and rags to do your cleanup. Just be careful because kerosene is flammable and its fumes can be dangerous. After washing everything with solvent, kerosene, or a good degreaser, shoot on a little WD-40 to keep things from rusting. Store all of your engine components in an orderly fashion so they won't get mixed up, lost, or damaged. Wrap big components in supermarket plastic bags to prevent rust and dirt from attacking them.

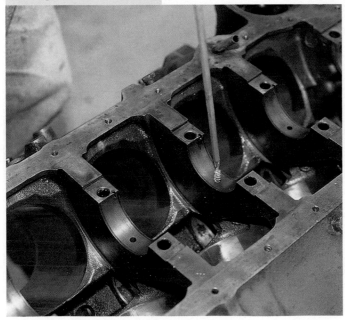

Measuring Tools: Taking The Measure Of Your Engine

Jim Richardson

Once, when I went to my favorite machine shop to drop off a 350 block and heads for some machine work, another guy was dropping his mouse motor off as well. The difference between his engine and mine was, his was still all together, right down to the carburetor and oil filter. It also appeared to be dripping a brown, thick, mixture of coolant and oil from somewhere. The fellow mumbled something about overheating as the engine was lifted off his truck.

It occurred to me that his bill might very well include an extra zero or two over what my trip to the machinist was going to cost because I had taken the time to tear my engine down, clean it up, and check it out. You see, it strikes me as folly to pay a high-end machine shop to degrease and disassemble an engine. Why would you pay skilled craftsmen the going rate to do work you can do yourself?

Judging from the chocolate pudding oozing from his engine's cooling system, the machinist's efforts may well have been for nothing. Besides, the block may have already been bored out as far as it can go. Oh, well. It's his money. Personally I would rather tear down an engine myself, figure out what it needs, and know what I am getting into before taking it to a machine shop.

I disassembled my engine completely, found out that it still had an overhaul left in it, and figured out what needed to be done before I ever dropped it off. I knew the block had been bored .040" over in a previous overhaul, and that the taper in the cylinders was beyond cleaning up with a hone and a drill. I also determined that the main bearings were still in alignment and that the decks (mating surfaces for the heads) and the

heads themselves were not cracked, but were nice and flat.

I verified that the crankshaft was in good shape, but not so with the cam—pretty much what I expected. You might think figuring out what an engine needs would require years of experience and that a novice would not be able to do it. Actually, the process is pretty simple. It just takes a few very precise hand tools and the know-how to use them. Here are the tools you'll use:

Calipers

These devices can measure any length up to 7.5 inches accurately to within .001" ($^1/_{1,000}$ of an inch). They are very handy and easy to use for a quick check of engine components, if you do not require more accurate measurements. There are three styles of calipers. Which style you choose depends on how much you are willing to learn, and how much

Calipers are great for taking quick measurements to .001" and are easy to use. Vernier calipers are the standard at machine shops, but a dial caliper like this one is easier to read.

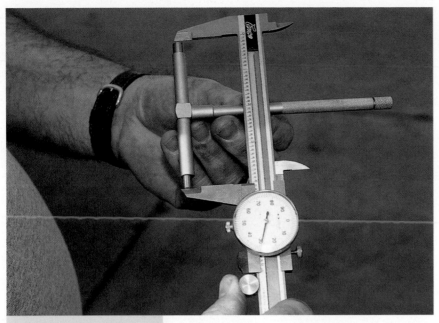

Snap gauges are only used to transfer an inside dimension to an outside micrometer or calipers.

you want to spend. If you need to measure beyond 7.5 inches, extended calipers are available, but you won't need such large ones for engine work.

There are smooth calipers that have no measuring scale on them at all, and those are just for transferring a particular dimension to another measuring device, such as an inside micrometer. They can be handy for getting into tight places, and when combined with micrometers, can provide accurate information. Using them does require some skill and experience, because two measurements have to be taken instead of

one. However, uncalibrated calipers are inexpensive, and can be a handy addition to your tool chest.

The most accurate and durable caliper is the vernier caliper. The device is called that because it has a vernier scale etched into it that tells you the dimension you are measuring to the thousandth of an inch. Vernier scales can be a little confusing until you get the hang of reading them. On the other hand, most professional machinists will use nothing else. We'll show you how to read a vernier scale a little later.

If you don't want to bother with the vernier scale, for a few bucks more you can get a dial caliper. As the name indicates, these have an analog dial built into them that will tell you dimensions in thousandths of an inch. You just zero out the dial with the calipers closed or zeroed on a measuring standard, then take your measurement. If you buy a quality dial caliper, accuracy will not be a problem and they are easy to use.

Then there is the new kid on the block—the digital caliper. This is the most expensive of the choices. It comes with a battery-powered digital readout that is simple to comprehend, but it becomes a paperweight if the battery dies. Digital calipers can also be confining in the same way that learning to drive a car with an automatic—but never mastering a standard shift—can cut down on your options. Someday you might be in a situation where all that is available to you is a vernier caliper, and you won't be able to use it if you have never learned how.

Micrometers

There are times when measuring engine components to one-thousandth of an inch isn't close enough. For instance, the stock, cast-aluminum piston clearance in a Chevy 350 is .0015" to .0025". This means a piston with a clearance of .0012" could seize in the bore when the engine warms up, and a piston that has a clearance of .0027" is in danger of developing piston slap when it wears in. If you can only measure to the nearest thousandth, you can't verify such clearances precisely enough. As a result, you could have a problem if you went ahead and installed new pistons without checking them.

Shown here are the parts of a micrometer.

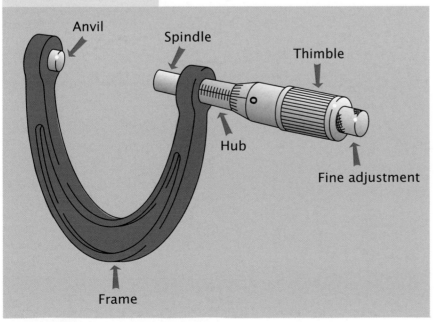

Anvil

Spindle

Thimble

Hub

Fine adjustment

Frame

Micrometers are what you need to measure your pistons. The most precise micrometers can measure to .0001" using a combination vernier scale. Such tools can be pricey if you want the finest, and even the less expensive alternatives aren't cheap. Sears sells a Craftsman 0- to 4-inch set of four micrometers for $279.99 at this writing, but Starrett, Mitutoyo, Fowler, and Mahr Federal—the brands favored by the pros—cost more.

Craftsman micrometers are excellent, as are many other less expensive brands, but beware of extremely low-priced, imported micrometers. Rather than buying those to save money, do as I did and pick up a set of micrometers at a pawn shop. You can sometimes find name brands for a fraction of what they cost new. Just make sure you get the proper measuring standards with them, and make sure the scale on each mic zeros out at the correct dimension.

Micrometers that are out of adjustment can be recalibrated professionally by the manufacturer, but that will cost money. To check the calibration, clean the measuring points (the anvil and spindle tips) and the measuring standard with a piece of paper or a lint-free cloth, then turn the fine adjustment on the end of the thimble in until it clicks. The scale should zero out at the dimension of the measuring standard.

Micrometers can measure to .0001" accurately and are essential for close engine work.

HOW TO READ A VERNIER SCALE

The scale shown in our illustration looks as if it were unwrapped from around the hub and thimble, and then placed flat on a table. In reality, you will have to rotate the instrument slightly to read the entire scale.

Adjust the thimble to a bit larger than the item to be measured, and then turn the fine adjustment slowly until it clicks. Make sure the item to be adjusted is not slightly cockeyed between the thimble and anvil, and then begin reading the scale.

Observe the number of lines revealed on the hub, or barrel. In the case of our diagram the thimble has moved out beyond the 2 mark, but not quite to the next mark beyond it. Note the number, which is 0.2000.

Next, note the number on the thimble, which most closely aligns with the line on the barrel. In this case, it is 22 or .0220.

Find the line on the vernier scale that exactly lines up with one of the marks on the thimble. In this case, it is the 3 line. This translates to .0003, or three ten-thousandths of an inch.

Barrel =   .2000
Thimble =   .0220
Vernier scale =   .0003
                  _____
Total reading is   .2223

Shown here is a vernier scale laid out flat.

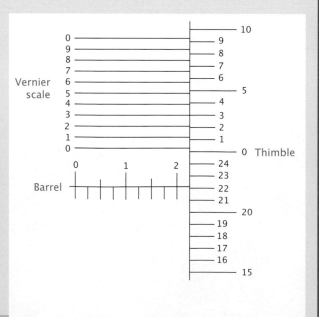

Reading a vernier micrometer

Clean the anvil and spindle tips of your micrometer after each measurement using a piece of paper or a lint-free rag. Clean the part to be measured too.

Snap gauges are a less expensive alternative to inside micrometers, but they take a little finesse to use correctly.

Never oil a micrometer, because doing so will cause it to read incorrectly. Also, treat your micrometers with the respect delicate measuring tools deserve. Avoid dropping them or treating them roughly, and never use a micrometer as a C clamp. This last bit of advice should be obvious, but every auto shop teacher can tell you stories about people who have done such things.

Ideally, your selection of engine-measuring micrometers would include inside and outside mics, but you can get by using a telescope gauge set and your outside micrometers. Telescoping gauges are also called snap gauges, because you insert them in the opening to be measured and snap them out against the surfaces. You then lock the snap gauge using the twist barrel on top and slip it out of the hole. Use an outside micrometer to measure the snap gauge and you have the dimension you are looking for.

Whether you use inside micrometers or snap gauges, the key to measuring correctly is having the gauge or inside mic exactly 90 degrees to the surfaces being measured. You can make a light pencil line on the extension of the snap gauge, and then watch the line move in and out when you rock the mic back and forth slightly. When the line is in as far as it will go before it starts to come back out, you are at exactly 90 degrees.

In the case of a cylinder bore, you can also push a piston up from underneath to help line up your mic or snap gauge. But the most accurate way to measure a cylinder bore is using a dial indicator mounted in a special jig that holds it straight while you move it up and down inside the bore.

A dial gauge mounted in a special jig is the most reliable way to measure for taper and out-of-roundness in cylinder bores.

Dial Indicators

These are invaluable devices that can perform all sorts of automotive tasks. For example, they can measure gear lash on a differential and run-out in a transmission or flywheel. And they are indispensable for checking crankshaft straightness, finding precisely TDC for pistons when you are degreeing in a cam, and determining cylinder bore taper. Dial indicators aren't terribly expensive, and they are vital for careful engine rebuilding. New indicators can run around $80, but, you may be able to beat this price at the pawn shop.

When you purchase your dial indicator, be sure to pick up a good magnetic base as well. You'll want one with a minimum 90-pound pull so it will hold firm to the part on which it is placed. A complete magnetic base with attachments from Craftsman retails for around $50.

Machinist's Straightedges

These are great for measuring valve spring height and checking flatness of heads and decks. They are also great for determining whether an engine needs its main bearing journals align-bored or not. Don't be tempted to use an ordinary straightedge, because it may not be straight enough to give you an accurate reading. A machinist's straightedge can be found for under $10.

You don't need all or any of these tools to build an engine. But the fewer measuring tools you have, the more you will be required to depend on your machinist to tell you what needs to be done, you will have to trust that the job was done correctly, and your machining bill will be much bigger.

Also, to really blueprint an engine and make it better than the factory original—something you will want to do if you are planning to pump more performance out of your small block—you will need to understand how to take precise measurements. We'll tell you what blueprinting means and how it is done in the next section.

Measuring: Lessons in Tolerance

Jim Richardson

TIME
3 hours

SKILL LEVEL
★★★☆

COST
$100–$500 (for tools)

APPLICABLE MODELS/YEARS
All

I hear some of the guys at meets tossing around the term "blueprinting" when talking about engines, but I don't think many of them know what the term really means. They usually use it to imply that an engine was carefully machined and assembled, and that's close enough to loosely fit the modern definition of the word blueprinting. But my sarcastic side sometimes tempts me to ask them to which blueprint they referred when they built their engines.

Back in the late 1950s, in the days of such drivers as Fireball Roberts and Marvin Panch, stock cars were really stock. The race car builders would go to the factories and rummage through the parts bins until they found pistons, rods, crankshafts, and blocks that were manufactured and machined as close to the specifications on the original blueprints as possible. Such components produced the best engines for the track, hence the term blueprinting.

Race car builders did this because the engines that came off Detroit assembly lines back then were only approximately within tolerance. When you realize that these cars were cranked out at about the rate of one per minute, you can understand why. That's not a lot of time to spend making sure everything is perfect. On motors, valves were manipulated to get them to seat, pistons were put in blocks by trial and error, and the assemblers worked at a brisk pace.

As a result, very few of our cars' engines performed quite to their potential, even from the factory. And that is why you can often make them better than new when you overhaul them. In addition, machining has come a long way in the past 50 years, and careful work can make a big difference in your engine's performance and longevity.

Also, most racers prefer blocks that have been around awhile because it means the stresses cast into them at the factory have had time to work themselves out, so they will be more stable and will hold their dimensions better. Some of the manufacturers of the great hand-made classics even let their block castings age for as long as six months before doing any machine work on them. We're talking clearances of only thousandths of an inch, after all, so any warping will throw them off.

The keys to having powerful, smooth, long-lived engines are good measuring, careful machining, and meticulous assembly. Most of us can't do our own machine work, but we can take careful measurements to determine what our engine needs, then verify that the machine shop did the job correctly. And we can do a top-quality job of assembly if we try.

Measuring in thousandths of an inch takes care and a little experience, but it is not as difficult as you might think. Read chapter 5 and spend a little time practicing before you try measuring your motor. If you're just refurbishing, and especially if you are building a performance engine, you will want to take such measurements. They can tell you what an engine needs, and even tell you if a trip to the machine shop is necessary. Sometimes all an engine needs is honing, new rings, and a valve job.

If your engine has a lot of miles on it and is well worn, or if it has been sitting for years, you will want to have a machine shop go through it to make it as close to optimum as possible. Whatever your particular situation is, if at all possible, you will want to check your engine yourself before and after having any machine work done to it.

Cylinders

At the top of each cylinder bore on a worn engine, you will find a ridge just above where the rings moved up and down in service. The ridge extends from the top of the bore down about ¼ inch. If it is thick (.003 or .004), or hangs up when you pass your fingernail over it, the engine will need to be rebored. In any case, you will most likely have used a ridge reamer to cut down this lip at the top of the cylinder to remove the pistons and rods.

If the ridge is thin or nonexistent, use a bore gauge or inside micrometer to see how much taper there is in the cylinders. Check at right angles and near the top and bottom of where the rings travel. Use an old piston to help get an inside mic perpendicular to the bore, as described in chapter 5. Cylinder wall taper develops when the compression and oil rings on the piston scrape along the upper parts of the cylinder bore, eventually causing it to wear and get larger in diameter than the lower area and top ¼ inch that the rings never touch.

Taper isn't the only problem. Be sure to use your bore gauge to check along the axis of the crankshaft, and then again at right angles from top to bottom, because cylinders wear out of round. If the taper is

Check each cylinder bore for taper and wear using a micrometer or bore gauge.

within .003 from top to bottom, and the cylinders are no more than .0025 out of round, you can overhaul your engine. Use its original pistons and new rings by cleaning the bores and knocking off the glaze with a cylinder hone chucked into a ⅜-inch multi-speed drill.

You can even clean cylinder bores without removing the crankshaft by carefully wrapping the crank with rags to catch any grit from the hone. Liberally coat the cylinder walls with kerosene or an oil-and-solvent mix,

An inside micrometer can also be used to check taper. Tip it back and forth until you have the minimum dimension and the gauge is at a right angle to the bore.

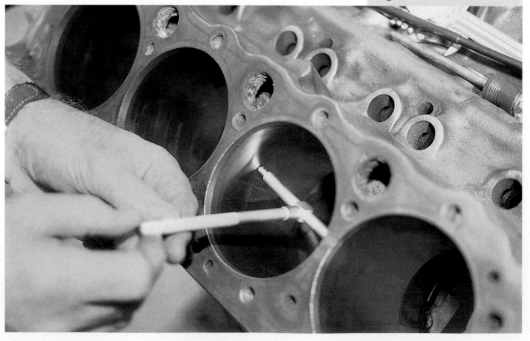

then run the hone slowly up and down in the bores. Make sure all of the glaze is gone and there is a faint cross-hatch pattern on all the surfaces. Be careful not to push the hone down so far that its stones come out down below the bores. You will ruin the tool and risk damaging the crankshaft. A ball hone is the best glaze breaker. A sunken stone hone is best left to a professional. Ball hones can be rented. After honing, clean the bores with soapy water and oil them. Solvent alone will not lift out the honing grit.

Pistons

Measure your old pistons top, bottom, and parallel to the wrist pin, as well as 90 degrees to it, using an outside micrometer. Next, check the figures against the pistons specifications. Pistons wear out eventually, and sometimes their skirts shrink or collapse if the engine seriously overheats. Worn and collapsed pistons wobble in their bores and cause an annoying clatter called piston slap. They will eventually fail, and their rings will wear unnecessarily too.

Rings

Even if you are simply putting new rings on your original pistons, you will need to use flat-stock feeler gauges to verify that the rings have the correct tolerances in their grooves and that the ring gaps are the correct width. Specs are supplied with the ring set. Make sure the rings are not too thick for their grooves and that the ring gaps are not too small. Otherwise, when the engine warms up and the pistons expand under running conditions, the rings will not be able to move in their lands and the engine will seize.

Connecting Rods

Your engine's rods must withstand a great deal of punishment because of the push and pull they have to deal with over the years. They can stretch, bend, and even crack, especially in performance engines. You can check length, and look for cracks at home, but it is pretty hard to accurately check for bending and twisting.

To check for cracks, use a Magnaflux Spotcheck Jr. kit. If you find cracks in any of your rods, it's best to replace them all. You can get away with changing out just one rod, but if an engine has been pushed to the point of cracking one connecting rod, chances are the others have been overstressed too. You can check rods for length using vernier calipers, and if any are stretched, replace them all. Stretched rods can result in spun bearings and will be prone to cracking and failure, often with catastrophic results for your engine.

On the other hand, also make sure the rods are not bent or twisted. If rods are bent or twisted, they can create friction due to mis-aligned bearings and pistons. Slightly bent or twisted rods can be straightened, and for general street use they will in all likelihood perform well for years. Of course, if you are building a nitrous-burning racing engine, even new stock rods may not suffice. Have your machine shop make all the same checks you did, just to verify your findings, and then decide whether you want to stay with your stockers or buy replacements.

Measure the piston at the wrist pin and perpendicular to it, top and bottom.

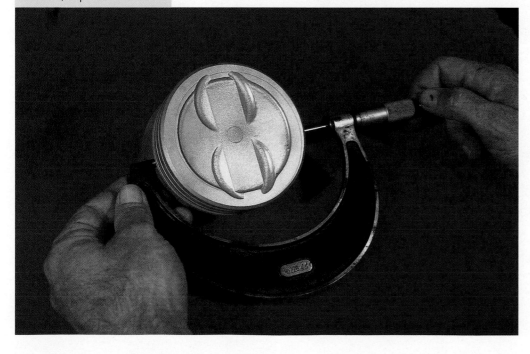

Check heads and decks for flatness along the length and diagonally, both ways.

Use a machinist's straightedge to determine if heads and decks are flat. If a .004" feeler gauge will slide under it at any point, the surface will need to be ground flat.

Use a machinist's straight-edge (not an ordinary metal ruler) and feeler gauge to check the alignment of your engine's main bearings. If they are out by more than .004" from one to another, have the block align-bored.

Checking For Flatness

Engine blocks and heads warp due to repeated heating up and cooling down during operation. If your engine's heads or block decks are warped, the head gaskets will leak. Then you will lose compression and you can easily damage your engine. The simplest way to tell if you have a warped head or deck is with a steel machinist's straightedge and flashlight.

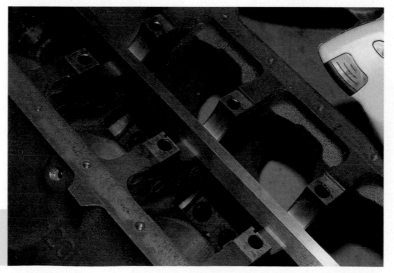

Be sure to check both the sides and bottoms of the mains to make sure they are in alignment.

Place the straightedge on its edge across each head lengthwise, then sight under it with a flashlight. Make several checks with the straightedge parallel to the head, diagonally across it, and across its narrow dimension in several places to make sure it is completely flat. Do the same with the mating surfaces of the block (decks).

If you see light under the straightedge, check the gap with a feeler gauge. If a .004"-thick gauge will fit under the straightedge, the block or head will need to be resurfaced. You can also check the main-bearing saddles for the crankshaft with your steel straightedge to see if they are aligned properly. If they are out of alignment more than .0015", the block should be align-bored.

Using a micrometer, check each of the rod journals for out-of-roundness.

Check The Crank

Put the crankshaft in the block with only the front and rear main-bearing shells in place, then turn it and watch for wobble at the center mains, or use a dial indicator to measure the wobble. Hold a feeler gauge (the thickness of a bearing shell) next to a center-bearing journal and see if you can spot any side-to-side movement. If you do, the crankshaft will need to be straightened.

Check the main- and rod-bearing journals for roundness and taper using an outside micrometer. You will need to take the following four measurements: two at the front of each journal at right angles to each other, and two at the back in the same manner. These measurements will tell you if the crankshaft needs to be machined and undersize bearings fitted. Bearings and journals wear out of round from the pounding they get in operation. They often wear more at one end than the other as they work back and forth in the block. If your crankshaft journals are more than .0005" out of round, or taper more than .0005", the crankshaft will have to be reground.

Check each of the crankshaft journals for out-of-roundness as well as taper using a micrometer.

Left: Cams on old engines can be reground, but if they are chipped and worn through the hard chrome surface like this, they should be replaced.

Center: It is important to measure the heel, or base circle, of the cam to make sure it is within tolerances.

Right: Cam lobes wear flatter as engines age. Check the height of each lobe to make sure it meets the specifications in your manual.

Left: If you want to reuse valve springs, you'll need to test them for correct height and make sure they aren't warped out of square.

Right: You must also test valve springs for correct tension. This is a device most machine shops have to do the job.

Cams

If you are doing more than a simple ring-and-valve job, remove your cam and check for wear and flattened lobes too. (I generally replace the cam as a matter of course during a complete overhaul because it takes a lot of punishment in service, and an uneven or worn cam can spoil an otherwise nice engine.) Verify the dimension across the heel, and from heel to toe of each lobe, using a micrometer. Replace the camshaft if it is not within specifications.

All of the valve springs should be inspected and measured using a steel straightedge. The springs should all be the height specified in your shop manual. If they aren't, replace them. Also, have a machinist measure the valve guides to see that they are in specs. If they aren't, they will need to

be machined out and bushings will need to be installed. Otherwise, oil will run down through the valve guides and your engine will burn oil.

These basic checks will indicate your engine's condition and can help you make choices that will be the difference between a motor that will run well only for another year or two, and one that will last a lifetime. Take your time, take notes, and work carefully. Then, when you make that trip to the machine shop, you will know what your engine's needs are. And when you get it back, you will be able to verify that the job was done properly.

1/16" Maximum

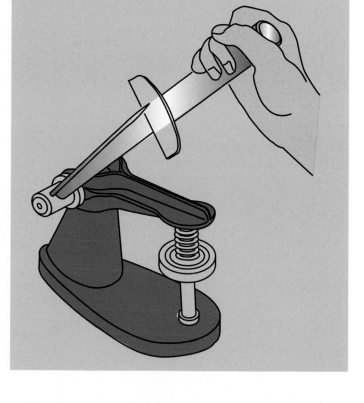

Heads: Have Your Heads Examined

Jim Richardson

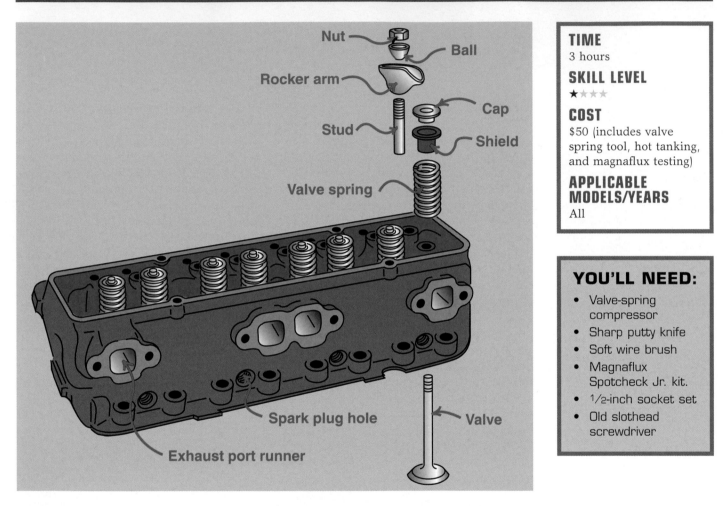

Nut

Ball

Rocker arm

Cap

Stud

Shield

Valve spring

Spark plug hole

Valve

Exhaust port runner

TIME
3 hours

SKILL LEVEL
★☆☆☆

COST
$50 (includes valve spring tool, hot tanking, and magnaflux testing)

APPLICABLE MODELS/YEARS
All

YOU'LL NEED:

- Valve-spring compressor
- Sharp putty knife
- Soft wire brush
- Magnaflux Spotcheck Jr. kit.
- 1/2-inch socket set
- Old slothead screwdriver

Whether you use the original heads for your engine or decide to go with a set that better suits your goals, you will need to know how to disassemble and inspect a set of heads to make sure they are useable. This is an easy task that can save you money. You get to keep what the machine shop would charge to tear down your heads, and you avoid having costly machine work done on defective ones.

To begin with, look over the faces of the valves and inspect them for cracks or missing bits. Check the valve springs for looseness or breaks. Also check inside the water passages for extensive corrosion. You will find crust and rust in heads that have been in service for any length of time, but if passages are extensively clogged, the interiors of the water jackets may be in bad shape.

If the heads are off of an engine you are overhauling, you can tell a lot about the general health of the engine by looking at the combustion chambers and valves. If a combustion chamber is rusty, you may have had a leaking head gasket. This can usually be verified by inspecting the head gasket itself. A head or cylinder block may be cracked, which would indicate a more serious problem.

A sturdy valve-spring compressor is required to decrease the tension of valve springs so that valves can be removed.

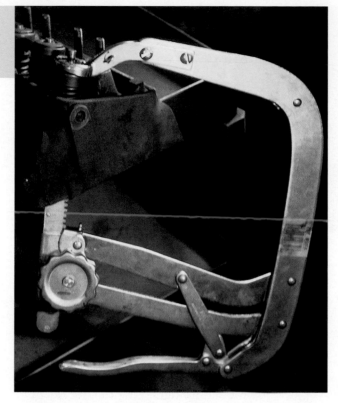

and filth. Another blast of degreaser followed by a little scrubbing and scraping with a soft wire brush and a putty knife will get most of the filth off. Later, after the heads are stripped for overhaul, you will want to have them hot-tanked and Magnaflux tested, but for right now a general cleanup will do.

Take Out The Valves

You'll need a good-quality, sturdy valve compressor to remove the valves. Cheap valve compressors won't have the capability to compress the valve springs adequately. Slide the cupped part of the tool onto the valve spring keeper, and then slip the flat part of the tool onto the center of the valve face. Adjust the tool so that when you push down on the lever, the valve spring will be compressed enough to allow you to lift out the split keeper. A small pocket magnet helps to do this job. Be careful not to let your fingers get pinched during this process.

Lift off the retainer, the outer spring, and the inner, flat harmonic spring if there is one, and then slide the valve out the bottom of the head. Keep the valves in order on a piece of cardboard, and put the springs, retainers, and keepers in a plastic bag and label it as to which cylinder it came from and whether it went to the intake or exhaust valve.

If a combustion chamber is particularly wet with oil and full of carbon, oil was probably leaking down the valve guides or blowing up past worn piston rings. Either condition means the engine should be inspected. Valve guides in Chevy heads are cast-in, and knurling them to curb oil consumption is only a temporary solution. Machining out old guides and installing bushings is a better solution to the problem. And rings should always be replaced when an engine is down for servicing.

Next, clean the heads of carbon, gasket residue, and caked-on grease

Left: Once a valve spring is compressed, keepers can be removed. Keep any parts that are to be reused separate from each other and labeled.

Right: Once a keeper is out of the way, let the tension off the valve spring and remove the rest of the assembly.

Clean up the valve seats with a soft wire brush and solvent and examine them for cracks. It is generally not worth attempting to weld up cracks in cast-iron heads because the process is very costly and the results are most often marginal. Aluminum heads are able to be welded quite easily by a professional.

Pull the rubber oil seal off and slip the valve out of its guide.

Remove The Rocker Studs

If they are not damaged, rocker studs can be left in place, but if you are building a performance engine, remove them and have new, threaded studs installed. The originals can work loose under stress and pull out of their mounts. Never try to cut new threads and replace the rocker studs yourself because it is easy to get them off-center or misaligned. Let a competent machin-ist do this job when the heads are being reconditioned.

The simplest way to remove rocker studs is to put spacers or a stack of washers on the stud and then tighten a nut down onto the washers to pull the stud out. As the stud is pulled up, you will need to add more washers so that you don't end up tightening the nut down to the limit of the threads.

If you plan to reuse them, leave the rocker studs in place. Otherwise, remove them by using spacers and a nut to press against the head.

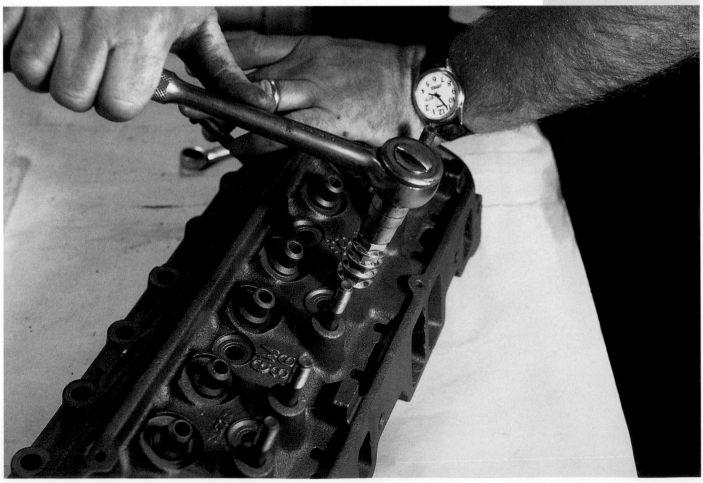

Left: One way to check for cracks is to use a Spotcheck Jr. kit from Magnaflux.

Center: Clean the area to be checked using the included cleaner. Be sure to check around the valve seats and bolt-holes.

Right: Shoot on a light coat of the red dye and let it soak in.

Left: Next, shoot a little cleaner on a rag—not the part—and wipe off the red dye.

Center: Spray on a light coat of the developing powder.

Right: Cracks show up as red lines. Cracked Chevy heads aren't usually worth fixing.

Check For Cracks

I like to do a preliminary check for cracks before I take a set of heads to the machine shop. If I find cracks, I can save myself a trip to the machinist, as well as the money it costs to have the heads hot-tanked and Magnaflux tested. You'll want to check around valve seats, combustion chambers, bolt-holes, and valve guides.

I use a little kit made by Magnaflux called the Spotcheck Jr. to do this inspection. It consists of a cleaner, a dye penetrant, and a developing powder. It will work on cast iron or aluminum and is very accurate, although I would still want to have cast-iron components Magnafluxed by a machinist before I did a lot of expensive work. Here's how to use the kit:

First, shoot on the cleaner and wipe down the part with a rag to rid it of dirt,

oil, and grease. The surface to be tested needs to be clean for the process to work. Next, shoot on a little of the red dye. (The little aerosol canisters are color coded so you can't get confused.) Let the dye soak in for a couple of minutes.

When the dye gets tacky, shoot a little of the cleaner onto your rag and wipe off the red penetrating dye. Do not put the cleaner directly on the part because it will cause the red penetrant dye to diffuse too much and wash deep into small cracks. Finally, shoot on the white powder developer.

Even tiny hairline cracks will become visible almost immediately as bright red lines. You can also use a Spotcheck Jr. kit to check engine blocks and connecting rods, which will be covered later. At this point, we want to make sure we have a good set of rebuildable heads for our engine.

Switching Heads

There are certain small-block heads that are better for performance applications than others. You'll hear lots about 68-cc versus 74-cc heads, bigger valves versus smaller, aluminum heads versus cast iron, and "camel hump" versus other castings. All of these factors have advantages under certain circumstances.

Chevrolet has developed hundreds of different small-block head configurations over the years for all kinds of applications, so the possibilities are mind boggling. An entire book could be written about Chevy small-block head castings alone, but many of them wouldn't interest anyone except the historians. So which heads are best for you? That depends.

Some heads lend themselves to modifications better than others, and some of them cannot be used at all on cars that must meet today's air pollution standards. Of course, aftermarket performance heads are available from a number of sources that will meet current pollution laws and give hotter performance. If you can afford them, they will save you the time and effort you would expend to modify a set of stock heads.

With a little work, the heads that came on your engine, or a set of used heads you find at a swap meet or wrecking yard, can be made to perform very well too. Just be careful when buying used heads. Make sure the vendor will allow you to exchange them for another set if the ones he sells you turn out to be defective. And use casting numbers to verify whether you are getting the heads you want.

Closed- Versus Open-Combustion Chamber Heads

Earlier, cast-iron small combustion chamber heads (64 cc) from the 1960s can be made to breathe very well and they can deliver more torque all across the rpm range. When they are surfaced and paired with flat-top pistons, they can easily bump your compression up over 10:1. At this point, your engine would suffer from detonation on pump gas, and that will ruin it in a hurry.

Aluminum closed-combustion chamber heads are better when combined

This is a closed-combustion chamber head with big valves installed. They'll make mighty horsepower but will probably make your compression too high for the street.

with flat-top pistons because of their superior heat-conducting capacity, but they are more expensive and harder to find. Even cast-iron small combustion chamber heads are becoming pricey and rare these days. Dished pistons, when combined with closed-combustion chamber heads, will lower your compression ratio to around 9:1, so if you do find a good set of closed-combustion chamber heads for a reasonable price, grab them while you can.

Open-combustion chamber heads (72–74 cc) are not as good for all-out racing, but can be made to breathe very well for street use, and they are much more common and less expensive to acquire. Unless you live in a cold cli-

Later on, open-combustion chamber heads can be made to perform by pocket porting and will still keep your compression in the pump gas range.

These heat-riser ports can be blocked to produce a cooler fuel-air mixture, provided you don't live in a cool climate.

mate, you will want to block the heat-riser ports that heat up the fuel mixture during cold starts because it also makes it less dense once the engine is warmed up, which cuts power. There is one caveat: These heat-riser ports were added partly to meet smog restrictions, so if you are going to put your engine in a later car that has to pass smog tests, you may not want to block them.

Bigger Versus Smaller Valves

Most small-block 350 heads came with either 1.94"/1.5" intake and exhaust valves or slightly larger 2.02"/1.6" valves for performance situations. If you are going with a more radical cam in a 350 or are building a stroker, you will definitely want to go with the larger 2.02"/1.6" valves. If you are leaving your engine basically stock you'd be better off leaving the valves at 1.94"/1.5" if that is how the engine was set up originally.

The bigger valves help you only at higher rpms, and then they only offer a significant increase in airflow if the intake valve is deshrouded and the head is pocket ported. The factory did this as a separate machining operation on heads in which bigger valves were installed.

Otherwise, by just installing bigger valves, you will only incur added expense and you might actually hurt your engine's performance.

Aluminum Versus Iron

Aluminum heads have the advantage of conducting heat better than iron heads, so an engine equipped with them can run a slightly higher compression ratio without detonation, but aluminum heads do not add horsepower per se. Aluminum Corvette heads from engines of the late 1980s to early 1990s breathe well, but because of their small combustion chamber (58 cc) they won't accept larger valves. However, if you find a set in good shape for a decent price, purchase them. With a little judicious porting, they will perform very well indeed.

Many people tout the weight advantage of aluminum heads. And at only 20 pounds each, they weigh less than half as much as cast-iron heads, but we're only talking about a savings of about 44 pounds altogether. Unless you are putting your engine in a very light, purpose-built race car, that doesn't mean much. I don't know about you, but I could go on a diet and lose that much weight for free.

You can tell what kind of head you have by looking at the cast-in symbol on the end. Double-hump heads are good street rod candidates.

Early, Small-Combustion Chamber Heads

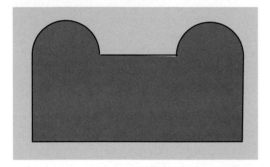

Casting No. 3782461

The 461 castings, produced from 1961–1966, were the first to have the double-hump symbol cast into their ends. Because, with few exceptions, they were made for and installed on fuel-injected Corvettes, these heads are sought after but not common, especially in rebuildable condition.

Casting No. 3782461X (1961–1963)

This is a very rare head because only a small batch was produced especially for drag racing. Strangely enough, a number of them wound up on truck engines. These heads are especially nice because they have larger intake port runners (175 cc as opposed to 158 cc) so they make more top-end power. The combustion chamber also has a quench pad next to the spark plug hole, which is unique to this head. These heads were made in either large or small valve configurations.

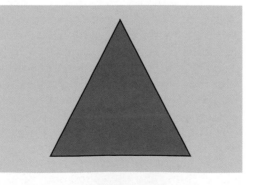

Casting No. 3795896 (1963–1965)

These were used on the 283 Power Pack and 327-ci 250-horsepower Corvette; 58-cc combustion chambers might make compression quite high.

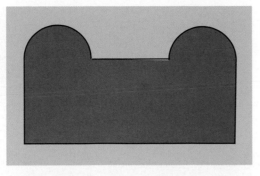

Casting No. 3890462 (1962–1967)

The double hump was also used to identify the more common 462 castings. Spark plugs are a little higher in the combustion chambers on these than they are in the 461 heads and that provides somewhat better performance. The quench pad behind the plug is relieved slightly. These somewhat more common double-hump heads came with large or small valves, depending on the application. One problem with these early heads is that they do not have accessory mounting holes in them.

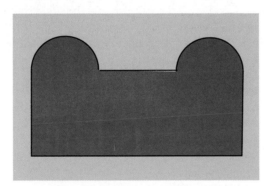

Casting No. 3917291 (1967–1968)

Almost identical to the 462 casting, these heads breathe well due to their larger port volumes. You'll find them on 302, 327, and 350 engines.

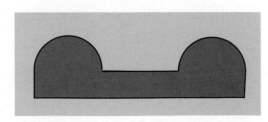

Casting No. 3927186 (1969–1970)

These were used on 302 and 350 high-performance engines and have small, 63-cc combustion chambers. These castings are very similar to the earlier 291s and 462s, but their big

advantage is that they have accessory bolt-holes in them, making them very desirable (as well as rare and expensive) for street rod use.

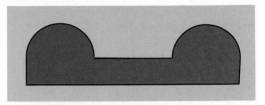

Casting No. 3991492 (1970 and up)

These heads came on LT1 350 engines and are available with a straight or angled plug. The combustion chamber is a closed, 64-cc type. Still available from your Chevrolet dealer, these heads can be purchased with screwed-in studs as part number PN3987376.

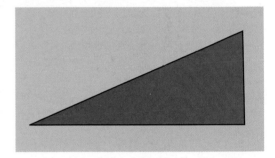

Casting No. 3947041 (1969–1970)

These are identical to the 186–187 heads and come in both closed (64 cc) and open (76 cc) when installed on the 400-ci engine. Both versions came with either 1.94"/1.5" diameter valves and 2.02"/1.6" valves.

Casting No. 3917292 (1968)

These are closed-combustion chamber, high-compression Corvette heads and came on both the 327 and 350 engines. They do have the accessory bolt-holes, so they are very desirable.

1970 And Later Open-Combustion Chamber Heads

Casting No. 3932441 (1969–1970)

These first smog heads are sturdy and can be made to perform well for street use with pocket porting. Compression ratios will be kept in a usable range with pump gas if you use this type of head with flat-top pistons.

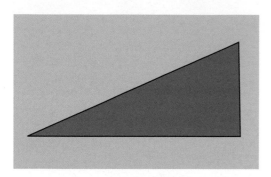

Casting No. 333882 (1974–1980)

Used on both the 350- and 400-ci engines, these heads are 76 cc.

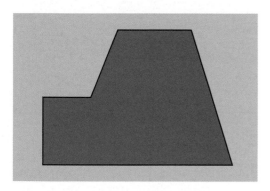

Casting No: 3998993 (In production)

Goodwrench 350 crate motor, made in Mexico.

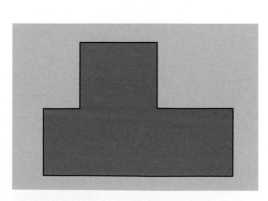

Casting No. 3986339 (1971)

307, 350; has 74.5-cc combustion chambers.

Head casting numbers are in the rocker arm area. The casting number tells us that these heads may be from a 350-ci motor.

Later Production Heads

Generally, castings made after 1987 are thinner, more prone to cracking, and will stand less porting than earlier heads, so keep that in mind when you are looking around. There are some notable exceptions to this rule of thumb. The tuned-port fuel injected heads from 1986 and later, used on the 350 high-output engines such as those in the Trans-Ams and Camaros, are excellent because they have smaller, well-designed combustion chambers that are suitable for performance applications.

This casting number indicates a later (after 1987) head. It won't take as much porting as an earlier head.

Porting: Open Up And Say "Aaah"

Jim Richardson

TIME
30 hours

SKILL LEVEL
★★★☆

COST
$70

APPLICABLE MODELS/YEARS
All

PERFORMANCE GAIN
More horsepower

YOU'LL NEED:

- Compressed air-powered or electric die grinder (An air-powered type is better because you can control its rpms, unlike electric die grinders.)
- Carbide burr-cutting tips
- Assortment of abrasive stones for high-speed motors (Don't use stones or burrs on aluminum heads.)
- Abrasive sandpaper rolls and tapers
- Manifold and head gaskets
- WD-40
- Beeswax
- Work gloves
- Particle masks

- 1¼-inch clear vinyl tubing (About 2 feet will do.)
- Small shop vacuum cleaner with filter bag
- Lamp or small light
- Safety shield/goggles
- Hearing protection
- 2x4 pieces of wood
- Machinist's bluing
- Coat hanger wire
- Clear plastic
- Graduated eyedropper
- Wood blocks
- Carpenter's spirit level
- Grease
- Dish soap

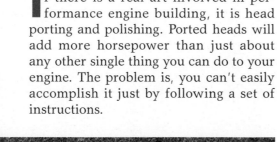
Area one benefits most from porting. Area two is next. Opening area three does little for all but radical drag-racing engines.

If there is a real art involved in performance engine building, it is head porting and polishing. Ported heads will add more horsepower than just about any other single thing you can do to your engine. The problem is, you can't easily accomplish it just by following a set of instructions.

If you really want to rework your engine's heads effectively without damaging them, practice on a set of scrap heads until you get the feel for what you are doing. Keep in mind that the point isn't to make the ports look pretty, or even to make them bigger. Rather, it is to allow more air to flow through them as quickly as possible.

Stock Chevy small blocks are great engines because they were beautifully designed to do the job they were intended to do. Yet, they were not made with the almost infinite care used to build a money-is-no-object racing engine. If they were, very few of us could afford Chevrolets. You see, machining and labor are the most costly aspects of building engines, and porting heads is a labor-intensive process, so the factory didn't bother. But with a little work you can. Here's how:

A scrap Chevy head suitable to learn on can be obtained from any large machine shop, or you can pick one up at a nearby salvage yard. Most of us will be working with cast-iron heads, but if you are lucky enough to be installing a set of aluminum heads, you may want to rework them too. In this case, you will want to practice on scrap aluminum heads first.

When doing cast-iron heads, try the different types of cutters such as stones, carbide burrs, and sandpaper rolls to gauge their effects. Practice working deep into the ports without damaging valve seat faces. You might also want to actually grind through into the water jacket in one port of your scrap head, just to see how much metal is there to play with. If you can see into the water jacket, you've ruined a head, and even if you only take off a bit too much, you will certainly shorten the life of a head.

The main reason for cleaning up ports and pockets in heads is that ridges and surface roughness cause turbulence that cuts down on airflow. Airplanes have flush riveting and retractable landing gear so air can travel over their external surfaces with minimal drag. Intake—and especially exhaust ports— in cylinder heads need to be as smooth and unrestricted as possible for the same reason. Making ports clean and smooth allows more air in and more air out of your engine, and a piston engine is really just an air pump.

Is Bigger Better?

Just cleaning up the ports in your heads can be worth 15 to 20 horsepower. The point of what we're trying to do isn't primarily to make the ports and pockets bigger, but to make them smoother and less restrictive. If the intake ports are too large on an engine intended for the street, it won't run well at low rpm. This problem is caused by the atomized fuel

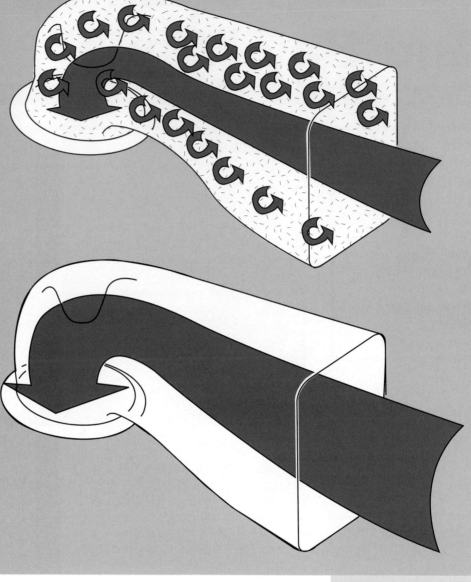

Cleaning up ports cuts down on turbulence, allowing more air in and out of your engine.

in the intake charge, which can actually slow down on its way to the combustion chamber, condense out, and run down the cylinder walls.

Ports that have been opened too much will also cut down on the velocity of the air going into the cylinder as the piston is on the down stroke, thus creating a weaker mixture. But if the velocity is right and the throat is opened to about 85 percent of the valve opening, the cylinder can actually fill to 110 percent of capacity because of the force of the air rushing in. And that means a denser mixture and more horsepower. But if you open the ports out to 100 percent of the valve opening, you will only get about 90 percent of

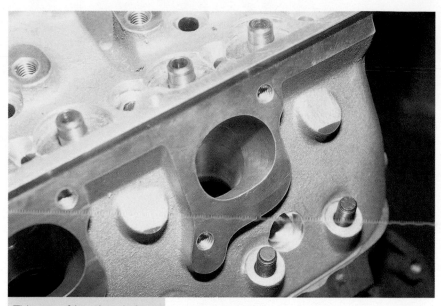

This set of late heads has had its exhaust ports done professionally.

to the larger valves can mean as much as 25 horsepower, and that's well worth the effort. Just remember, success when building engines depends on which combinations of things you do. Keep in mind that the tricks needed for a few seconds of awesome power in a funny car generally have no place in a street engine.

Radically ported heads can really pump out the ponies at high rpms (50–60 extra horsepower), but then there will not be enough air velocity at low rpms for the engine to perform properly for street use. If you want your cylinder heads reworked for maximum racing performance, take them to a professional porting facility that has a flow bench and experienced technicians.

Setting Up Shop

You will need to work in an area where you can make a mess, because iron filings will drift everywhere. Many people port their heads outdoors because the work area can then be hosed down afterward, and there is also usually plenty of light so you can see what you are doing. I chose to work inside because I have a workbench that fits my 6-foot, 2-inch height so I don't have to stoop or bend over. Comfort is an important factor to consider when choosing your work area, because porting heads takes a fair amount of time. It is safe to say that no one likes to be uncomfortable for hours on end.

Staying Clean

One little trick I learned from a professional colleague named John Jaroch is to hook up about 2 feet of 1¼-inch-diameter clear vinyl tubing to a shop vacuum with a filter bag so you can suck the swarf out the back of the chamber while you're grinding. Without this setup, it doesn't take long for powdered black iron to blow everywhere. The stuff gets into and under your skin, and if you don't wear a particle mask, you will taste iron for days afterward.

Another clever innovation Jaroch taught me is to hook up a small desk lamp or other type of light and shine it into the vinyl tubing from behind. When you do that, the clear plastic tubing acts sort of like fiber optics because it directs light into the port from behind, allowing you to check your progress easily.

the potential air fuel mixture due to lack of velocity, and you'll actually lose power.

Also, lots of rodders think that going to bigger valves in Chevy heads will produce more horsepower. Not so. A set of heads equipped with 1.94/1.50-inch valves won't necessarily produce more power if the smaller valves are replaced with larger, 2.02/1.60-inch valves. In fact, doing so can actually hurt power output because of the restricted area immediately below the valve called the throat. Tests have shown that this configuration is actually detrimental to airflow unless you go to a lift of .600″ or greater.

On the other hand, if you do a good job of opening the bowl area behind the valve (this is called pocket porting), switching

Use a shop vacuum, clear plastic tubing, and a desk lamp to remove swarf and allow you to see what you are doing.

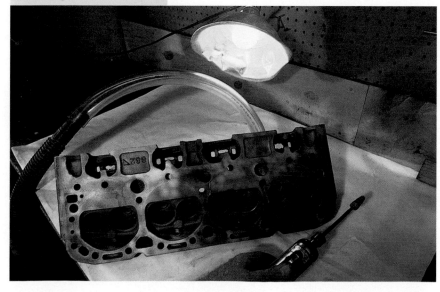

Tools And Rules

You will need a high-speed die grinder, and by that I mean one that can put out 20,000 rpm. A Dremel tool won't suffice. If you have a source of compressed air that can put out 4 cfm at 90 psi or more, go with an air-powered grinder because air grinders are smaller and lighter than electric grinders, and you will be able to control the speed with an air tool. Also, you will not risk the electrifying experience of having fine metal shavings get into the motor of an air tool and short it out, as is possible with an electric grinder. Don't forget to protect your lamp from metal particles as well.

You will also need an assortment of carbide burrs, stones, and abrasive rolls and tapers. Carbide burrs and cutting stones remove a lot of material in a hurry, so be careful when using them. And don't use stones or burrs on aluminum at all. Everything you need to do with aluminum heads can be done entirely with abrasive rolls.

If you can afford a nice assortment of carbide burrs, you can forget the abrasive stones, because they change shape as they are being used up, so they can be a bit erratic if you aren't careful. Long cylindrical burrs are dangerous, too, because the ends can make deep grooves that are hard to grind out. Personally, I prefer oval-shaped burrs for corners, and tapered burrs for flat areas. Keep beeswax nearby to clean carbide burrs, and use a little WD-40 to clean stones and abrasive rolls and tapers.

When you are working, wear a long-sleeve shirt and close-fitting gloves to protect your hands. This is especially important when using carbide burrs and until you get the feel for what you are doing. A carbide burr can easily hang up in the port and whip the die grinder loose from your hands, causing injury.

Also, wear a particle mask to prevent the inhalation of iron filings, and put on a safety shield or goggles to keep the stuff out of your eyes. Finally, the porting process can get pretty noisy with port grinding and a shop vacuum going all at once, so it would be a good idea to wear hearing protection or muffs too.

Paint on the machinist's dye liberally to create an easily read scribe line.

Getting Started

Before you begin, make sure you have plenty of light and that you can move around the head you are porting to get at everything. Long bolts can be loosely installed to hold the head up off the bench and at different angles too. A few short pieces of 2x4 are also good to support the head.

The best way to determine how much you can enlarge the ports is to spray on a little machinist's bluing, let it dry, then install a couple of manifold bolts. Place the gasket that will be used to seal the manifold on them. Hold the gasket carefully in place and, using an awl, scribe around the inner edge of the gasket opening for the port.

If you can't find machinist's dye, you can use a fine felt-tip marker to outline the gasket openings.

Open ports to the gasket edge and clean them up, but don't get carried away. Opening these areas does little to improve power in street engines.

Left: On the left is a finished port runner. Radical porting in the runners is a waste of time. Never go beyond the gasket line.

Right: Don't take much off of the port runner floor. There is nothing to gain and you could weaken the head.

corners first, then smoothing the flat surfaces level with them. All you are trying to do is clean up the long, straight area and open it out a little to match the gasket.

Removing Roughness

Intake ports should not be polished, but all the roughness should be gone. Exhaust ports and combustion chambers can benefit from polishing to a satin finish because doing so will help prevent carbon buildup. In any case, the most difficult area to get at is where the port makes a right-angle turn into the valve pocket. This is an area that will benefit greatly from smoothing and cleaning.

The area that will benefit the most from porting is the pocket, an inch or so behind the valve. The more easily that air can swoop around the valve in a perfect cone, the more power your engine will have. All roughness, ridges, and abrupt changes of angle should be smoothed to allow maximum flow and minimum turbulence.

An air-powered die grinder is easiest to control and you'll get your best results at around 10,000–12,000 rpm. Carbide burrs tend to chatter at high speeds, and stones can cut away too much before you realize it. Even after practicing on your scrap head you will want to work carefully and check your progress frequently.

As you are smoothing and cutting, shoot a little WD-40 on the stones or burrs periodically to keep them from gumming up. Also, check your progress

The gasket will be as little as 1/16-inch and as much as 1/8-inch bigger in places than the port opening. This will give you a good index as to how much to cut away, because you will want to remove material until the port is flush with the gasket. Don't remove any more than you have to from the floor of the port to clean it up. You can remove more from the top and sides. If you have followed the recommendation about practicing on a scrap head, you'll have a good idea about how much you can grind away without causing damage.

Getting aggressive in the port area leading up to the valve pocket is not very productive because the air has a pretty straight shot in this area, and you could actually make the head too thin in the pushrod area. Start by doing the

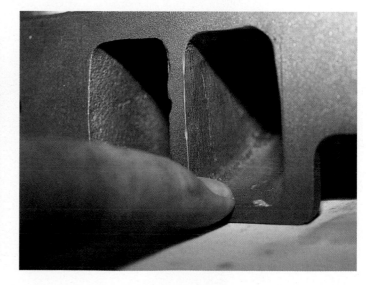

frequently by wiping the port surface with a rag dampened with WD-40 to get the swarf out. Then run your finger inside on the surface to check for ridges, slag, or roughness. Your fingertip (unless it is very callused or damaged by chemicals) is actually quite sensitive and can feel differences as slight as a couple thousandths of an inch.

Small, ball-shaped stones and burrs are great for corner areas, and ball shapes are good for down in pocket areas. Use large sandpaper cylinders for long, round sections, and valve pocket work. Slightly rounded cone-shaped stones or burrs are good for the slight ramping on the bottom surfaces of the inlets to ports.

Cleaning up around the valve guides is a little tricky because you don't want to grind too much away and leave a knife-edge at the opening, but you do want to smooth and round off all the

edges. Another thing John Jaroch taught me is to install long, Allen-head bolts through the guides and attach nuts on the bottom to hold the bolts in place. The Allen bolt heads help to preserve a little area around the valve guide. Be very careful in this area not to create deep grooves or take too much metal away. And check your work frequently, both visually and by using your fingertip.

Use sandpaper rolls and tapers to do your final finishing.

Check your progress frequently using your finger. You can feel roughness with your fingertip to within a few thousandths.

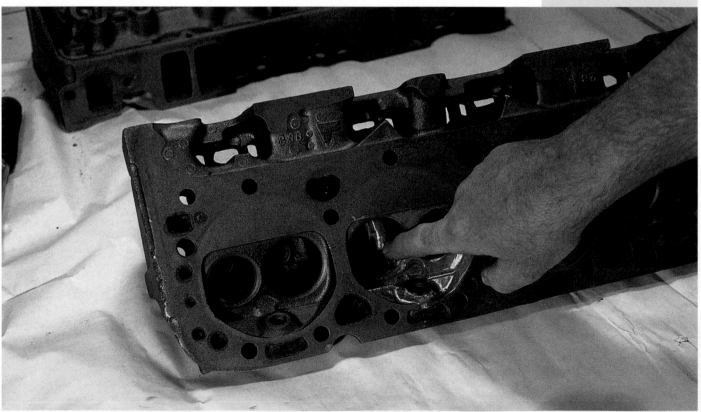

Abrasive sanding cylinders and bits are available at hardware stores and make pocket porting easier.

Polishing

Once a port is cleaned of slag, ridges, and roughness, switch to the sandpaper rolls and tapers. You could actually do a complete porting job with these on cast iron, but it would take quite a few of them. Even if you start out with burrs or stones, by all means use sandpaper disks to do your final smoothing and cleaning. Shoot a little WD-40 on them once in a while so they won't get clogged. Also, replace the sandpaper rolls when they get dull rather than trying to press harder.

Fine polishing of combustion chambers can be done by hand using #400 grit

MATCHING PORTS

Once you have opened your intake ports and smoothed them, you will want to clean up and open the intake manifold to match it—but not exactly. In the old days we used to go to extraordinary measures to line up the intake and exhaust manifolds with their ports exactly, but it has since been demonstrated that the intake manifold should be just a tiny bit smaller (.050" smaller at the port floor) at its mating surface, and the exhaust header openings should be a little bit larger all around by the same amount.

The reason is that, with the intake port just a tiny bit larger, a small amount of turbulence will be created in the incoming mixture that will help keep the fuel charge in suspension and mixed properly. On the exhaust side, a slight vacuum is created between exhaust pulses when the headers are slightly larger. This helps with scavenging and avoiding fuel mixture dilution.

It can easily take 30 hours or more to port a set of heads, so don't become impatient and try to hurry the process. If you are not the patient type, drop your heads off at a porting service and let them do the job. Otherwise you could ruin a good set of heads and cost yourself even more money.

You can use bent coathanger wire to make sure the port runners are even.

wet and dry sandpaper, or if you want to go for a truly shiny finish, you can use felt bobs and polishing compounds on your die grinder. Once again, the purpose of our efforts isn't to create a thing of beauty, but to make it as easy as possible for air to enter and exit the head.

When you have one port done, make templates of its inside dimensions using coat hanger wire. That way you can verify that each port is opened to the same size as the others. If the port sizes and combustion chamber volumes differ, your engine won't operate at its optimum performance level.

Combustion Chambers

After you have all the ports clean and smooth, place the head on your bench so its mating surface is up, shoot on a little machinist's bluing, then put a head gasket in place and scribe around the opening in the gasket for the combustion chamber. Slip a couple of old valves in place to protect the valve seats, then clean and smooth the combustion chamber area. Flat grinding disks are good for this, as are sanding disks and flapper disks of sandpaper.

You won't want to polish the combustion chambers if your engine is intended for the street, because doing so could cut swirl and actually lower performance. Just get the slag and roughness out, and chamfer any sharp edges, such as around spark plug openings and the edges of combustion chambers.

Also, be careful not to remove too much material because if you get too aggressive you could end up lowering your compression. If you are going to install 2.02" valves in a head that was equipped with 1.94" valves originally, you will need to de-shroud the area around the periphery of the valves in the side of the combustion chamber. Just don't go out beyond the gasket opening, which will result in gasket failure.

Checking Combustion Chamber Volume

If your combustion chambers are different sizes, they will have different volumes, which means that your engine will have higher compression ratios in some cylinders than in others. If your engine is to function well, you won't want a difference of more than a couple of cubic centimeters between cylinders.

You will also want to take into account how much metal will have to come off the surface of the head to make it flat. Don't go over 9.75:1 on compression if you want to be able to run pump gas on the street. This figure will put you as close

to detonation as you will want to go, and with that, ignition timing and fuel mixture will have to be pretty accurate to avoid problems.

The easiest and least expensive way to check the volumes of the combustion chambers is by using a sheet of clear plastic and an eyedropper or graduated beaker. The piece of clear plastic needs to be bigger than the diameter of the combustion chamber, and it needs a hole drilled into it to allow you to feed liquid into the combustion chamber with an eyedropper. You can pick up a graduated eyedropper, marked off in cubic centimeters, at most drugstores.

Use machinist's dye and the head gaskets you will be running in your engine to scribe around combustion chambers. Never enlarge the combustion chamber beyond the edge of the head gasket.

On the left is what a well-ported set of closed-chamber heads should look like.

FIGURING COMPRESSION RATIOS

Compression ratio is simply the volume of the cylinder compared to the volume of the combustion chamber. To determine the volume of one cylinder in a Chevy small block (or any engine for that matter), you merely divide the displacement by the number of cylinders, which in our case is eight. For example, 350 divided by 8 is 43.75 cubic inches, which is also the amount of air the piston displaces when it moves from bottom dead center (BDC) to top dead center (TDC).

If we convert that figure into cubic centimeters we then get 716.94. Then, if we divide that figure by the size of the combustion chamber (let's assume it is 68 cc) we get 10.54, or nearly 11:1, which is a compression ratio that is too high for pump gas. However, if we use an open-combustion chamber head with a volume of 74 cc, then divide that into our cylinder volume of 716.94, we get a compression ratio of 9.8:1, which is more viable.

If we then use a 1/8-inch (.125") dished piston, we increase the size of the combustion chamber enough to get our compression ratio down to roughly 9.5:1, which is comfortable for street use. Of course, there are lots of other little variables that can come into the equation as well, such as how high the piston comes up in the cylinder and how far up the piston ring package rides. Quite simply, if you are taking .030" off the heads and another .040" off the block decks, you could be bumping the compression up dangerously.

The mating surface for the head must be clean and the head must be propped up so it is absolutely horizontal. Use blocks of wood to support the head and use a carpenter's spirit level to adjust it to perfectly level. Lightly smear the valve seats with grease so they will seal, then install a couple of valves.

Mix up a little dish soap and water (you can add a little food coloring for higher visibility if you like) and slowly fill the combustion chamber, keeping careful track of the number of cubic centimeters it takes to fill the combustion chamber to the bottom of the piece of plastic. Repeat this process for each combustion chamber and note down the results. All of your figures should be within a couple of cubic centimeters of each other. Make fine adjustments as necessary.

If you find any significant difference, try juggling valves around in the heads. No matter how carefully made, your valves will vary in height slightly. Mixing and matching can often correct any difference in relative combustion chamber volumes. Only take more material out of a combustion chamber as a last resort to get volumes to agree.

This is a professional rig, but you can determine combustion chamber volume using a graduated eyedropper from the drugstore and a piece of flat clear plastic.

Camshafts: Getting A Lift

Jim Richardson

Back in the 1960s, while I was filling up at a gas station on the way to Lions Drag Strip in Long Beach, California, a little 1941 Studebaker Champion two-door sedan pulled in. Its driver rolled to a stop in the street, then in a series of roaring jumps, got up next to the pumps and shut the engine off. He filled the tank with high-test, paid the bill, and then roared and jack-rabbitted the car back out to the street. As the traffic light changed, he took the engine up to about 3,000 rpm, slipped the clutch, bogged down a little, and then blasted away in a thunderous roar.

The fellow had no choice but to drive like that. The small-block Chevy in his Studebaker had such a radical cam in it that it could not get out of its own way until it got up into the higher-rpm ranges. But once it did, it went like stink. As I recall, later that night the guy turned 147 miles per hour. Of course, the car's gas mileage would have been awful, the engine wouldn't have lasted long in street use, and the car's heavy-duty clutch would have given the driver a sore leg in minutes, but those were, and still are to a great extent, the trade-offs.

Back then, when I was in my early twenties, I was just crazy enough to want to build myself a car like that. These days I want a machine that is a bit more streetable. I like a car with impressive performance and a sexy rumble, but I also want a clutch that doesn't require both feet to depress it, and I want to be able to get away from traffic signals without having to break the tires loose.

I tell this little story because it illustrates a very important point. You must decide what you want your engine to do, and what kind of vehicle you want to put it in before you choose a cam. Just going for the most radical cam you can find is a big mistake for street use, even if you build the engine around the cam. You could wind up with big flat spots in acceleration, short valve train life, and a car that is not particularly fast or even fun to drive.

These days, with the advent of computers, the selection of cams is endless, so with a little thought and care, you can get whatever you want, if it is within reason. In the last 20 years, computer research has produced cams that can give you such awesome torque at low rpms that your Malibu will accelerate like a bullet from 0 to 60. You can also get cams that will give you awesome horsepower at high rpms, lower those E.T.s in the quarter mile, and shut down the competition. The stock cam is in between these extremes, though nearer the low-rpm end.

The people who developed your small block's original camshaft were no fools. They had a tough job to do. They needed to come up with valve timing that would provide a smooth idle, decent gas mileage, and low emissions. Yet it had to give you good performance at all rpm ranges and allow your engine to last for 100,000 miles and more without needing major work.

Quite simply, the camshaft in a conventional, four-cycle engine opens the intake and exhaust valves at just the right time so the fuel/air mixture comes in on cue, is burned, and then the exhaust gasses are cleared from the combustion chamber in time for the next event. The cam also turns the distributor, which causes the spark plugs to ignite the mixture at precisely the right moment. It turns the oil pump and drives the mechanical fuel pump too. In a way, it is the brains of the engine.

The challenge for cam designers is that the optimum time for each combustion event varies with engine speed (rpm). Some cams do their best work at low rpm, others at high rpm, and others,

TIME
4 hours

SKILL LEVEL
★★★☆

COST
less than $200

APPLICABLE MODELS/YEARS
All

PERFORMANCE GAIN
Customize engine characteristics to meet your needs

like your engine's stock cam, are a compromise between the two. Many people would say, "Just give me the cam that makes the most horsepower." But it isn't horsepower that makes it possible for a car to hit 200 miles per hour from a standing start in a quarter of a mile. It takes torque to do that.

A simplified explanation of torque versus horsepower is that torque is a measurement of the amount of work your engine can do, and horsepower is an indication of how quickly it can do it. An Indy Champ car engine can produce upwards of 900 horsepower, but you wouldn't want to put one in your 18-wheel Peterbilt because it wouldn't make enough torque to move the vehicle, even without a load in it.

On the other hand, a 600-ci Cummins diesel only puts out about 400 horsepower, but it can move 10 tons of cargo with ease all day long because it makes in the neighborhood of 1,200–1,400 foot-pounds of torque. The small 900-horsepower Indy car engine can do less work, but the work it does is done VERY quickly. A huge diesel engine can do an awesome amount of work, but it does it slowly. Of course,

the cam is only one factor in the equation. Stroke, bore, displacement, and engine and vehicle weight, along with a number of other factors, are also involved.

A low-rpm engine makes the maximum possible power in the combustion chamber because the chamber has more time to fill with the fuel/air charge. A bigger charge means a greater force exerted on the piston when the charge is ignited. As rpms go up, there is less time for the cylinder to fill, and less time for the exhaust to be pumped out, so the amount of work the cylinders can do goes down. However, at high rpms, the total amount of work that gets done in a given interval of time goes up.

So, what's your choice? It really depends on your intentions. Do you want to move a lot of weight off the line in a hurry, perhaps sacrificing a little top-end performance, or do you want a little street rod to blow through the traps in the low nines?

Of course, there are other factors you need to consider as well. For example, you need to decide whether you will be running a standard transmission or an automatic, what your transmission and

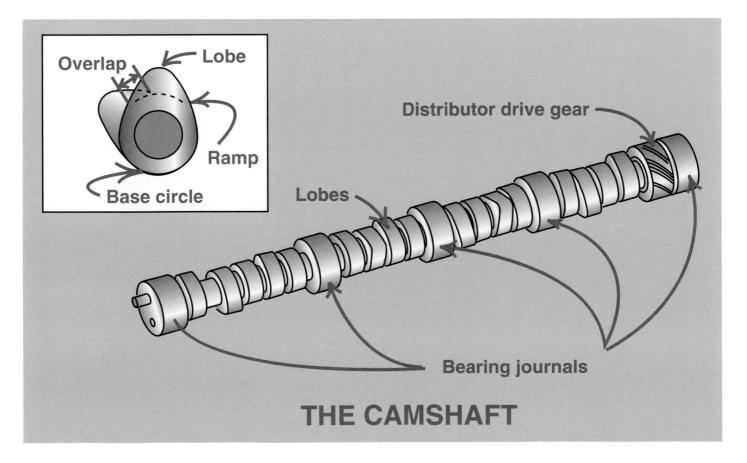

THE CAMSHAFT

differential gearing will be, how many rpm your engine can handle, and how well-behaved you want your car to be on the street.

You can do all the homework yourself to determine what duration and lift you might need for your application, or you can simply call a reputable cam manufacturer with your requirements. For instance, recently when I was building a stroker motor for my 1958 Chevy pickup, I called Ron at Ed Iskenderian Racing Cams in Gardena, California, and gave him all the stats. Ron noted down the data I furnished and determined that their 270--280 dual-pattern Megacam would do just what I wanted.

I wanted impressive bottom-end acceleration and a fairly broad working rpm band, but reasonable gas mileage. I didn't care about screaming high-speed performance because my old hauler doesn't have the sophisticated suspension and steering required for a triple-digit top end.

I called Iskenderian because they are one of the oldest and largest racing and specialty cam makers in the world. There are lots of cam grinders, but Isky cams are tops, and they don't cost much more than no-name cams for most applications. Also, the folks at Isky are willing to answer your questions and help you with problems. And their catalog contains a section that tells you just about everything you need to know to install a cam and get it timed correctly.

History Lesson

Early automotive engines were designed with no overlap. That is to say, when the piston reached BDC on the induction stroke, the intake valve opened and let in the fuel/air mixture. The exhaust valve would be completely closed at this point. On the compression stroke, both valves would be closed. Then when the gas fired, the piston would come back down to BDC, the exhaust valve would open, then the gasses would be pushed out.

CAM TERMS

BASE CIRCLE: This is the round part at the bottom of the cam lobe. Normally you don't need to think about it unless you are building a stroker engine, in which case you may need to run a small base-circle cam to avoid interference with the connecting rods. The base circle is also where the lifter should be riding when the valve lash is adjusted.

CAM PROFILE: The actual shape of the cam lobe. It varies greatly from cam to cam, and in some cases from intake to exhaust lobes.

CAM FOLLOWER: Device that rides on the cam and actuates pushrods and valves.

DURATION: The amount of time the valves are off their seats during the lifting cycles of the cam lobes.

HEEL: Same as the base circle

LIFTER: Same as the cam follower

LOBE: The eccentric part of the individual cam that opens the valve.

LOBE CENTER: The distance (measured in degrees) between the centerline of the intake lobe and the centerline of the exhaust lobe of the same cylinder.

NOSE: The highest portion of the lobe measuring from the base circle.

SPLIT OVERLAP: The point where both intake and exhaust valves are off their seats the same distance at the same time. At this point, the TDC mark on the vibration damper should be at the zero mark on the indicator.

Early designers thought that if the valves were even partially open at the same time, there would be a loss of power. Later it was determined that a little overlap added to the engine's power because the slug of escaping exhaust gasses actually created a vacuum behind it that helped pull in the fuel/air mixture, thus providing a mild supercharging effect.

Ed Iskenderian started experimenting with the use of this effect back in the 1940s and developed overlapping cams that increased power dramatically. Isky referred to this overlap as the "fifth cycle" and set about developing cams to make the most of the effect. Then in the 1950s, he came up with his famous Isky Five Cycle cam that made awesome horsepower. The sound alone from an engine equipped with one of these was enough to intimidate the competition.

Of course, there is a limitation as to how creative you can get with valve timing on a single-cam engine. And there is a limit to how long a cam with conventional lifters and pushrods can hold a valve open. Dual-overhead cams permit much more flexibility. Also, a stock grind cam has rather pointed lobes so the valves stay fully open only for a short time.

To get the valves to stay open longer, the tips of the lobes must be made wider, but this can only go so far before it has a negative effect on valve timing. Also, the ramps on the sides of the lobes get so steep that it causes rapid cam and lifter wear unless you go to roller lifters, and even then there are limits. Finally, flat tappet lifter diameter is limited, so there is only so much area to work with before the valve starts to override the lifter.

There is also a limit to how much overlap a cam can stand. It is overlap that causes that rough idle with radical cams. At low rpm, some of the unburned intake gasses get passed into the exhaust manifold where they ignite, causing that popping, rumbling sound. At higher rpm, a more radical cam comes into its own and the engine can produce prodigious amounts of horsepower.

Most street rod applications are best set up with hydraulic lifter cams. Back in the early 1960s, hydraulic lifters could cause a dangerous situation called lifter pump-up at high rpms, but that is large-ly a thing of the past if your lifters and valve train are fresh and properly set up, and you keep your small block below 6,500 rpm. Also, the big advantage with hydraulic lifters is that the valves are kept in constant adjustment at zero lash, so they are much quieter in operation.

Disadvantages to radical hydraulic lifter cams are that they produce a rougher idle and they contribute to low intake manifold vacuum. The latter can be a problem in cars equipped with automatic transmissions and power brakes. A radical hydraulic lifter cam can actually cause you to lose your brakes unless you have an auxiliary vacuum booster tied into the power brake system.

Solid (mechanical) lifters can handle higher rpms and more radical cams, and they do produce a smoother idle, but the rockers must be adjusted frequently and carefully if your engine is to perform to specs. For most street applications, a hydraulic cam is the best choice, but if you really want radical performance for weekend bracket racing, go with a solid lifter cam.

Making It Better Than New

Once you have made your cam selection, buy new lifters, pushrods, and rockers to work with it. Try to buy all from the same manufacturer to ensure compatibility. Roller lifters and rocker arms cut down on valve train friction because they have rotating rollers riding on the cam and valves.

Roller lifters are great for any application, and they can allow you to run a more radical cam without durability problems. The only catch is cost. Roller rockers and lifters are many times more expensive than the stock ones. Of course, the latest generations of Chevy small-block V-8s already come with roller lifters.

Roller lifters are more expensive because they are made of steel rather than iron, and they are much more difficult to manufacture. If you can spring for roller lifters and rockers, by all means use them, but make sure the cam you buy is designed to work with them. Solid lifter cams work only with solid lifters, hydraulic lifter cams must have hydraulic lifters, and roller lifter cams only work with roller lifters, so don't try to switch them around.

Installing A Cam

You can install a cam in a small block without tearing the engine down, and in most cases you can even install a cam without removing the engine from the car. However, the best way to put in a hotter cam is to do it when you have the engine down for overhaul. Cams (stock or hot) are not expensive, so even if you are just overhauling your stocker, replace its cam with a new one. Lobes wear flat and your engine will never be at its best with an old cam in it. Also, always install a new timing chain and new timing gears if they are notched or worn where the chain rides on the teeth of the gears.

To install your cam, find a long bolt with the same threads as the holes on the end of your cam and use it to help guide your new cam into place. Or you can attach the timing gear to the end of the cam to make handling it easier. Coat the cam bearings and journals lightly with a suitable assembly lube. I like Isky's Rev Lube for this task.

As you slip the cam in from the front of the engine, be careful not to bark the lobes against the block, and be very careful not to smear or mar the cam bearings. You can turn the cam slightly to work it through, but make sure you support it at both ends with your hands as you work. Once the cam is seated in the back bearing, try turning it. The cam should turn easily and shouldn't bind.

Smear a little assembly lube on the cam bearings before installing the cam.

Smear each cam lobe with assembly lube. You should be able to reach the cam. Smear the lobes with lube before

Screw in a long bolt at the front of the cam to use as a handle while installing the cam. Slip the cam in carefully, so you do not smear the bearings or bark the cam lobes against them.

Notice the special crankshaft gear with three keyways. One is straight up, one is 4 degrees advanced, and one is 4 degrees retarded to help degree in the cam.

Left: Slip the timing chain around the crankshaft gear, then over the cam timing gear. Line up the timing marks, then attach the cam gear.

Right: Timing marks must align straight across as shown here. If they are out by even one tooth on the gears, your engine will not run right.

ing mark, or at 6 o'clock. Take the cam timing gear off again, smear the gears with assembly lube, dip the timing chain in clean motor oil, and slip it over the crankshaft timing gear and the cam timing gear.

Now hold the cam timing gear in place with your hand while you install its attaching bolts. The keyway in the crankshaft and the locator pin in the camshaft gear take the guesswork out of orienting the gears. Make sure you don't slip and get the timing marks out of orientation with each other, because if they are off even by one tooth, the engine will not run correctly.

What we have just described is the standard way to install a stock cam, and it will work fine for a performance cam most of the time. Since you are going to all this trouble, you might want to make sure your valve timing is spot-on. It is not unusual for cams to be out 1 to 4 degrees, and if they are, the cam won't perform to specs. That's why you should read the corresponding sidebar about degreeing in a cam before going any further.

installation if you are only installing the new cam with the engine still in the car. This is a crucial step to avoid rapid lobe wear when the engine is in its first few minutes of running before the oil gets up into the galleries in quantity. Lifters are held against the cam under a lot of pressure by the valve springs, so without a good assembly lube, the cam lobes will self-destruct in minutes.

Turn the crankshaft until its gear's timing mark is straight up, or at 12 o'clock, pointing directly toward the cam. Slide on the cam timing gear and turn the cam until its timing mark is immediately opposite the crankshaft tim-

DEGREEING IN THE CAM

Most street cams can be installed as described in the text, but no matter how carefully each engine component was made, there is still the possibility of tolerance stacking. That is to say, your cam may well be machined right on the money, but the keyway in the crankshaft may be cut in the wrong place, the gears may not line up exactly as marked, and the timing chain may be a little tight or loose. All of these variables, added together, could make a difference to your engine's performance.

You can use a magnetic base and a dial indicator to find top-dead-center (TDC) on the piston.

Cams also can be installed in the advanced or retarded position on purpose, to produce a little more power at the bottom end or more at the top. That goes for stock cams too. If you have to move a cam more than 4 degrees to get what you want, you are better off installing a different cam. If you advance the cam a little, you'll get a little more bottom-end power at the expense of the top end. If you retard the cam a little, you will get a little more top-end power, but lose at the bottom end.

Most cams are intended by the manufacturer to be installed at exactly split overlap, or right in the middle between the precise center of the intake and exhaust lobes, because that is where they will do the job they were designed to do. The trick is to find the exact center of each lobe, then split the difference to determine how the cam should be oriented. It is actually easier than it sounds. To do it, you need a degree wheel and a magnetic base. A positive piston stop is a good idea because it is more accurate than a dial indicator for determining TDC.

Magnetic Base Method

To begin with, it helps to keep in mind that the camshaft in your small block turns at half the speed of the crankshaft, so the cam only does one revolution for every two of the crankshaft. Each cycle (induction, compression, ignition/power, exhaust) of the engine amounts to 180 degrees on your degree wheel.

Oil the number one piston lightly, and then slip it (without rings installed) and its rod assembly into its bore. Pop in a set of rod bearings, oil them, and attach the rod to the crankshaft. You don't need to torque the bolts to specs. Just snug them up. Rotate the crankshaft in the direction of engine rotation until the piston is at approximately TDC.

Left: When degreeing in your cam, put a washer on top of the hydraulic lifter to support and center the dial indicator extension.

Set up your magnetic base and dial indicator so that the needle plunger on the dial indicator is compressed by about $1/2$ inch on the center of the piston. It is important that the gauge needle be centered as close as possible to the piston's center because without rings on the piston, it can wobble and cause faulty readings if the dial indicator needle is nearer the edge.

Right: At TDC, zero out the dial indicator, then move your degree wheel to zero it out as well. You can tweak your pointer a little to align it precisely.

Attach your degree wheel loosely to the crankshaft gear using a fine-threaded $3/8$-inch bolt in the crankshaft snout. Next, make up a pointer out of coat hanger wire that reaches out to just in front of your degree wheel. You could use a stock, sheetmetal pointer, but a thin wire pointer can be bent into precise alignment rather than fussing with rotating the crankshaft to

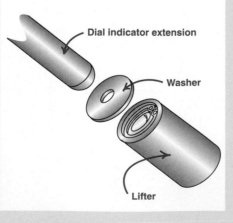

Dial indicator extension

Washer

Lifter

Install a lifter and then determine lobe center on the intake lobe first. Cams are correctly installed at perfect split overlap.

exactly the right spot. You'll see why this is important in a minute.

Slowly and smoothly turn the crankshaft until the dial indicator reaches its highest reading before starting to go back down. You don't need to be 100 percent on TDC because this method of degreeing in the cam compensates for any slight error. When you have determined the highest point the piston reaches to the best of your ability, set the dial indicator so it reads zero at that point. Now turn the degree wheel (but not the crankshaft) until it reads zero on your wire pointer.

It is best to use solid lifters for this task, but if you don't have any, you can put a washer on top of a hydraulic lifter to keep it from compressing while you perform your measurements. Lightly oil a couple of lifters and put them in their bores. Press them against the cam gently with your thumb. Now place a pushrod in the intake lifter. Relocate your magnetic stand and place the needle of your dial indicator in the upper tip of the pushrod so it has about 1/2 inch of downward travel. Zero out the dial indicator.

Now turn the crankshaft in its normal rotation to exactly fifty thousandths as indicated on the dial indicator. Note the reading indicated on your degree wheel. You can turn the crank with a wrench using the bolt you put into the crankshaft snout, or you can move it with your hands.

Next, turn the crankshaft all the way around to fifty thousandths before zero on the dial indicator. Again, note that reading of your degree wheel. Add these numbers together and divide the result by two, which will give you the exact split overlap figure. Assuming your cam is at exact split overlap at 108 degrees, you'll know whether it is installed in an advanced or retarded position. You should get a figure somewhere in the neighborhood of 104 to 112 degrees. The idea is to get it exactly in the middle.

To double-check yourself, check the exhaust lobe next. You'll know if you've measured accurately because, assuming, for instance, that the intake is opening at 104 degrees, the exhaust should then be opening at 112 on a cam that is at precisely split overlap at 108 degrees when installed correctly, indicating that the cam is 4 degrees advanced. If your figures from the intake and exhaust lobes don't result in the correct number at split overlap, you haven't got your dial indicator zeroed out at exactly TDC on the piston.

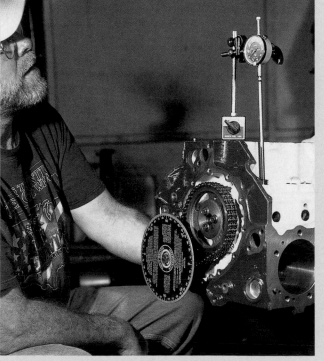

Turn the engine to determine the exact lobe centers on the cam. Make sure there is no slop at the lifter.

Positive Stop Method

A more foolproof way to determine TDC is to install a piston stop. You can make one of these out of 1/4–inch-thick steel strap by drilling a couple of holes in it to coincide with head bolt-holes, then drilling and tapping a hole in the center and installing a bolt. The strap attaches to the deck of the block over a piston. The bolt is installed so the piston will bump against it before it reaches TDC. Then you turn the crankshaft until the piston just bumps the bolt on the positive stop and note the reading on the degree wheel.

Next turn the crankshaft back the other way once again until the piston just bumps the stop, and note your reading. Add these numbers and divide by two. This will give you exact TDC for the piston. From there you can accurately measure the lobe centers on your cam. If your cam is within specs plus or minus 1 degree, I would leave it alone, because cams are ground a little out to account for wear in the timing chain. If your cam is 2 to 5 degrees out, you should correct it.

You can do that by using a crankshaft gear that has extra keyways cut in it 4 degrees (8 crank degrees) apart. Or you can drill out the holes in the cam timing gear to 11/32-inch and install an eccentric bushing to nudge the gear just a few degrees (no more than 3) in the right direction. Install the bushing with a little Lok-Tite, and swage it in so it won't fall out. Moving the cam in the direction of engine rotation retards the cam, and moving the cam against the engine advances the cam.

If you are degreeing in a cam for the first time, be patient, double-check your work and your figures, and get an experienced friend to help. As I said before, it sounds more complicated than it is. Gather the tools, follow the instructions step-by-step, and you'll soon get the hang of it. Your engine will run the way it was intended and perform at its maximum potential.

Top: A more accurate way to determine TDC is to make yourself a piston stop out of steel strap and use that rather than a magnetic base and dial gauge.

Center: Holes in cam drive gear can be drilled out and an eccentric washer (available from speed shops) can be installed on the locator pin to locate the cam exactly at split overlap.

Bottom: Finally, secure the cam with a locking device like this. Just bend up one tab on each bolt.

Installing Valvetrain Roller Rockers And Poly Locks

Colin Date

TIME
3 hours

SKILL LEVEL
★★☆☆

COST
$250–$450

APPLICABLE MODELS/YEARS
All

PERFORMANCE GAIN
Drastically reduced friction and heat in the cylinder heads, significant power increases (10–30 horsepower advertised)

YOU'LL NEED:
- Standard socket set
- Allen wrench set
- Breaker bar
- Crankshaft socket
- Clean engine oil
- Set of roller rocker arms
- Set of poly locks

Rocker arms, in conjunction with the pushrods, actuate the opening and closing of the valves. As the camshaft rotates, the lifters continuously ride up and down on the ground lobes of the cam. Atop the other end of the lifter sits a pushrod. It serves as the bridge between the lower rotating assembly and the upper portion of the valvetrain. Naturally, as the lifter is thrust upward, so is the corresponding pushrod. Coming up through the bottom of the cylinder head, the pushrod engages the machined recess in the underside of the rocker arm. By translating this repetitive up-and-down motion, the other end of the rocker arm (placed at the tip of the valve) will open and close the valves accordingly.

There are three basic parts of the rocker arm assembly—the body, the fulcrum, and the tip. Each one plays a significant role in your car's valvetrain operation. Most factory rocker arm bodies are stamped steel. Although fine for stock or mildly enhanced performance applications, these units are prone to distortion and failure when mated with larger cams and heavy-duty valve springs. The results can be devastating. If you install a radical high-lift cam, switching over to a quality set of aftermarket rockers is a must. Not only does the flexure and bending of stamped steel pose a serious threat to the rest of the valvetrain, it also produces inconsistent ratios from one rocker arm to the next. To fix the dilemma, most aftermarket high-performance companies, such as Comp Cams, use high-strength investment-cast chrome-moly steel, cast-aluminum, or even stainless-steel bodies for accurate readings and rigid strength.

The rocker arm fulcrum is the center pivoting point on which the rocker moves back and forth. As the arm slides down over the stud, the fulcrum ball and adjusting nut follow. Once in motion, the fulcrum becomes a concentrated area of intense friction and relies purely on engine oil for lubrication. In fact, most performance rocker arm kits come complete with upgraded, grooved fulcrum balls. The small passages grooved into the outside of the balls trap and retain oil to help reduce the friction. A full-roller rocker arm is designed with a "rollerized" fulcrum of needle bearings to further reduce excess wear and heat.

The tip of the rocker arm is positioned to sit evenly on the top of the valve. Over time, however, sloppy and inaccurate stock-style rockers can cause substantial damage to both the valve tips and the guides. This is where roller-tip rocker arms enter the picture. The roller tips of

Although compatible with the rest of the valvetrain, the two rocker arms have a distinctly different body from one another (note the machined roller tip on the right).

the rockers help reduce the constant friction and scraping of the valve ends. By replacing your factory rockers with quality roller-tips, you can preserve the life of your valvetrain and pick up more than a few extra ponies at the same time.

In addition to changing out the stock rocker arms in your motor, think about investing in a set of poly locks. Most engines with an adjustable valvetrain left the factory with a standard rocker arm nut. This nut threads down on the rocker arm stud to locate and retain the arm in relation to the valve tip. Under load, the rocker nuts can work themselves loose and even come off of the stud altogether. Constructed of high-strength materials, poly locks are designed with a small jam screw in the top of the nut to place added tension on the stud. Again, if you run a high-lift cam, buy the extra insurance and protect your valvetrain from possible disaster. Poly locks are fast and easy for setting valve lashes as well.

When the time comes to decide on what style of rocker arms to purchase, think practical. What is the primary function of the vehicle? Not every motor will benefit from having the biggest, baddest (not to mention the most expensive) rocker arms on the market. You want the rockers to complement your existing camshaft and valvetrain without having to change everything around. Regardless of your car and engine, there are plenty of choices. Keep in mind that you have the option of increasing the rocker ratio. On a small-block Chevy with a stock 1.5:1 rocker ratio and a 0.500 lift cam, upgrading to a 1.6:1 ratio rocker arm with the same cam would yield a valve lift of 0.533—you basically trick the motor into believing it has a larger cam than it actually does. Although most performance engines would respond favorably to the swap, it does present a new set of concerns regarding clearances. In this case, technical hotlines of major valvetrain companies can prove to be extremely helpful and informative.

Now that we better understand the components and how they operate, let's get to work. Up first are the valve covers and anything else that may restrict access to the inside of the cylinder heads. With a socket and wrench, loosen the nut and remove the rocker arm and pivot ball from each stud.

When using poly locks or any similar locking rocker nut, first tighten the nut itself followed by the setscrew. This keeps the constant vibration of the valvetrain and engine from backing off the rocker nut.

Always follow the manufacturer's specs on lubrication prior to installing the new arms. This is very important for breaking-in the new components. It is also recommended to replace the pushrods when installing new rocker arms. Pushrods and rocker arms tend to wear together much like a camshaft and its lifters. Installing new rockers on old pushrods can result in premature failure.

Install the new arms and pivot balls onto the rocker studs. Hand-tighten the rocker nuts or poly locks to the body of the rockers and begin to set the required valve lash or lifter preload. For hydraulic cams and lifters, the steps are similar and equally straightforward. Turn the engine over by hand in the direction of rotation using a breaker bar and a crankshaft socket. As the exhaust valve begins its upward travel, the intake valve is ready to be set. Slowly tighten the rocker nut while spinning the pushrod of the intake valve with your fingers. When you feel a slight drag or resistance in the rod, the clearance has been taken up, reaching the zero lash point. Approximately 1/2 turn on the wrench past this point will provide the proper preload for the valve.

On the exhaust side, turn the engine until the intake valve of the same cylinder reaches its highest point of travel. Continue to rotate the motor, allowing the intake valve to return 3/4 of the way back down. The exhaust valve can now be set to zero lash and snugged down 1/2 turn. This completes preloading the valves for one cylinder; repeat for all.

TIP

Be sure to check all of your existing valvetrain clearances before purchasing new rocker arms.

Replacing Rocker Arm Cover Gaskets

Richard Newton

TIME
2 to 3 hours

SKILL LEVEL
★★☆☆

COST
$10-$20

APPLICABLE MODELS/YEARS
Corvettes 1984-1996

PERFORMANCE GAIN
None

YOU'LL NEED:
- Metric socket set.
- Brake Clean
- Torx drivers
- 90 inch-pounds for center-bolt style

There are two types of stock Corvette rocker arm covers—actually three if you count the LT5 engine. From 1984 to 1986, the Corvette used the cast-iron cylinder heads that had been first designed in 1955. These early rocker arm covers all leak and will continue to leak despite your best efforts. You can slow the leaks down, but don't expect that you can eliminate the leaks.

When the small block was designed in 1955, the idea was that only one side would be machined. Obviously this saved money. The only problem was that the mounting surface for the gasket was left as a rough cast surface. The gasket could never totally seal this area.

From 1984 to 1986, the Corvette used a magnesium rocker arm cover. This fixed most, but not all, leakage problems. The issue really wasn't solved until the aluminum cylinder head was introduced.

In 1987 Chevrolet released the new aluminum cylinder heads which incorporated a new gasket and mounting system. This system uses a center-bolt mounting system and a U-shaped gasket where the cover joins the cylinder head. These aluminum heads seldom leak.

The first round of valve covers for the aluminum heads used a magnesium casting. These are almost indestructible, and you should have very few problems with them. In 1993 the construction was switched to a polyester resin. This switch was done in the interest of noise dampening, since no weight was saved. All you really need to know is that the magnesium covers and the polyester rocker arm covers are interchangeable.

When you install a new gasket, whether it's for the steel heads or the aluminum heads, make sure that everything is as clean as you can possibly get it. Any little particles left on either the cylinder head or the rocker arm cover will be potential starting points for leaks.

Be careful when you're removing the old gasket material. You're dealing with soft materials here. If you get a little too aggressive with your cleaning, you're going to remove material. This is really a case where it's important to take your time and do it properly.

The holes for the oil filler cap and the PCV hoses on this aftermarket cover just aren't right for the Corvette. You have to use a push-in oil filler cap, and then you have to rig a new system for the emissions plumbing. As beautiful as they are, they make you wonder why companies just can't make things correctly.

COMPLEMENTARY MODIFICATION

After you've completed installing the new gaskets, you should warm up the car and change the oil. No matter how careful you are, some particles will fall into the rocker arm area.

When it comes to replacing the gaskets, the most important part of the process is removing everything that gets in the way of getting to the gaskets. Clearing the right side is usually a walk in the park. Removing everything from the left side will test your drive for perfection. There's just a whole lot of stuff you have to remove in order to get at the actual valve cover.

The best procedure is to take several pictures so you can have a visual record of where everything goes. Then take a couple of additional pictures of the process as you go along.

Several companies make aftermarket rocker arm covers for the engines with the aluminum heads. While most Corvette owners prefer to keep the stock appearance, there's a growing trend toward the use of high-quality aftermarket parts.

Make sure you get this ridge very clean. Any old gasket material here could be the source of a future oil leak.

> **TIP:**
> Use Brake Clean to clean the valve covers.

There's one giant issue with these aftermarket parts, however. Most of them will not meet emission standards. If you look at your standard rocker arm covers, you'll notice that there are usually two lines attached to the cover, and the oil fill cap seals solid to the rocker arm cover. This means that your rocker arm covers are really a part of the total emissions system. I haven't found one yet that really meets emissions standards. If you live in a tough place for emissions tests, they'll fail you in a second. If you don't have emissions tests in your area, you can install these aftermarket covers.

You should use a torque wrench on the rocker arm cover bolts. Remember, it's 90 inch-pounds of torque – not 90 foot-pounds. This is a case where tighter is not necessarily better. If you get the bolts too tight, you're squeezing the gasket and just asking for a leak. This is much more critical on the old four-bolt steel cylinder heads than it is on the aluminum heads. Of course, you should use caution regardless of which type of rocker arm cover is on your Corvette.

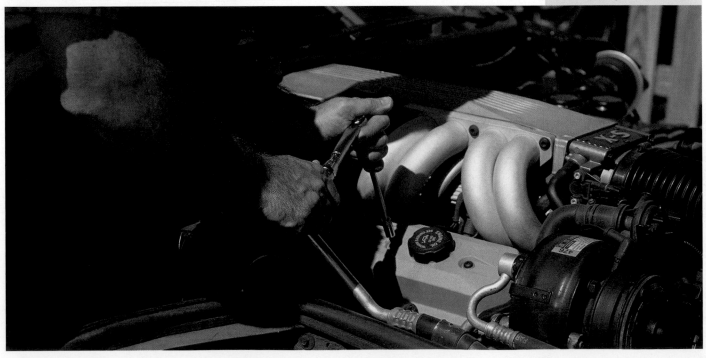

Hygiene: Cleaning Up The Mess

Jim Richardson

TIME
2 hours

SKILL LEVEL
★☆☆☆

COST
$20 – $30

APPLICABLE MODELS/YEARS
All

YOU'LL NEED:
- Paint thinner (mineral spirits)
- Solvent sprayer
- Latex gloves
- Face shield
- Concrete mixing tub
- Bottle brushes and clean rags
- Lacquer thinner
- Epoxy paint (color optional)
- Engine enamel (Chevrolet V-8 red or color of choice)
- Thread taps

Wash the block thoroughly when you get it home, and make sure to shoot solvent down in all the little oil galleries too. Then clean your engine again thoroughly after you have detailed and painted it.

A few months ago, a young fellow across the street from my shop was overhauling the small-block engine out of his red 1969 Camaro. He was just finishing up when I walked over and had a cup of coffee with him. While we talked he went through the list of what he had done to the engine, and it included a rebore, new bearings throughout, a mild cam, forged pistons, headers, and a Holley double pumper. It sounded like a great combination. A couple of days later he had the engine in the car and it sounded sweet.

Then a week later I saw him with the Camaro's engine torn down on a stand again out in front of his garage. I strolled over and asked him what had gone

wrong. He told me that he had neglected to clean out the oil galleries when he got the engine back from the machine shop, so metal shavings had been washed by the engine's oil right to the crankshaft bearings and had scored the crank to the point where it had to be replaced. I told him not to be too hard on himself, because I had made the same mistake once and had suffered the same fate as a result.

That was a long time ago, but it was a costly lesson I never forgot. So in an effort to help others avoid the same calamity, I'd like to share the benefits of my expensive education. The number one thing to remember is to keep it clean. Dirt, grit, and machinist's metal shavings (swarf) are the enemies of engines. And dirt can be introduced at any stage of assembly.

In fact, the top racing engine builders assemble their engines in "clean rooms" where you could eat off the floor, and where there is a positive atmosphere at all times thanks to filtered air being pumped in. That way dust can't even drift into the room. You don't need to take it that far yourself, but you do need to make sure your engine, shop, tools, and hands are surgery-room clean.

Sweep and mop your shop before you even unwrap your engine parts. Just shooting a lot of compressed air around accomplishes nothing. Wipe down all your tools, and get rid of any sandblasting media, metal shavings, or other grit that could drift into your work area. Finally, keep your hands and clothes clean. Many top engine builders these days use dispos-

Chase all threaded holes with the correct tap to remove dirt and metal filings.

able latex gloves while working to prevent oil and moisture on their fingers from attacking engine parts. I don't take it that far, but it isn't a bad idea.

Next, run a tap (make sure it is for the correct threads), down each bolt hole in the block and heads, and chase the threads for any dirt, rust, or metal shavings. Use compressed air or a rifle cleaning brush to clean out the holes. Also, inspect the block and heads for any burrs or casting slag that might interfere with assembly. Often a burr is not easy to see, but if you run your fingertip along edges you can feel them. Remove burrs with a bearing scraper.

The oil return holes in the lifter valley often have a ridge of slag that should be removed with a die grinder or files. Any last-minute deburring, chamfering,

Left: Remove any slag around the oil drain holes using a die grinder and carbide bit.

Right: An old-fashioned bearing scraper is great for deburring machined edges such as lifter bores and bearing journals.

Once your engine is clean, wipe it down with clean rags so the oily residue won't attract more dirt.

Clean out the cam-oil galleries, the galleries going to the main bearings, and the galleries in the crankshaft using a rifle bore cleaning kit. Keep working until a cotton swab comes out clean.

your engine down with lacquer thinner, shoot it with a little WD-40, and then wipe it down afterward to prevent rust.

I like to use a big, clean plastic concrete-mixing tray to wash things in. For safety's sake don latex gloves and a face shield while you are doing your washing. Put the block on an engine stand and put the concrete mixing tray under it to catch the drippings. If you have a source of compressed air, hook up a solvent sprayer, set it at fairly low pressure, and shoot the paint thinner down into lifter bores, bolt holes, oil galleries, and such.

Bottle brushes, small scrub brushes, and clean rags are all necessary for the next task. With a small container of thinner, go around and scrub away any dirt or scale that is stuck in the nooks and crannies of the block. When you are finished, everything should be clean, bright metal. Be especially fussy about areas where oil flows through the engine, such as the lifter valley, the timing gear and chain compartment, and the tops of the heads.

Next, use a rifle cleaning kit to wash out all the little oil galleries in the block. Remove any plugs, then dip a rifle bore brush in paint thinner and work it back and forth in the galleries to loosen any residue and pull out any metal chips left over from machining. Just as you would with a rifle, keep working until you can shove a white cotton swab in the gallery and have it come out clean. Take out the pipe plugs you had installed at the ends of the cam galleries and clean them out too.

Don't forget to clean out all of the oil passageways in the crankshaft as well. Use a rifle bore brush of the appropriate size and keep working until you can push in a cot-

or dressing should be done now. Be sure to do it before you clean the engine because you will not want metal filings blowing around and scoring pistons, bearings, and crankshafts after your engine is clean.

As soon as you get your engine back from the machine shop, wash everything down with paint thinner. It's cheap, it doesn't leave an oily residue (though it does leave a thin protective film), and you can reuse it. Lacquer thinner is also good, though more volatile. If you wash ton swab and have it come back out clean. Any swarf in the crank will go right to the bearings in the first few minutes of operation and become embedded in them. They will then score the crankshaft, often to the point where it must be replaced. And that could be an expensive situation if you've just dropped in a new stroker crankshaft.

Finally, check everything one more time before moving on to the next step. Once you are sure everything is meticulously clean, wrap each component in a plastic bag, and set it aside where it won't get dropped or bumped. Store the crankshaft vertically so it won't warp. Strap it to a vertical garage stud or the leg of a workbench so it won't fall over and fracture your toes.

Blow air through your solvent sprayer until it runs clear of liquid. Pour the mineral spirits out of your concrete-mixing tray back into a can using a funnel. You can use it again for washing parts, but if you don't, be sure to dispose of it according to local environmental regulations. Wash out your concrete tray using dish soap and hot water, then use it under your engine during assembly to catch dropped parts.

Paint Your Parts

This step is not an absolute must, but it comes under the category of making things better than new. Professional engine builders paint the inside of the engine as well as the outside. Even though you don't see it, it makes a big difference. When you paint the lifter valley and the tops of the cylinder heads with epoxy paint, engine oil will run down out of these areas more easily, and there will be less tendency for the engine to build up sludge.

Painting the inside of the engine also makes it easier to clean up and work on too. Use only epoxy paint because ordinary spray enamel will just heat up, flake off, and become part of the sludge.

Don't forget to check the timing gears and other components for burrs too.

Wash the areas you are going to paint with lacquer thinner to remove any oily residue. Mask off rocker studs, bolt holes, and other items you don't want to paint, and use pieces of cardboard as masks while spraying. Put old spark plugs in the plug holes to protect their threads from paint. Don't use any primer because it will burn. Just shoot on a thin tack coat, let it get sticky, then shoot on a full wet coat of paint.

Now is a good time to paint the exterior of the block, heads, and any other items you want painted. Unless you are doing some custom color, you can just use engine enamel in aerosol cans that is mixed to match Chevy red. Again, don't prime, because it will cause the

Mask off the areas you don't want painted, then shoot epoxy primer in the lifter valley, timing gear compartment, and rocker arm areas of the heads so oil will run back quickly and sludge won't build up in service.

Mask off the gasket mating surfaces for the gaskets, or wipe them clean with lacquer thinner.

Use a rag dipped in lacquer thinner to clean out lifter bores. Nothing must interfere with smooth lifter operation.

ry), but I prefer not to paint over gaskets and such.

If you are going to paint your intake manifold, shoot on a little silver high-temp manifold paint, let it dry, then shoot on the orange enamel. That way the engine enamel won't burn off as it often does when applied directly on the intake manifold. Keep paint away from gasket surfaces, as it might not interact favorably with sealants. And while your paint is drying, now is a good time to polish any aluminum manifolds, water pumps, timing gear covers, and valve covers because you can't do the job once they are on the engine.

Finally, clean and wipe down your block, heads, and other components again and store them carefully. A dropped crankshaft or cam will most likely bend or even fracture, rendering it useless. Other components can gather dust, rust, and contaminants. Mop your shop every time you work on your engine, and keep your hands clean. Habits of care and precision are basic to proper engine building.

enamel to flake off. Just shoot on a tack coat, then shoot on a couple of full wet coats, and let the parts dry for a day or so before working on them. If you are doing a strictly correct restoration, you may want to paint the engine after it is assembled (just as they did at the facto-

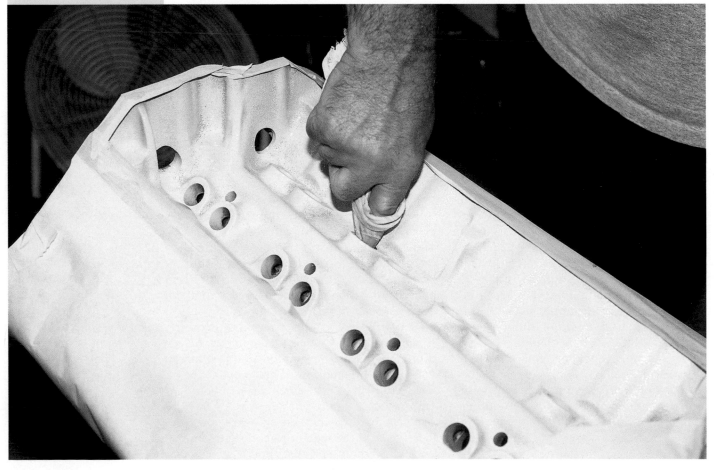

Preparing For Assembly: Basic Training

Jim Richardson

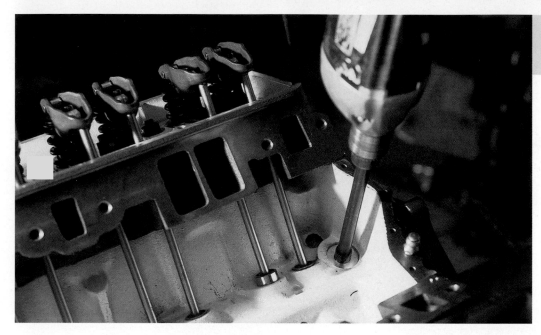

Taking the time to pump up the oil in the lifters using a priming tool is a useful professional tip.

Auto shop wasn't offered where I went to high school, so I learned to work on engines the hard way. When I was 16 years old, a grumpy mechanic named Dutch took me under his wing and taught me a few tricks. Rather than clutching me gently to his bosom, he usually slapped my cap off my head from behind when he wished to counsel me. Then, only after proceeding to tell me how worthless my entire generation was, he would point out what I had done wrong.

At first I helped him for free, just to learn. The fact that he didn't run me off was my only affirmation. The truth is, he may have been grumpy, but he had a good heart, and he took the time to teach me some things. Dutch is gone now, but for those of you who are novices, I'll share some of what he taught me. You'll have to come up with your own trick to help you remember things. Keep in mind that the sooner you make good techniques into habits, the better.

Putting an engine together is not like putting together a jigsaw puzzle, or at least it shouldn't be. By the time you are ready to assemble your engine, you should know where every piece goes and what it does. You can accomplish this by taking notes and photos when you take the engine apart, and by reading as much as you can about what each component does before you put your engine back together.

Putting together an engine is all about precision, such as getting tolerances right and making sure pistons are installed facing the right direction. Keep in mind that a couple of thousandths of an inch can make a huge difference, and that even particles of dust are that big, so you have to keep everything clean. Also, even if you aren't a novice, make notes of dimensions you have measured, what you have finished, and what you have left to do. When you come back to your engine later, you'll know exactly what you have to do next. Make sure you don't lose the card the machine shop gave you with all of their work listed on it.

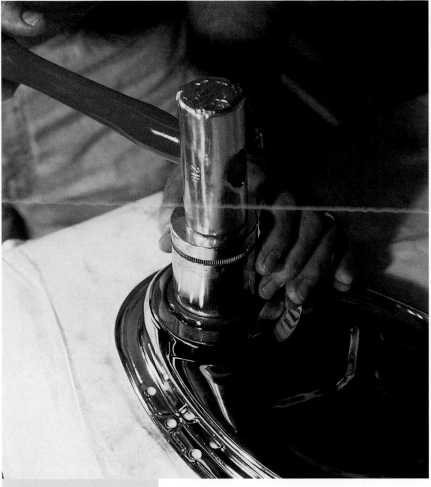

Use the right tool for the job. This soft brass hammer will not damage steel components.

Use the right sealant for each task to avoid leaks and seal failure.

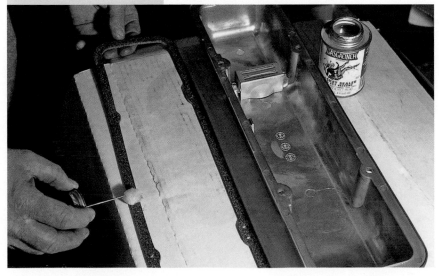

In The Beginning

When assembling engines, use the right tool for the job. Most tasks are easy if you have the right tools, but are nearly impossible if you don't. For example, some beginners will use a crescent wrench for everything just because it is

handy. This is a good way to round off bolts and nuts and damage your hands. A set of open- and box-end wrenches are basic necessities. A decent socket set is required too. And for anything beyond a tune-up, a quality torque wrench is imperative.

I prefer the type with a rotating handle and a scale to which you can adjust the wrench. The old-style, needle-and-arm-type wrench is pretty crude and hard to read precisely. If you buy one of the adjustable-type torque wrenches, be sure to set it back to zero after each use so the spring inside won't lose its tension. Open your wallet a little wider when you buy your torque wrench, and get the best one you can afford. It could make a difference in your engine's longevity.

Other specialty tools are also important for engine work, such as a ring compressor for installing pistons, vernier calipers, and micrometers for accurate measuring. An engine stand to make your work convenient and to save your back is a good idea too. Some tools, such as engine hoists, can be rented from tool rental yards, but you may have to purchase gear pullers and other specialty tools if you can't rent or borrow them. Nonessential tools that will make your life a whole lot easier include a parts-washing tank, an air compressor, and a solvent sprayer.

Swap meets and garage sales are great for picking up used tools, but make sure you buy quality items. Sears Craftsman automotive tools are top-notch and are not as costly as tools from some of the specialty companies. For specialized tools that will only be used now and then, cheap imports will work, but they are not generally as durable or precise as domestic, professional-quality tools.

And don't neglect the small stuff. Squeeze-type oil cans and plastic ketchup squeeze bottles make shooting on oil or cleaner easier. You will also want to buy some good hand cleaner, and collect a bundle of clean, lint-free rags. Before you start assembly, gather together assembly lube, cam lube, silicone sealant, Lok-Tite, anti-seize compound, and lacquer thinner as well as paint thinner for cleaning.

ALL ABOUT TORQUE WRENCHES

Quality torque wrenches have a micrometer-type adjustment built into their handle to adjust the applied torque. Just dial in the specified torque for the fastener, select the correct-sized socket, and tighten the fastener. This type of torque wrench will make a snapping sound when it reaches the selected torque. Do not tighten any more beyond the click, because doing so will overtorque the fastener and may cause it to fail. Never jerk or force the wrench abruptly. Just gently pull it to specs.

When you are given a value range, such as 85–100 foot-pounds for attaching the vibration damper, for example, tighten all of the fasteners evenly in three stages to the same value, whether it be 85, 95, or 100 foot-pounds of torque. When torquing larger items such as intake manifolds and heads, follow the proper sequence for that component.

When attaching cast-iron cylinder heads, follow the torque diagram in your shop manual or in chapter 26. Start in the middle of the head and run each fastener down in three stages. First, tighten all the fasteners to 50 foot-pounds. Then, starting in the center again, adjust the torque wrench to the setting for the second stage, or 60 foot-pounds. Then retorque the fasteners again. This time, start in the center, and torque them to the final spec of 65–72 foot-pounds.

If you do not tighten engine bolts and nuts to the specifications in your shop manual, they could work loose or become overtightened and break. Reputable hardware manufacturers have arrived at torque values for each type of fastener. This is usually stated in foot-pounds, or occasionally in inch-pounds (120 inch-pounds are the same as 10 foot-pounds). The assembly manual for your engine will have a torque specification section that will list the torque values for all of its fasteners, but here are the critical ones:

TORQUE LIMITS IN FOOT-POUNDS	
For A Chevy Small Block	
Main bearing cap bolts	60–70
Damper to crankshaft	85–100
Connecting rod nuts	19–24
Oil pump to block	12–15
Flywheel to crankshaft	75–85
Valve rocker supports to head	30–35
Fuel pump to block	12–15
Cylinder Heads (Iron)	
Stage 1	50
Stage 2	60
Stage 3	65–72

The scale on a torque wrench is in pounds and is at the base of the handle in most cases.

A Clean, Well-Lighted Place

As we pointed out in chapter 14, cleanliness is critical. Grit in oil galleries or around a bearing shell can ruin the bearing and possibly your engine as well. Keep your engine and its components covered with plastic trash bags when you are not working on them. Sweep and mop your shop before you begin each work session, and wipe down your tools after you use them.

A dry garage with a concrete floor is a good place to work, but never work

Use a solvent sprayer and drip tray to make sure everything is clean.

Always pull wrenches toward you to avoid accidents and injury.

Habits of precision are critical to building a high-performance engine.

directly on the floor. You can also work outdoors on still days when there is no dust in the air. Make sure you have plenty of light where you choose to work. Fluorescent fixtures are available for a nominal price at home improvement centers and they require very little energy. Install several in your workspace, and keep a good trouble light handy too. Finally, a small flashlight is great for peering into dark crevices.

Break It Up

When disassembling or assembling an engine, break the job into tasks. Then look over each task and think it out. Lay out the tools and other things you are going to need ahead of time. As you take things apart, place components on your bench in the order they came apart. You may think you'll remember, but unless you are quite exceptional, you probably won't.

If you are putting an assembly together, pause and think about what sequence the job will require. Lay out the components in order. You don't want to have to take things apart again just because you didn't remember to install something vital. If anything seems unfamiliar, read the chapter on that item again before going to the next step.

Resign yourself to the idea that you will most likely have to assemble some things two or even three times before you get everything right. Racing mechanics dry-assemble entire engines just to make sure everything fits and works together, and that they have the tolerances right before building the engine in earnest. If you are a novice, I highly recommend that you do the same thing. You don't need to put rings on the pistons during dry assembly, and you don't need to put a lot of lube or oil on things either because you will be taking everything apart again anyway.

It's About Time

Seasoned mechanics with all the right tools can build performance engines in as little as a few hours, but it can take weeks for a novice to do the job correctly—especially if you are installing a cam from one manufacturer, a crankshaft from another, connecting rods from someone else, and pistons or heads from yet another company. All of these items are likely to be well made and within specs, but they may not have been designed to work together. You can easily wind up with tolerance stacking and an engine that is too tight, too loose, or binding somewhere. Take the time to measure and find out before problems blossom.

If this is your first engine, it would pay to have the machine shop assemble the valvetrain for the heads before giving them back to you. They can do the job in a lot less time than you can, and they will have all the tools necessary. You may want to have the machine shop hang the pistons on the rods too. They can ream and fit them much more accurately than most of us can do at home.

Keep Records

When you check clearances, write them in a small spiral notebook. You'll be surprised how useful this kind of information can be as you go along. In addition, keep track of what you were doing before you quit for the day, to ensure that nothing is forgotten. For instance, you may have torqued the main bearings into place, but not the rods before you called it a day. If you don't take note of such things, you may come back and think you have done the rods too. Aside from avoiding catastrophe, such records also help refresh

Install gaskets only with the correct face up. It's easy to get sloppy and create problems for yourself later.

your memory if you have to work on your engine later.

There will always be more to learn no matter how long you play with engines, so don't try to master everything all at once. If any procedure seems daunting, practice putting together old parts until you get the picture. The main thing is not to get in a hurry and damage things. Also, don't be afraid to ask for advice from pros, or people who have more experience than you do. If you approach professionals with respect, they will usually be more than generous with their advice and aid.

Also be sure to use the correct lubricant for each task.

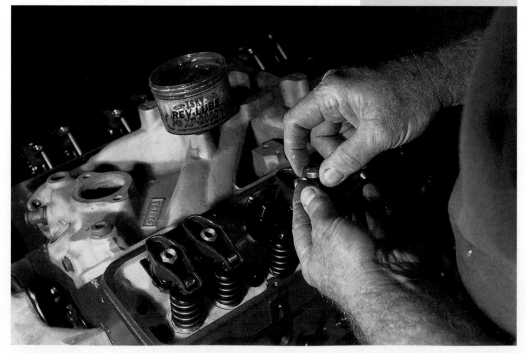

Start-Up: Lighting It Off

Jim Richardson

Attach the brackets and be sure to fill the oil filter and install old plugs to keep dirt out before putting your engine in the car.

Fill your engine with oil. A good-quality 10W-30 will do just fine unless you will be running synthetic oil, in which case you will need special synthetic break-in oil.

ightning flashes; thunder crashes. The platform is slowly lowered from the opening in the roof of the laboratory. Dr. Frankenstein rushes over, looks down, and sees his creation twitch its pinkie. "IT'S ALIIIIIIIIIIIIIIIIIVE!" screams the doc in maniacal glee as he dances a hideous gavotte. I know the feeling. In fact, I've been known to shout the same line after starting an engine that I have just built. For a motorhead, there is nothing quite like hearing what has been a 600-pound paperweight cough and roar to life.

All that care and hard work finally pays off. It is the single most exciting moment for a street rodder. Of course, it can also be the single most disheartening one, too, if you haven't prepared for the event by checking everything out carefully before you start your new engine. That's because in its first critical moments of life, things have to settle in. Parts that have never been introduced to each other before now have to work together as a team.

Hook up the temperature gauge and oil pressure sending unit. Make sure all of the vital fluids are topped up. Good-

START-UP CHECKLIST

- Check the oil. Use a good grade of 10W-30 detergent oil and make sure you fill the oil filter before installing it. (A special break-in oil is strongly recommended for synthetic oils.)

- Use only water as coolant for the initial run-in. It makes fixing any leaks much easier and you can just dump it out. Afterward, put in the correct amount of 50/50 coolant-to-water mixture.

- Check the ignition static timing, and make sure that you have the distributor wires in the correct order in the distributor cap.

- Make sure the valves are adjusted to the cold setting indicated in your shop manual or to the specifications provided by your cam manufacturer.

- Verify that the fuel lines are connected properly and tightened securely, and that you have fresh gas in the tank. Gasoline has a shelf life of six months. If the gas in the lines has been sitting for longer than that, drain it out.

- Make sure the throttle linkage works without binding, and that the throttle butterflies are fully open when the throttle is wide open.

- Make sure the throttle return spring is properly connected at the carburetor.

- If your car has an automatic transmission, make sure it is in "Park." If your car is equipped with a standard transmission, make sure it is in neutral before starting the engine.

- Check to see that all accessory belts are tight, but not too tight. They should flex about 3/4 inch in either direction when pressed in the middle using your thumb.

- Make sure no tools, electrical cords, or other items are left in the engine bay where they could fall into the fan or cause other problems.

---

quality 10W-30 motor oil is all that is required to break in your engine. However, if you plan to run your motor only on synthetic oil, you will need a special synthetic break-in oil. Otherwise, the piston rings will take quite a long time to seat properly.

Slip an oil pump priming tool (TD Performance Products makes a good one) into the hole where the distributor goes and pump the oil pressure up until it reads on your dash pressure gauge if your car has one. Otherwise, just spin up the pump for at least one full minute so oil will fill all of the little galleries and top up the lifters. Then reinstall the distributor.

Gentlemen, Start Your Engines

Be sure to start your new engine outdoors where there is plenty of ventilation. Carbon monoxide is insidious, odorless, and deadly. I remember a tragic accident that happened locally a couple of years ago where a fellow started his van, which was backed into his attached garage, to warm it up before the

family left for church. Sadly, he left the door to the kitchen open. The fumes filled the house and killed the entire family. It sounds incredible, but it's true. And even if you hook up a hose to the exhaust system to take the gasses outdoors, leaks from manifolds, headers, or mufflers can be deadly.

Make sure you fill the cooling system with the correct coolant and water mixture. Also, make sure your pressure cap is the correct one and in good repair.

This handy device, available from tool stores, makes engine installation easier and safer.

Use a timing light to adjust the timing of your new engine. Move the distributor a few degrees at a time until you get it just right, and then tighten the distributor clamp.

an oil squirt can and a small amount of fuel.

If the engine doesn't start after several revolutions, go around and recheck everything on the checklist earlier in this chapter to make sure you haven't missed anything. You may have forgotten something obvious in your excitement. Once the engine fires, take it slowly up to about 2,000 rpm, and then run it up slowly to 2,500 rpm and back down to 2,000 rpm for about 20 minutes. But don't let the rpm fall below 2,000.

The valvetrain components (cam, lifters, pushrods, and rockers) need to seat and wear in together. If the rpm is left at idle, these parts, as well as the cylinder bores, may not get enough oil to sustain them for these first critical moments. Of course, if there are any strange sounds or roughness, shut the engine off immediately and find the problem. Also, keep an eye out for oil, fuel, and coolant leaks. A helper to cycle the engine while you check these things out is a must.

Hook up a remote starter and an engine tachometer, or have a friend stand by and watch while you start the engine. Electric fuel pumps are nice in this situation because they will fill the float bowl quickly without you having to crank the engine and further discharge the battery. A fresh engine with an empty carb will have to turn over several times to fill the carb float bowl before it will fire. Priming the carb can be dangerous, but if you choose to do so, use

Trapped air in the water jacket can be dangerous, so if your engine took less coolant than is called for, make sure you top up the coolant as soon as possible after the engine gets going. In fact, a good way to avoid this problem is to leave the thermostat out of the engine for the first 20 minutes of running. That way the coolant begins circulating immediately and trapped air can't heat up, cause steam, and damage the engine.

If you spot a leak, slowly lower the rpm to idle, then shut the engine off and make the necessary repairs. Keep an eye on your temperature gauge at all times too. If the needle drifts up very far past normal, ease back on the throttle and shut the engine off. Check to see that your engine still has enough coolant. If the radiator is low on coolant after the engine has been run for a few minutes, it's proba-

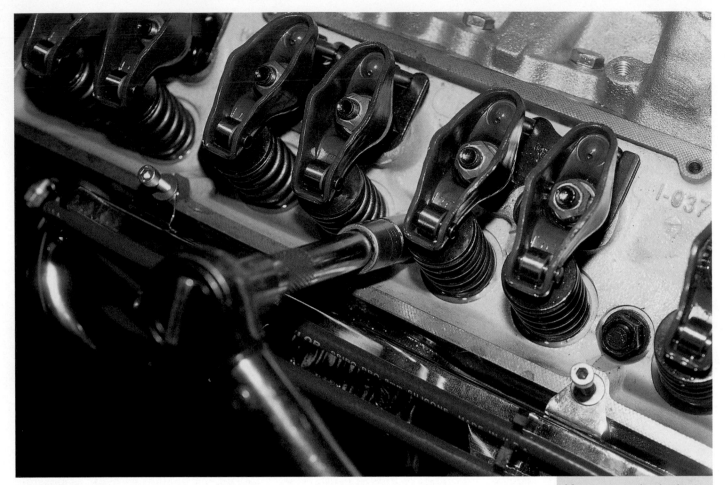

bly because trapped air has finally escaped.

As soon as the engine has warmed up for 20 minutes, fine-tune the timing and the carb. If your engine has mechanical (solid) lifters, adjust them now. Be sure to wear heavy gloves that come up your arms so you won't get burned by hot oil. With mechanical lifters the valves must be hot, with the engine running at a fast idle before you adjust them. Set them to the cam grinder's specs. You will need to adjust them again every 6,000 miles for your engine to run its best.

If your engine has hydraulic lifters, now is the time to fine-tune them too. Just take each adjuster in (or out) until you can barely notice the clicking, take it down to no click, then take it down ½ turn further. No further adjustment should be necessary, but check them every 20,000 miles or every 24 months. Just change your oil regularly and use a good quality of detergent oil to keep the lifters healthy.

Extra Care

If you do not experience any problems, keep your engine between 2,000 and 3,000 rpm for a full 20 minutes, then back the throttle down slowly, and shut it off. Let it cool for an hour or so, then check the torque of the head and manifold bolts. Many of the head gasket makers these days say you need not re-torque the heads, and if that is the case with the head gaskets you purchased, defer to the instructions with the gaskets. I still check

After your engine is thoroughly warmed up, then allowed to cool, re-torque the heads, intake manifold, and headers.

After running in and changing oil, check your oil frequently in the first few thousand miles to make sure you don't have a leak or another problem.

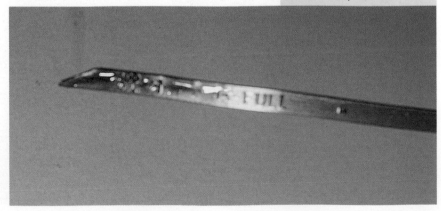

the head and manifold bolt torque just to make sure I didn't get a false torque reading due to a burr or something else during my first reading. I would also recheck these items with the first real oil change. Gaskets can compress with the cycling of hot to cold.

Also, change the oil and take a look at what comes out of the pan. You should see nothing at all in the oil and certainly not feel anything in it. If there are bits you can see, you will certainly want to drop the pan and check the bearings. However, if you cleaned the engine thoroughly before assembly and checked all the clearances, this should not happen.

Shakedown Cruise

If everything checks out and there is no overheating, take your car around the block. Keep an eye on the gauges and listen carefully for untoward noises. When you get back home, check your spark plugs. They should be dry, with a little soot on them. If any are wet with oil or coolant, pull the head and find out why. This would normally be accompanied by steam or blue oil smoke at the tailpipe. If everything functions fine, congratulations!

Routine Maintenance

Be sure to change the oil and filter after 1,000 miles, and don't push the engine while you are letting it settle in. Also, check the coolant, and take another look at the spark plugs.

It is also a good idea to take your car to a shop that has a chassis dyno and let them dial it in and make sure it is in proper tune. Dyno tuning can get the carb mixture and, more important, the ignition advance curve spot-on. And don't forget to keep an eye out for oil and coolant leaks. Chances are you will only need to tighten a bolt or two a little to fix them. Good luck and happy hunting at the bracket races.

Be sure to adjust rockers with the engine running and hot. Hydraulic lifters only require that you take them down until they stop ticking, then 1/2 turn further.

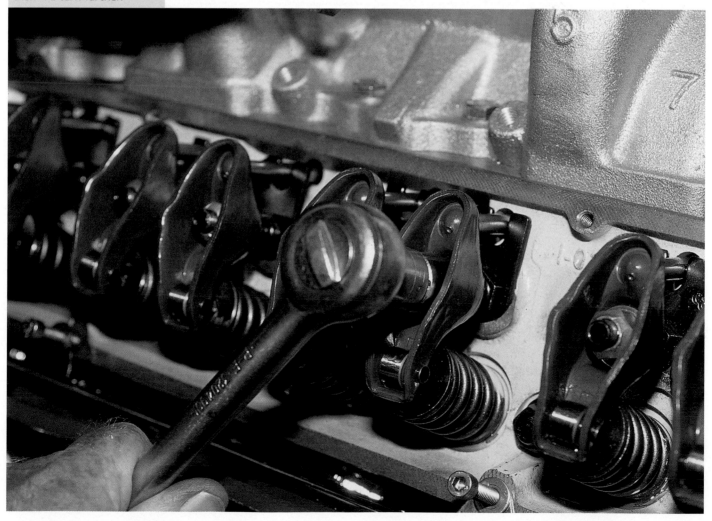

Dynamometer Testing: Give Your Engine A Physical

Jim Richardson

YOU'LL NEED:

- Gasket set
- Torque wrench
- Socket set
- Screwdrivers
- Carburetor parts including jets, metering rods, needles, squirt can of gasoline
- Spark plugs, distributor cap, rotor
- Alternate components such as carbs, manifolds, headers
- Leather welding gloves (for changing hot components)
- Gasket scraper
- Spark plug socket
- Oil and drain pan
- Ear plugs

TIME
6–8 hours
1–2 hours; for chassis dyno

SKILL LEVEL
★☆☆☆

COST
Approximately $450 for engine dyno; $150 for chassis, dyno

APPLICABLE MODELS/YEARS
All

PERFORMANCE GAIN
Optimize your engine's power and driveability

Nine hundred horsepower! That's how much the small block was making on the Vrbancic Brothers' engine dyno. I read the computer myself so I knew it was true. Of course, this engine didn't produce such unbelievable power when they first hooked it up earlier that morning. It took some tweaking and changing out of components to get everything just right. They also fixed a couple of minor oil leaks. But there it was—close to 1,000 horsepower out of a Bow Tie mouse motor.

How about 900+ horsepower out of this normally aspirated Chevy small block? Dyno tuning can help do that.

George at Vrbancic Brothers Racing in Ontario, California, watches the monitor as he runs up the engine.

The engine is set in a test jig and its flywheel is bolted to a device that looks a lot like a pair of heavy-duty torque converters. Attached to them is a torque arm and strain gauge that measures torque. Horsepower is extrapolated from the torque figures. The engine attempts to overcome resistance in the stators. Water under pressure is used to create the resistance. There are also dynos that use your car's engine to drive a big electric generator, but they are less common.

Of course, this monster mill was built for the strip. It would never grace a street machine. And it was well worth the owner's money to have this mighty mouse dialed to perfection because doing so could mean the difference between taking home a trophy and going home broke. But what about the street rodder building a milder motor? Is putting it on an engine dynamometer worth the trouble? The answer is yes. Like many aspects of engine building, if you can afford to get your engine dynoed, it's well worth the $450 a day it costs to have it done.

A Real Eye-Opener

Most people think of engine dynamometer testing solely as a method of establishing horsepower, but it can do much more than that. Putting a fresh engine on a dynamometer before installing it is a prudent safety measure because it allows you to break it in correctly, fix any oil leaks, and most important, get the timing and carburetion set up exactly as they need to be. And yes, you can do all of that with the engine in the car, but it is much more difficult.

Besides, the first few minutes of any engine's life are critical to its longevity.

The guys try some different component combinations and check for oil leaks between pulls.

Lifters can eat up a cam in a hurry if they don't get a healthy oil supply. And poor ignition timing and a lean mixture can damage a piston in no time, if undetected. Lack of oil pressure to bearings and oil leaks from mating surfaces can be dangerous, too, and are hard to spot on an engine installed in a crowded engine bay.

All of these problems are easily remedied on an engine dyno because you can get to everything easily, and you can hook the engine up to sensors that can monitor everything including exhaust gas temperature, rpm, fuel/air mixture, and ignition timing. Lambda (oxygen) sensors can also be tied into primary exhaust tubes and tell you which cylinders are running leaner and hotter. And they can be fitted farther down near the collector tubes to let you know how the engine is performing overall.

Try It, You'll Like It

You can also try various components, such as intake manifolds, carbs, headers, and even camshafts to see which ones perform best for your needs. For example, you can see first-hand what kind of

This is an oxygen sensor. It indicates whether an engine is burning its fuel correctly.

torque and horsepower a dual-plane manifold makes versus a single plane at any given rpm, and what kind of power your engine puts out with tri-Y headers versus four-into-one collectors or stock, cast-iron manifolds.

A day on the dyno will allow you to tune your engine to its utmost before putting it in your car. That way you won't have to wait in long lines to make

If anything, such as an oil leak, shows up on an engine dyno, it's easy to fix.

those runs at the strip and then somehow factor in shifting errors, ambient temperature, cold tires, and all of the other variables that can render your performance figures invalid.

On a dyno, the first moments of life for your new motor will be presided over by trained technicians who have had lots of experience breaking in engines so their cam lobes don't get galled and their lifters damaged. They will also make sure that oil pressure is where it needs to be before they even start the engine, and that the operating temperature is kept within strict parameters once it is running. In the unlikely event that anything breaks on the dyno, it most likely would have broken anyway. Fixing an engine out of the car is much easier than trying to deal with it once it is installed in the chassis.

Then there are the bragging rights. At the end of the day, you'll have a printout proving exactly what your carefully crafted powerplant can produce. And you'll be able to tailor your engine's performance to your particular ride too. When

you set it in the car, you'll know everything is as it should be, and that the engine will perform as you intended it to.

Come Prepared

If you are interested in testing different cams, an engine dyno is really the way to go, because changing cams with the engine in the car is time-consuming and difficult to get right. Of course, you'll be expected to bring along any components you want to try, and you will also need to bring your own tools. It is unprofessional—not to mention uncool—to borrow tools from the dynamometer shop. Besides, when it comes to custom components, the shop is not likely to have them on hand for you to try.

The ultimate setup for tuning is to have a set of headers with an exhaust gas temperature sensor or an oxygen sensor in them as well, unless the dynamometer shop has headers to fit your engine. The Chevy small block is easily the most popular engine to race-tune, so they might just have what you need. Exhaust gas temperature can be important because engines make the most power when running very lean just before they melt down. It is very important that internal temperatures don't get too high, or too low.

It may be possible for your dyno shop to hook up lambda (oxygen) sensors at each exhaust port to really get an accurate picture. These tests aren't critical unless you are a serious racer, because you aren't going to be seeking ragged-edge performance. But if you're the type that likes to take things to the max, this is one good way to do it. For the street, as long as your ignition timing is right all through the advance curve, your carb is set up properly for the secondaries to kick in when they should, and the mixture is optimum through the rpm range, you'll be fine.

Chassis Dynamometers

An engine dyno will tell you what an engine can do in terms of brake horsepower with no accessories hooked up to it. That means no clutch, transmission, driveshaft, or differential. But it won't tell you what your car can do out in the real world because an engine dyno only

Newer chassis dynos can tell you much more, and everything is displayed on a computer monitor or printout.

tests one component. To test what an entire car can do, you need a chassis dynamometer. A session on one of these is less expensive than an engine dyno, depending on how much time you spend on it. The average session runs about $100 plus labor for an hour, and can do many of the things an engine dyno can do.

There are two kinds of horsepower figures commonly quoted. The first is brake horsepower, which is what a totally unfettered engine can produce on an engine dyno, and the second is rear-wheel horsepower, which is less impressive, but more critical to your success on the strip. Accessories such as fans, pulleys, and air-conditioning compressors eat up more horsepower than you might think. And then there is all that heavy driveline to turn in addition to the weight and diameter of your tires and wheels.

Not only can you figure rear-wheel horsepower, but you can easily deter-

A chassis dyno tells you horsepower at the wheels, and that can be a real eye-opener.

Randy at Don and Harold's in Long Beach, California, runs up a 1955 Nomad with a 327 in it for its annual physical.

mine what rpm you'll be turning at your favorite cruising speed if you don't have a tachometer, and even calculate your likely mileage. You can do most of the engine corrections that you can do on an engine dyno, though the corrections may not be as accurate. Of course, fixing

Type of transmission, tire size, and rear-end gears determine rpm at cruising speed.

Here is an old-style chassis dyno. It shows rpm, vacuum, dwell, amps, volts, and exhaust gas composition.

things can be a lot more trouble with the engine in the car.

Chassis dynos are less expensive and more commonly available, so I recommend that if you are building a small block for the street, have the engine checked out before you put your foot in it at the local drag strip. All of those

expensive components and your hard work could come to a tragic end if something isn't right.

Also, if you've built a bottom-end torque engine for a big, heavy car, you will most likely want a differential with slightly taller gears than you would want if you had a high-rpm screamer in it. Gearing is as important to speed as the engine is, and your stock gearing may be all wrong for the engine you've built. Check it out on a chassis dyno.

Larger-than-stock-diameter tires have the same effect as higher gearing; smaller-diameter tires mean that your engine has to spin faster to go the same distance in the same amount of time. Also, fat, heavy tires create more rolling friction and eat up more torque, so you will want to work with various combinations here too. And if you are running an automatic transmission, you will want to establish its stall speed and its shift points. Setting your car up based on data from a chassis dyno can make all the difference to its real-world performance.

Chapter 2
CHASSIS & DRIVELINE

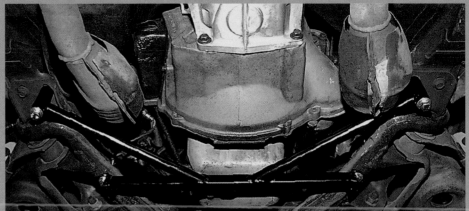

E ven if you've got the ultimate motor, it's not worth much if you can't get that power to the ground effectively. This chapter provides advice for dealing with your transmission and rear end—vital components in any street machine—as well as other chassis tweaks that can help redistribute weight and prepare your chassis for more horsepower.

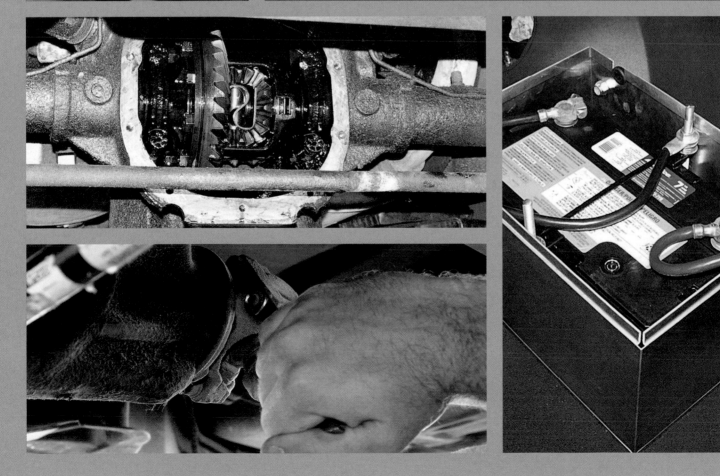

Installing A Strut Tower And g-Load Brace

Huw Evans

YOU'LL NEED:

- Impact gun
- Adjustable torque wrench
- Sockets, drill
- Sharpie marker
- Portable MIG welder
- Strut tower brace
- g-load brace
- Bolts and fasteners

TIME
2 hours

SKILL LEVEL
★★☆☆

COST
$80–$150

APPLICABLE MODELS/YEARS
All 5.0 Mustangs

PERFORMANCE GAIN
Increased chassis strength, better handling, steering response, agility

---

Not as fundamental for chassis stiffness as subframe connectors but still an important piece in the unibody strengthening puzzle are strut tower and g-load braces. These two items become particularly important if you plan on serious corner carving in your 5-liter Mustang, but even on street cars (particularly the 1979–1993 variety), they're worth considering, because they'll help tie the unibody down and make your Mustang handle better in the turns.

Strut Tower Brace

If you own a Fox-body car, the best way to start is with the strut tower brace. On the SN95 cars, Ford has already done half the chassis stiffening for you—among other things, these cars came from the factory with strut braces. Therefore, unless you're planning to build a serious road-race handler from your 1994 or 1995 V-8 Mustang, you don't really need to replace your stock strut brace with an aftermarket one.

The purpose of the strut tower brace is to reduce torsional chassis flex, which it does by joining the shock towers and the firewall. Combined with subframe connectors, the brace will make a noticeable difference in the overall stiffness and driving characteristics of your older Fox 5-liter, especially those convertibles, which have considerable cowl shake from the factory. However, as with many other upgrades for the 5.0, not all strut braces are created equal. When looking to install one, it should have two or more attachment points to the shock towers on

each side and preferably be triangular or trapezoidal, with sizable area where it attaches to the firewall. The larger and more numerous the attachment points, the stiffer the result. Companies such as Eibach, HPM, MAC, Steeda, Saleen, and Jamex all offer good-quality strut tower braces, with the Steeda pieces in particular being popular.

Installing a strut brace is relatively straightforward—it simply bolts up to the shock tower and firewall. Also get a backing plate that attaches between the brace and the firewall, to further increase stiffness (some strut braces, such as HPM's, come with these).

Before you begin the installation, test-fit the brace and backing plate. If your Mustang already has a modified engine with a bigger and taller aftermarket intake, you may face clearance problems with a prefab brace. In this case, it might be best to fabricate your own, in conjunction with an experienced Mustang shop.

If you like going around corners in your Fox Mustang, installing a strut tower brace is a great idea. It will help stiffen the flimsy unibody. Many types of strut braces are available, including chrome ones to complement dressed-up engine bays. Most come supplied with bolts and fittings.

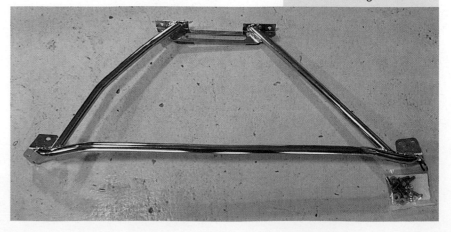

Shown here is a strut brace installed on a 1992 Mustang GT. Even if you drive your car only on the street, the difference in stiffness and handling is quite noticeable. The owner of this car drives it every day and takes it road racing once in a while. *Evan Smith*

If all appears well up to this point, have a colleague hold the brace in position while you mark the attachment points. Next, where you've marked, carefully drill holes for the strut mounting bolts on the firewall and each of the front strut towers. Make sure when you're done that they correspond in size to the bolts themselves. The best way to get an exact result is to trace around the inside of the bolt hole in the brace, set the brace aside, then strike directly in the center of the circle with a punch. This will make an impression to guide your drill bit.

Start with a bit that's smaller than you need and work up gradually to one that's the same diameter as the mounting bolt. Doing it this way allows you several opportunities to check that the hole you're making is dead center on your mark. If it isn't, when you change to the next bigger bit, point it slightly in the direction you need to go to get it back to center.

Most prefab strut braces include all mounting hardware, so in most cases it's

simply a matter of securing the brace and accompanying bolts in place and torquing them to the recommended specifications. It's also a good idea to pinch-weld the attachments at the firewall, to maximize the brace's stiffening ability.

g-Load Brace

A g-load brace, while not as fundamentally important as frame connectors or a strut brace, can still contribute significantly to overall chassis stiffness. In fact, some companies, such as Eibach, often sell this and the strut tower brace together, for maximum effectiveness. Saleen Motorsports coined the term g-load for its own chassis steering brace, though several manufacturers offer comparable products. These braces work by bolting to the two front frame rails, thus reducing the tendency for the rails to deflect inward under hard cornering or braking. They improve steering precision and aid front-end alignment (particularly on the 1979–1993 Mustangs).

These chassis braces fall primarily into two categories: basic metal tubes with twin attachment points at each end, or more complex pieces with angled arms that link up to your Mustang's frame in four locations instead of two. The latter provide bracing over a greater area and are thus more effective.

Installing these will, like the strut brace, be a bolt-on affair, requiring you to drill holes at the attachment points. Therefore, you'll need to test-fit the brace and mark the holes correctly before installation, to prevent poor alignment. Because you'll be working underneath the car, you'll need to put it on a lift or support it on axle stands and remove the front wheels. This will provide much easier access and flexibility when installing the g-load or chassis steering brace. Check fit and alignment of the brace first, then carefully drill the holes for the brace bolts. Make sure you tighten all the fittings correctly. Once you're done, reinstall the two front wheels and carefully lower the car.

Along with a strut brace, installing a chassis steering brace or g-load brace (as it's often referred to in Mustang circles) will help, because it prevents the frame rails from flexing and keeps your car pointed in the direction you want to go. This brace has angled arms in addition to the tubular crossmember, for greater stiffness and improved steering precision. *Evan Smith*

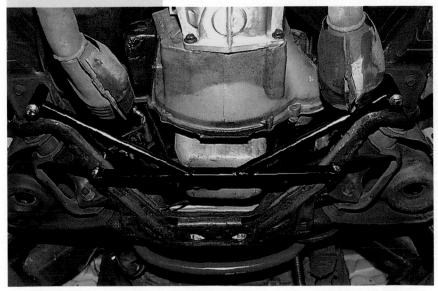

TIP:
Pinch-weld your strut brace at the firewall for best results.

Moving The Battery To The Trunk

Huw Evans

YOU'LL NEED:

- Flat-blade screwdriver
- Phillips-head screwdriver
- Wrench
- Torque wrench
- Sockets
- Battery relocation kit

COMPLEMENTARY PROJECT

Ignition upgrade

TIME
5 hours

SKILL LEVEL
★★☆☆

COST
$200

APPLICABLE MODELS/YEARS
All

PERFORMANCE GAIN
Improved weight distribution, handling, better starting

With the engine mounted almost directly over the front wheels and the vehicle's tendency to understeer if pushed hard through corners, yielding poor traction on all but the driest of pavement, moving weight rearward on almost any muscle car is a great idea. One of the most cost-effective methods is to relocate the battery to the right side of the trunk. Not only does this help redress the balance of weight, it also frees up space in the engine bay, should you wish to install an aftermarket ignition box or hide the underhood wiring for a custom look.

One of the best ways to relocate the battery is to purchase a kit, such as the one from MAD Enterprises. This includes a case for the battery, fasteners and bolts to secure it to the trunk floor, a brace to keep it in place, and special, long positive and negative cables that are routed from the trunk through the floorpan, right to the starter solenoid and motor.

When you perform this task, also consider replacing your battery. The heavy-duty Optima units, with their colorful plastic tops and distinctive spiral cells, provide sealing qualities far greater than most traditional batteries, so they won't leak and contaminate or corrode the inside of the trunk. These batteries are also suitable for high-power engines that place more of a strain on the alternator and electrical system, so they go hand in hand with modified cars.

TIP:

Mount the battery on the right side of the trunk if possible for better weight distribution.

When you're thinking of adding an aftermarket ignition box or installing a supercharger, the battery can get in the way. This is a good time to relocate it to the trunk, which frees up space and improves weight distribution in your nose-heavy car. Mount the battery on the right side of the trunk or hatch for best results.

Installing Steeper Rear-End Gears

Huw Evans

TIME
4 hours

SKILL LEVEL
★★★★

COST
$350

APPLICABLE MODELS/YEARS
Mustangs 1986–1995

PERFORMANCE GAIN
Improved torque multiplication and acceleration

YOU'LL NEED:

- Impact gun
- Adjustable torque wrench
- Sockets
- Screwdriver
- Lithium high-temperature grease
- Special Ford service tool
- Dial indicator
- Shims
- New ring and pinion
- Clutches
- Gear oil
- Differential

During the 5-liter Mustang's long production run, two styles of rear end were employed. In the early days (1979–1985), Ford mated its trusty 7.5-inch solid axle to the rear control arms. Given that the 1979 302 couldn't muster more than 240 ft-lb of torque in stock form, and even the 1983–1985 four-barrel engines made only 245 to 270 ft-lb, this fairly small rear was perfectly adequate. To provide better offline bite, Ford offered 3.08, 3.27, and even 3.45:1 axle ratios (yes, on manual transmissions) and, thankfully, from 1981 a Traction-Lok limited differential. This uses internal gear

Swapping your stock final-drive ratios for a steeper replacement ring and pinion, such as this one from Precision Gear, is one of the best bang-for-the-buck projects you can do on your 5-liter Mustang.

friction to direct more torque to the rear wheel with the most traction, reducing wheelspin and increasing off-the-line bite (just ask anybody who's driven a powerful V-8, rear-drive car with an open diff, particularly in the wet).

For 1986, when Ford switched the 5-liter Mustang to sequential fuel injection, among the parts to be upgraded was the rear end. In place of the old 7.5, FoMoCo substituted the 8.8, also found on its Ranger compact pickup truck. This was distinguished externally by a differential cover that was flat on all sides, whereas the 7.5 was flat only on the top and bottom. The new rear was more than 30 percent stronger than its predecessor, but alas, the final drive ratios were dropped—2.73 and optional 3.08:1 for five-speed cars. Automatics, in part to compensate for the gentle tranny shift calibrations and greater parasitic power loss, got steeper 3.08:1 as standard, with 3.27:1 optional. You can tell what factory gears your Mustang has by looking at the data tag on the driver's door. M identifies 2.73, while Z and E are for 3.08 and 3.27:1, respectively.

The tall 2.73:1 axle ratio found in the majority of stock 5-speed 302 Mustangs is a major Achilles' heel for lightning-quick takeoffs. Just replacing it with steeper axle ratios can make a huge difference in acceleration. However, the 2.73 was chosen largely on the basis of fuel economy and fast highway driving, particularly for law enforcement agencies, which snapped up thousands of 5-liter Fox Mustang coupes in the 1980s and early 1990s.

When considering a gear swap, the general rule is that the higher the numerical ratio, the greater the acceleration but the lower the top speed. More gear is nice, but you need to match it to your engine's operating range and the transmission's gear ratios. While some people say that the shorter the ratio the better, too much can be a pain, especially on a street car. Gearing that's too low causes premature wear on the engine and other driveline components, not to mention making your Mustang a chore to drive, particularly on the highway—no one wants to be cruising at 65 mph with the engine turning at 5,000 rpm.

The aftermarket, including companies like Ford Racing Performance Parts, Precision Gear, Pro 5.0, and Richmond, offers a huge selection of axle ratios—the most common being 3.27, 3.55, 3.73, 4.10, 4.30, and 4.56 through 4.88, and even 5.13:1. For most street-going 5.0s, especially those using essentially stock engines and stock transmission ratios, consider going with a set of 3.55 gears in five-speed cars and 3.73 for automatics, to get the most bang for your buck. This will usually provide the best balance between acceleration, drivability, reliability, and fuel economy. If you plan on going road racing, where higher speeds and aerodynamics are more important than off-the-line grunt, you'll probably want to select ratios between 3.27 and 3.55, because many classes permit limited engine modifications as well.

Many street enthusiasts will step up to 3.73 on stick applications and 4.10 for automatics, but these increase the risk of breakage and are best suited to cars that spend a considerable amount of time at the drag strip, where torque multiplication and quick acceleration are the name of the game, top speed be damned. They're also best suited to cars using power adders or seriously modified high-revving engines, because these steeper ratios can more effectively exploit the engine's power. Many 5-liter pilots have destroyed a sizable number of transmis-

sions (particularly AODs) by putting 4.10 gears in essentially stock Mustangs.

Anything above 4.10 is best left to quarter-mile thrashers. However, if you install a T56 six-speed transmission, you can still technically run 4.10s or 4.88s on the street, though engine longevity on most pushrod 302s and gas mileage will be questionable at best.

Although a rear-end gear swap represents tremendous performance per dollar, especially compared to other mods, it's quite tricky to do right and is best left to a professional shop mechanic who has considerable experience working on rear ends and all the proper tools. Even so, it's worth watching, because it will give you an insight into what goes into this process.

What a Rear Gear Swap Entails

To begin with, a special press is required for installing the bearing on the pinion gear. You'll also need to check the depth of the pinion, using a special Ford service tool for rear ends. If it's not in spec, the pinion will need to be shimmed until it is. Once installed, the pinion will require proper torquing to set preload. Also, clearance between the ring gear and pinion must be precise and should be checked with a dial indicator and adjusted with shims. The clearance, known as backlash, is generally set loose to achieve quiet, smooth gears. Unskillful gear installations will often result in considerable rear-end axle whine and premature

When you pull off the stock differential cover, this is probably what you'll see—the Traction-Lok differential. Because you'll be pulling out the ring and pinion for a gear swap, this is also a good time to check the condition of your Traction-Lok and replace it if necessary.

Many things need to be addressed when doing a rear gear swap, including making sure your speedometer is properly calibrated with the change in final drive ratio. Ford supplies replacement plastic speedo gears, though you need to make sure you select the right ones to correspond with your new rear gears.

wear, in part from too tight a backlash between ring teeth and pinion.

Another thing that goes hand in hand with a gear swap is recalibrating the speedometer gears in the transmission, which requires removing the tranny from the car. The factory plastic speedo gears on five-speed cars can wear out quickly (if your speedometer needle bounces up and down, the gear is probably on its way out). Not only that, correct speedo calibration also requires considerable math, for although Ford supplies replacement speedo gears, you need to work out which one is compatible with your new rear-end ratio.

The speedo gears are housed inside the transmission. Although they're not too tricky to access on stick-shift 5-liters, getting at them requires pulling off the tranny tail shaft. On automatic Mustangs, the drive gears are integrated and machined with the tranny output shaft, so the whole transmission has to be pulled apart to replace them. From this, you can see that a gear swap is not for the fainthearted.

The stock 8.8 rear (you shouldn't use a 7.5 with a modified engine) found in most 5-liter Mustangs isn't bad. From the factory it had 28-spline axles with either four or five (1993 Cobra and 1994–1995 Mustangs) lugs, held in place by C-clips and turned by the fairly reliable Trac-

tion-Lok differential. The differential itself works by pushing side gears and uses layers of clutch packs to engage and turn the axles. When pulled out of the axle housing, the stock Traction-Lok can be identified by the S-shaped spring in the middle section.

When upgrading the rear-end gears, pay special attention to the differential and the axles. Over time, especially if the Mustang is subjected to numerous hard drag launches, the differential clutches can wear out, causing it to slip. If your 5-liter has a generous number of miles under its belt, it would be worth inspecting the Traction-Lok when doing the gears. If you want to replace it, the Auburn High Torque and Torsen Traction-Lok differentials are good, slightly more durable substitutes and support both the factory 28-spline and bigger 31-spline axles.

Speaking of the stock axles, the factory 28-spliners work okay on a stock 5-liter but become susceptible to breakage once you start putting significantly more power to the ground. (Go to a drag racing event and chances are you'll see a street-driven Mustang break one of them.) A cost-effective way to remedy this problem is to install the stouter 31-spline axles from Ford Racing Performance Parts that originally came in Ford trucks.

If you're shooting for the low 12-second zone at the drag strip, you'll have to eschew stock axles, because the C-clips that hold them in place can fail, causing the axles to work their way loose—not something you want while racing down the strip. The most popular solution for drag cars is stronger axles that work with C-clip eliminators, such as those available from Moser. These eliminators feature bearings mounted inside an aluminum case to keep the axles in check, though for regular high-power street cars and road racing, consider stepping up to stronger 9-inch bearings, which can handle both straight line and side loading (the others can handle only drag launches).

Companies like Currie Enterprises, Strange Engineering (and, of course, Moser) are experts in the field of rear ends and will steer you in the right direction when you're looking to upgrade your solid axle.

TIP:
Unless you're really experienced, leave this job to a pro.

Replacing The Universal Joint And Driveshaft/ Installing The Driveshaft Safety Loop

Colin Date

YOU'LL NEED:

- Standard socket set
- Standard wrenches
- Set of heavy-duty performance U-joints
- Driveshaft loop (optional)

TIME
2 hours

SKILL LEVEL
★★☆☆

COST
$50 for new U-joints, $50 for driveshaft loop

APPLICABLE MODELS/YEARS
All

PERFORMANCE GAINS
a stout, rigid drivetrain capable of handling the high-torque loads of performance motors

Driveshafts and their ever-important joints are solely responsible for transferring the power and torque of your engine and transmission to the rear-end unit. Most GM muscle cars have conventional, open-type driveshafts. This means there is a U-joint (universal joint) at each end of the driveshaft assembly. The U-joints allow the driveshaft to move freely up and down to match the travel of the rear end. The forward U-joint connects the shaft to a slip-jointed yoke that slides into the back of the transmission. The inside of this yoke is splined and designed to mate with the splines of the transmission output shaft, creating a smooth, gear-like connection. The rear U-joint is located at the rear drive axle assembly and is held in place by two long, U-shaped bolts. At each end of the joint is a bearing cup or cap that houses the needle bearing internals and grease. The caps are secured by conventional snap rings in the recessed groove of the yoke.

Using both a socket and a boxed wrench, loosen and remove the U-shaped bolts from the joints.

The crossmember mount will serve as the locating point for the new driveshaft loop.

Many novice car crafters fall under the assumption that because U-joints and the driveshaft are integral parts of the driveline, they are difficult to replace and should only be handled by a professional. In reality, universal joint and/or driveshaft replacement is one of the easiest projects you can tackle underneath your car. All you need are some good jack stands, a 1/2-inch socket wrench, and a 1/2-inch boxed wrench.

First and foremost, raise the rear of the car to a suitable working level and support it with a pair of jack stands. Try to pick out the flattest open area in which to do so. Before disassembly, mark the location of the driveshaft in relation to the rear-end yoke to ensure the same positioning during reassembly. Loosen and remove the two nuts from each U-shaped bolt. You may need to lightly tap the U bolts back out of their respective through-holes, as they fit pretty tightly. With the bolts out of the way, the rear universal joint can be removed from the car. If you plan on reusing the same U-joints for whatever reason, tape the bearing caps shut to avoid spilling and losing the needle bearings inside.

At this point, you can slide the driveshaft out the back of the transmission. Place a small container at the front of the yoke to catch any spilled or leaking oil. You can also wrap a plastic bag with a rubber band around the end of the transmission to keep the oil off of the floor. Once the driveshaft is disconnected and out of the car, you can easily remove the front U-joint from the yoke.

Although it is possible to overhaul universal joints, I recommend replacing them. For the relatively low cost of new joints and the ease of removal, it's really a no-brainer. If it's necessary to clamp the assembly down in order to remove or install the joints, secure the ends of the yokes for stabilization. Never clamp the shaft with a vice or any other object that could dent or damage it.

The joints and the shaft will return in reversed order. As long as the driveline components are already removed from the vehicle, consider a driveshaft loop for high-end street use or racing applications. A driveshaft loop is engineered to retain and support the rapidly rotating shaft in the ill event of front U-joint failure. If the rear joint breaks, the shaft will most likely slide out of the transmission and exit the back of the car. However, if the forward U-joint gives way, the front of the shaft will drop, and can very easily stick or plant itself into the pavement. With the rear of the shaft still fixed and mounted to the differential assembly, the likely results can be catastrophic, if not fatal.

Installing a safety loop is relatively simple and only requires two bolts. In fact, you end up using the same two bolt holes in the transmission at the crossmember mount. First, remove the bolts securing the transmission to the crossmember. Using a floor jack, support and slowly raise the transmission just enough to allow ample clearance to slide the mounting plate of the loop between the crossmember and the top of the mount. After the plate is in position and the bolt holes are realigned, insert the new mounting bolts into the mount. The bolts will tie the crossmember, driveshaft loop, and mount to the transmission as one rigid assembly. Contact any aftermarket performance company for the correct driveshaft loop for your vehicle.

Transmission Removal And Replacement

Colin Date

YOU'LL NEED:
- Standard socket set
- Standard wrenches
- Torque wrench
- Torque converter holding tool (optional)
- Floor jack
- Transmission jack (optional)
- Transmission fluid
- Transmission tailshaft plug

TIME
4 hours

SKILL LEVEL
★★★★

COST
$10–$25 for materials/fluids

APPLICABLE MODELS/YEARS
All

PERFORMANCE GAIN
A finely-tuned transmission is a cornerstone of performance

Removing the transmission assembly from any vehicle is a delicate procedure. It requires time, open space, and plenty of patience. Located smack dab between the engine and the rear drivetrain, the transmission and its various counterparts literally serve as the middle man in the forever-valuable transfer of power. Whether you prefer manual domination or the creature comforts of an auto-pilot, the basic principals and operation of the transmission remain constant. The same goes for removing and installing as well. Although there are many modifications to be made on individual components, this project narrows the focus to getting the beast safely in and out of the car.

As covered earlier in the engine removal process, you can make the swap as one complete assembly (engine included) or opt for the transmission alone. It's really just a matter of preference. Regardless, start by disconnecting the negative battery cable from its terminal post. Drain any fluids (e.g., coolant, engine oil, power steering fluid, etc.) from the engine that may result in a spill during the process. Disconnect any and all electrical connectors from the engine/transmission assembly. This may include the engine harness, the neutral-safety and back-up light switches (if applicable), and the throttle valve detent switch. The order and approach may vary slightly from one tranny to another, as GM produced and offered more than a handful of different designs over the years. Continue the disassembly by removing the air cleaner and the throttle linkage cable or rods; you want to create as much room as possible for easier access to other areas. Unbolt the shifter linkage at the steering column and remove any retaining clips (see photo 1). Floor-shift cars will require the removal of the shifter boot and housing, the center console (if so equipped), and the shifter mechanism. On a four-speed, disconnect the Z-bar rods and springs. Be careful—these pieces may still be loaded under high spring pressures.

Before going any further, raise and support the car using a floor jack and a sturdy pair of jack stands. You will need to loosen and remove the lower shifter and/or clutch linkage from the side of the

Release the transmission shifter linkage from the steering column.

Depending on the application, most of the transmission-to-engine mounting bolts can be accessed from the top of the vehicle.

transmission case. Anything that may obstruct a clean removal must go. Keep track of and label all of your hardware, clips, and retainers to make the reassembly a much smoother operation. The speedometer cable and oil cooler lines (if applicable) should be next on the list. The speedometer cable will simply unthread from the case and slide right out. Label the cooler lines for pressure or return and tie them back out of the way. Be prepared for a little oil spill when disconnecting the lines. On some models, it may be necessary to unbolt the exhaust pipe(s) from

the collector for additional clearance. Sometimes, it's easier just to remove the whole system from the collector rearward, including the mufflers. This is especially true when crossover bars or X pipes are implemented midway in the exhaust system. At the rear of the car, unbolt the U-joints and disengage the driveshaft from the transmission tailshaft. Refer to the U-joint/driveshaft removal and replacement project for instructions on the disassembly.

Pulling the transmission out and away from the back of the engine requires the torque converter to be loosened from the crankshaft flexplate. Start by removing the flywheel/torque converter cover at the front of the transmission. You should then have sufficient clearance to access the converter mounting bolts. Remove the converter from the plate and secure it to the body of the transmission. Be sure to mark the orientation of the torque converter in relation to the flexplate for reassembly.

Support the transmission housing with a floor jack and remove the transmission-mount-to-crossmember support bolts. Loosen the bolts securing the crossmember to the frame and slide it toward the rear of the vehicle. With the engine properly supported, the transmission-to-engine/bell housing mounting bolts may now be removed. Manual transmissions may be pulled with or without the bell housing. The case is typically mounted to the housing by four bolts. With the transmission isolated, slowly slide the assembly rearward and lower to the ground.

To install, realign the proper marks and lubricate all bearings and shafts with clean engine oil. Raise the transmission with the floor jack and secure it to the engine block. Reattach the remaining components, linkage, and hardware, and set them to the proper torque values. Refill the transmission case with fresh fluid if necessary.

Loosen and remove the transmission-mount-to-crossmember support bolts (two bolts).

Chapter 3

BRAKES & SUSPENSION

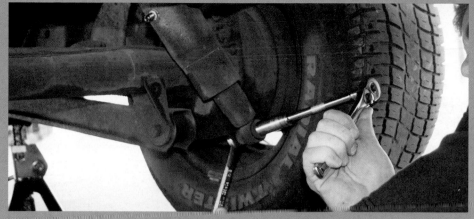

If there's any one area that often needs attention in a muscle car, it's the brakes and suspension. After all, most of these cars were built to go fast in a straight line—not stop fast or handle well. This chapter features projects that will help you remedy this situation.

Replacing Front Brake Pads

Richard Newton

COMPLEMENTARY MODIFICATION:

Flush all the old brake fluid from the system after the new pads have been installed.

YOU'LL NEED:

- ¹/₂-inch metric sockets
- Caliper mounting bolts – 165 foot-pounds

TIME
1 hour

SKILL LEVEL
★★★☆

COST
$75-$150

APPLICABLE MODELS/YEARS
Corvettes 1984-1996; other disk-brake-equipped cars

PERFORMANCE GAIN
Your car will stop faster, and, more importantly, it should stop smoother

You can always pay someone to do this job. But, since it's so easy, you may as well do it yourself. Plus, you can usually do a better job than most shops. Most shops make very little money if they simply replace brake pads. The only way to improve the profit margin on brake work is to complete the job as quickly as possible, or sell you a bunch of extra parts.

Doing a brake job at home is simply a matter of checking everything carefully and taking your time. One thing to remember is that you should only take one side apart at a time. That way, if you get confused, you'll still have a good sample to examine.

Before you start taking your brakes apart, you should decide what brand of brake pad you want to purchase. In order to do this, you'll have to decide what's important to you in a brake pad.

If you only drive your car on the street, your biggest concerns are going to be about brake dust and noise. Almost every brake pad on the market will stop your street-driven car, and most of the major brands come with a lifetime warranty.

When it comes to brake pads, the important thing isn't the composition of the pad, but rather the preparation of the rotor. People seem to forget that stopping involves the brake pad rubbing against the rotor. The rotor and the brake pad are equally vital.

You should make sure you break in your new pads very carefully. Take the car for a drive and get it up to about 40 miles per hour. Then bring the car to a complete stop. Now drive a mile or so and repeat the process. Once you've done this about fifteen times, you've started the bedding process. Now just be careful for the next hundred miles, and you'll have a great set of brakes.

Left: The first thing is to check the condition of the rotors. Don't just replace them. Take a minute and measure them. Notice how I've used the lug nuts to hold the rotor firmly to the hub to measure for rotor warping. The dial gauge should be at a right angle to the hub and near the outer edge. If the dial moves more than 0.006 inches, you should pick up the phone and order new rotors.

Right: Now scrub the rotor with soap and water. This should be done with new brake rotors as well as used ones. You'll need a stiff brush and lots of soapsuds. Finish the cleaning process by spraying down the brake rotor with Brake Clean. After all this effort, you should be able to rub a white paper towel on the rotor surface and not get it dirty.

Now that you've checked for run-out, or warping, you should check for thickness. The brake rotor is really one giant heat sink. If it's too thin, it's not going to pull enough heat away from the pads, and you risk boiling the brake fluid under hard braking. In addition, your caliper pistons will have to extend too far when the brake pads wear. Pay attention to the manufacturer's specifications. The minimum thickness is usually stamped inside the rotor. If you can't find this information, just call your local machine shop, and they will tell you the specification. Take a measurement in several places and compare the numbers you find. If the numbers vary by more than 0.013 inches, buy some new rotors.

You should put a proper finish on both new and used brake rotors with an orbital sander and 100-grit paper. This gives the rotor a non-directional finish. You should sand it until you've removed the usual high spots, especially the areas at the outer edge. There should be a series of little scratches and swirls in the surface of the rotor when you're done.

Another reason for doing this is to ensure you remove all the remnants of the old brake pad material. Your brake rotor is coated with the material from that earlier brake pad. By sanding the rotor, you're ensuring that the new pads make contact with the rotor, not with a surface layer of the old brake pad. A lot of the squealing problems come from the new pad material being exposed to the old pad material.

TIP:

This is an easy task that just requires time and attention to detail. The most important step is preparing the brake rotors for new pads.

Before you put the brake caliper bracket back on the car, clean the area where the caliper slides across the bracket surface. When you push down on the brake pedal, the piston(s) push the brake pad into the rotor. This forces the whole caliper to move toward the center of the car and pull the outer pad against the rotor. Every time you push down on the brake pedal, the caliper moves. Opinions vary on the need of lube on this area of contact. If you use lube, make sure that's it a very high temperature lube designed for the brakes.

Inset: No one ever talks about brake caliper hardware. When you remove your calipers, take time to examine these pins very carefully. If you see any wear, replace them. If you can't remember the last time you replaced these pins, just order a new set when you order your brake pads. I found that the most expensive place to purchase these pins was the local Chevrolet dealer. I actually walked out without my parts because the price was so outrageous. I ended up getting a better deal from Baer Racing. Even with the shipping cost, it was only a fourth of what my local dealer wanted to charge me. When I ordered the pins, I also ordered about a dozen of the little circlips that hold the pins in place. You should use new clips every time you replace the brake pads.

Bleeding And Flushing The Brake System

Richard Newton

YOU'LL NEED:

- Pressure bleeder
- Brake fluid
- Vinyl tubing

These pressure bleeders are available for around fifty dollars. One real advantage is that they use a hand pump to build pressure. This means you don't need to have a compressed air source in your home garage. Secondly, they'll never build enough pressure to damage your hydraulic system. You only need about four to five pounds of compressed air to effectively flush or bleed your brake system. The thing to remember is that you never want to let the tank run dry of brake fluid. Also, when you're done, throw all the unused brake fluid out. Every time you flush the brake system you should start with new cans of fluid. Open cans of brake fluid around the garage do nothing but collect moisture. That's exactly what you're trying to avoid by flushing the brake system.

Although very few people do this, you should be bleeding and flushing the brake system once a year. If you run track events with your car, you should do it before every event.

Your brake fluid actually sucks the moisture out of the air. After a year or two, there's bound to be a pretty high moisture content in your brake fluid. This happens even if you never take the caps off the master cylinder.

Once your fluid gets contaminated with a lot of moisture, you have two problems. First, the water can set up rust problems in your brake system. This is minimized by all the aluminum components in some brake systems, but the problem still exists in the steel brake lines.

The other problem is that water boils at 212 degrees Fahrenheit. That's a pretty common temperature for your brake system. Knowing that my calipers run around 550 degrees at the track, you'll realize that 212 degrees is no big deal. All that moisture in the brake system will turn to steam. As a result, you'll have water vapor, or steam, in your brake lines, which is compressible, unlike the brake fluid.

Bleeding Is NOT Flushing

Flushing your hydraulic system is a little different than simply bleeding the brake system. When you bleed the brake system, you're simply trying to get all the air bubbles out of the system. When you flush the brake system, you're getting rid of all the fluid that's been in the system since the last flush. More accu-

rately, you're replacing the current brake fluid with brand-new, fresh brake fluid. You might think of a brake system flush as being more complete than a simple bleeding of the system.

If you kept on bleeding the hydraulic system even after you had expelled all the air in the system, you would be doing a complete flush of the braking system.

Four Ways To Flush The Brake System

There are four methods of bleeding the brake system. It really doesn't make much difference which one you use since they all accomplish the same thing. It's mostly a matter of which tools you have available and how much time you have.

Pressure Bleeding: With this system, you have a reservoir of brake fluid in a

TIME
1 hour

SKILL LEVEL
★★☆☆

COST
$10-$100

APPLICABLE MODELS/YEARS
Corvettes 1985-1996; other cars with hydraulic brake systems

PERFORMANCE GAIN
You'll improve the braking force and have far less of a chance of experiencing brake pedal fade

COMPLEMENTARY MODIFICATION:

Check your brake pads for wear. You should consider replacing the brake pads anytime they're below half of their original thickness.

pressurized tank. You then place a positive air pressure force on the opposite side of the fluid, forcing it into the brake system, pushing all the old brake fluid out of the system.

Vacuum Bleeding: This is where you fill the reservoir and then apply a vacuum at the caliper bleeder nipple. The vacuum pump pulls the fluid through the system.

Family & Friends Bleeding: This is a system where you recruit a family member or friend who owes you a favor and have them push on the pedal repeatedly until the entire system is bled.

Gravity Bleeding: This is a unique procedure where you simply open all the bleeder screws and let the fluid run out. The key point here is that you never let the master cylinder run dry. A lot of race teams use gravity bleeding when they have completely rebuilt the brake system.

I prefer bleeding the system with the pressure tank because most folks don't really know how to push the brake pedal during the bleeding process.

From The Bleeder To The Bottle

It's really not a good idea to simply let the fluid run all over the shop floor. The

best way to deal with these fluids is to take a couple of feet of vinyl tubing and push one end onto the bleeder screw and place the other end in a bottle. This minimizes the mess on the floor and on the car. Brake fluid is the best paint remover on the market. You don't want it on any painted surfaces unless you intend to strip the paint. There is no such thing as being too careful with brake fluid.

Pushing The Pedal

During normal use, the piston in a master cylinder only goes into the cylinder about one-third of its possible travel. New master cylinders have clean and smooth pistons, but pistons on older master cylinders are dirty and corroded.

As the piston is depressed into the bore of the master cylinder, the seals and fluid help to keep that smaller portion of the piston bore clean, smooth, and well lubricated. The remaining two-thirds of the bore is exposed to dirty brake fluid and doesn't get the benefit of regular cleaning. When your friend or family member depresses the piston during the bleeding process, the cylinder is pushed into this dirty, corroded area and drags across the seals. This is a perfect situation for tearing and nicking the little O-ring seals.

The more dirt or corrosion on the interior of the master cylinder, or the more frequently and vigorously the person pumps the pedal, the worse the damage will be. The net effect is a leaky master cylinder. The best way to prevent this is to place a block of wood under the brake pedal so the person in the seat can never push the brake pedal all the way to the floor.

The person pumping the pedal should do so with slow, even strokes. There is no need to go crazy on the pedal. Over the years, I've seen unskilled people do more damage to master cylinders than to any other item. With this in mind, I prefer a pressure bleeder to any of the other systems.

Vinyl tubing is great for bleeding and flushing brakes. When you insert the other end of the tubing into a bottle, it keeps all the brake fluid off both the car and the garage floor. This also allows you to see any air bubbles that might have been trapped in the brake system. I suggest that you keep flushing fluid through the system until you see new, clean brake fluid coming out of the caliper.

TIP:

This is a necessary task and should be done once a year.

Drum Brake Rebuild

Colin Date

YOU'LL NEED:

- Lug wrench
- Flat-blade screwdriver
- Rubber mallet
- Needle-nose pliers
- Specialty brake tools (recommended)
- Brake shoes
- Drum brake hardware kit

TIME
3 hours (per pair)

SKILL LEVEL
★★★☆

COST
$100

APPLICABLE MODELS/YEARS
All

PERFORMANCE GAIN
Better brakes and increased chances of seeing old age

Let's face it—the brake system is the single most important set of components on your vehicle. Drum brakes are often regarded as safety hazards and marginal performers by street enthusiasts and racers alike. The stopping power and control of a drum fails to meet up to the ever-increasing standard of its favored sibling, the disc. However, with the right selection of quality parts and a little massaging, you can cheaply transform your factory binders into rock-solid performers.

The mechanical principles of drum brakes are fairly basic. The design consists of two brakes shoes mounted on a stationary backing plate. The spring-mounted shoes are positioned inside the drum, which rotates with the wheel assembly. The shoes move toward the drums while braking and maintain proper alignment of the linings and the drums. At the top of the backing plate is the wheel cylinder. When the brakes are deployed, hydraulic pressure forces the actuating links of the wheel cylinder outward and against the top surface of the brake shoes. The tops of the shoes are then forced against the inner linings of the drums, causing the revolution of the wheels to be slowed. When the pressure is released from the brake pedal, the return springs pull the shoes back away from the drums.

To access the drum and brake assemblies, you must first remove the wheel from the hub. Safely raise and support your vehicle with a floor jack and jack stands. Loosen the lug nuts before lifting the tire off the ground. Once the wheel is removed, the drum is fully exposed and can be eliminated. Remove the cotter pin and spindle nut from the front of the hub assembly. It may be necessary to retract the adjuster on the back side of the drum. Remove the plug from the back side of the drum and turn the

Once the tension has been released and the cotter pin and spindle nut removed, simply pull the drum from the hub assembly.

Although a spring puller is highly recommended, the job can be done with a set of needle-nose pliers.

TIP:

When doing your brakes, only disassemble one side at a time. The other side will serve as an accurate point of reference when putting all of the pieces back together.

connect the parking brake cable. By releasing the primary hold-down pin and spring, you can extract the leading shoe. Check the condition of the seals on the wheel cylinders for any leaks or cracks and replace if necessary. Inspect the wheel bearings, wheel seals, and hydraulic brake hoses too.

The reinstallation requires only a few special details. Lightly lubricate the backing plate contact points before positioning the new shoes. Be sure the right- and left-hand adjusting screws are not mixed up during the process. Focus on one side at a time, using the opposite side as a visual reference. When installed correctly, the star-wheel adjuster should be closest to the secondary shoe. When complete, properly adjust the drum brakes and bleed them if necessary.

adjuster with a small flat-blade screwdriver to release any excess tension between the shoes and the inner linings of the drums. Using a rubber mallet, tap the rear edge of the drum forward over the wheel studs. Inspect each drum closely for any cracks, scores, or grooves in the surface. If the unit is cracked, replace it. Deep scores and grooves can be handled by any automotive machine shop on a lathe. If the damage is minimal, try using some fine emery cloth to smooth out the roughness or burrs.

Before digging into the mess, spray the shoes, springs, and hardware down with brake cleaner. Do *not* use compressed air—brake shoes contain cancer-causing asbestos. One at a time, remove the springs, screws, pins, and levers from the inner brake assembly. Specialty tools are readily available at any parts counter to make this chore a little easier. When approaching the shoes, notice the difference in size of the primary and secondary linings. The primary (leading) shoe has a shorter lining than the secondary (trailing) shoe and is mounted to the front of the wheel.

To remove the shoes, pull back on the secondary lining and disengage the parking brake strut and strut spring (rear drum brakes). Remove the shoe and dis-

To adjust the drums, remove the rubber plug from the adjusting slot on the backing plate. Insert a brake adjusting spoon into the slot and engage the lowest possible tooth on the star wheel. Lower the spoon to move the star wheel upward and to extend the adjusting screw. Continue this movement until the brakes lock, preventing the wheels from turning. Using a small screwdriver, push and hold the adjuster lever away from the star wheel. Now engage the topmost tooth on the star wheel with the spoon and begin backing off the tension until the tire and wheel spin freely with a minimum of drag. Keep track of the number of turns the star wheel is backed off to create an even balance between both sides. Perform this method of adjusting the brakes while the car is supported on jack stands and the wheel is installed.

In addition to the drums and brake shoes, rebuild kits are often sold and installed to enhance the performance of tired drum brakes. The kits typically include all of the springs, screws, pins, and miscellaneous hardware needed for the job.

Installing A Front Sway Bar

Colin Date

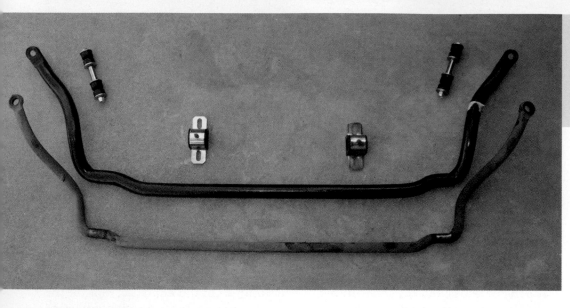

When upgrading or increasing the size of your sway bar, you must also buy a pair of matching bushings (1¼-inch versus ⅞-inch stock in this case). We decided to replace the end links with a quality polyurethane set as well.

Many factors contribute to creating a well-balanced and tuned suspension system. From braking, cornering, and steering to tire traction and various weight transfers, the highly detailed equation of suspensions can be overwhelming and often leaves us in the dirt.

Traction is at the top of the list in any application. Whether you rely solely on the bite of the rear meats for quick quarter-mile action or the four-wheel gripping force in heavy side-to-side cornering, the traction of the tires ultimately determines how your car handles. You can invest thousands of hard-earned dollars into expensive handling components, but if the car will not hook on the pavement, what good is it really doing?

Most of these cars were factory-equipped with a fairly marginal suspension system. Although well-designed and durable, they were not built with high-performance handling in mind. Even when new, they pale in comparison to the standards of performance and safety that we know today, leaving us plenty of room for improvement.

Enter the front anti-roll bar. The primary function of the front sway bar is to limit and control the side-to-side body roll of the vehicle. Attached to both the frame and the lower control arms, the sway bar rigidly ties both sides of the suspension together, naturally decreasing its flexibility. In addition, it contributes to balancing the rolling front-to-rear weight transfer.

Most GM A-body cars were shipped with a stock ⅞-inch sway bar. Considering the sheer size and weight of these machines, the pencil-thin bars and their rubber bushings (see photo above) have seen more than their share of stress and abuse over the years. Constant flexure, road grime and debris, and extreme temperatures all play a part in the deterioration of these pieces.

With so many aftermarket suspension companies now offering complete upgrade kits for almost every GM product, the process of beefing up your existing front end is relatively painless. We decided to swap out the stock sway bar with a monster 1¼-inch bar and matching polyurethane bushings. For an extra

---

TIME
1 hour

SKILL LEVEL
★★☆☆

COST
$125

APPLICABLE MODELS/YEARS
All

PERFORMANCE GAIN
A tighter, better-handling front end and longer lasting components

---

YOU'LL NEED:

- Standard socket set
- Standard wrenches
- Lubrication grease
- Front sway bar
- New sway bar bushings

The end links slide up from the bottom side of the lower control arm. The sway bar is sandwiched between a series of bushings and washers on the top side and is secured with a single nut.

$20, we also replaced the sway bar end links.

Starting with the front end in the air, loosen and remove the end link bolts and bushings. Note the proper sequence of bushings and washers to help during the reassembly. With the end links gone, unbolt the brackets from the frame. At this point, the sway bar should literally drop down into your hands.

After loosely fitting the sway bar into place at the control arms, tighten the sway bar brackets to secure the bar to the frame. Thoroughly grease the insides of the bushings prior to installation.

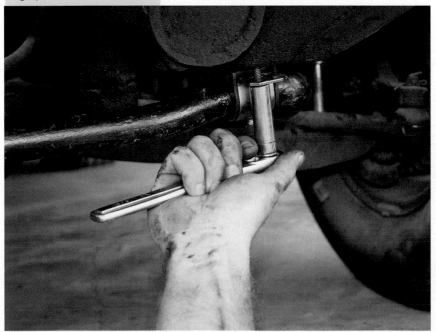

The install is just as easy. Be sure to apply plenty of grease to the bushings before installing them on the bar. Slide the new end links through the bottom of the lower control arms, followed by the nut on top. Attach the sway bar brackets to the frame and loosely snug them down, allowing for slight adjustments before final tightening.

You'll immediately notice results from upgrading the front sway bar and bushings. A positive, more responsive front end will increase the overall handling and performance of your vehicle without question. Furthermore, polyurethane bushings will far outlast their rubber counterparts and will help reduce suspension deflection. Changing the diameter of your front sway bar is one of the most dramatic changes you can make in your front-end suspension.

TIP:

Before removing anything from the car, take note of the sequence of the bushings in relation to the lower control arm and the sway bar.

Installing A Rear Sway Bar

Colin Date

TIME
30 minutes

SKILL LEVEL
★★☆☆

COST
$100

APPLICABLE MODELS/YEARS
All

PERFORMANCE GAINS
A solid, well-planted rear suspension that works in unison with your front-end components

The rear sway bar is an often-overlooked piece of the rear suspension. Most of these cars were built and sold sans rear anti-roll bar. Back in those days, only the special high-performance vehicles were granted rear reinforcements. Even a large number of Chevrolet's factory Super Sports did not have a rear sway bar. The reason? The factory was mainly interested in production and keeping all costs as low as possible. Since many General Motors manufacturers shared the same or similar platforms (and parts), it made more sense to utilize the parts available from each other than to make each rear-end assembly different. And as we all know, the vast majority of assembly-line cars at the time were not performance vehicles. Truth be told, most car buyers were not interested in the performance arena or plainly could not afford it.

And what am I getting at? When used in any high-performance application, the poor geometry and flexibility of the stock rear suspension needs work. In addition to control arms and bushings, the rear sway bar is one of the first improvements that comes to mind and one of the easiest.

If your car was not originally equipped with a rear sway bar, chances are you will need to drill two holes in the sides of your existing lower control arms to mount the bar. Making sure you have marked the arms to be drilled evenly and symmetrically is key. If your measurements are even slightly out of whack, it can hurt your car's performance. Don't take any chances—double-check your work.

The easiest way to obtain the correct placement of the sway bar mounting holes is to measure a pair of pre-drilled factory lower control arms. If you are unable to use a factory template, carefully measure the distance from the forward end of the control arm to the location of the sway bar. Have a friend or two help you out with the mockup. Once its position is determined, remove the arms from the vehicle and place them on the workbench. Scribe a mark in the same location on each arm, representing the sway bar. Transfer the hole

Most aftermarket rear sway bars complete with mounting hardware sell for around $100. This is one of the best nominal investments you can make for your car's suspension and handling capabilities.

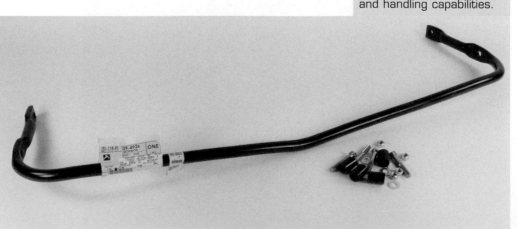

In this photo, we show the sway bar bolting right up to a fully boxed control arm. If you use a stock (unboxed) control arm, the supplied spacers will fit right inside the arm, adding strength and rigidity.

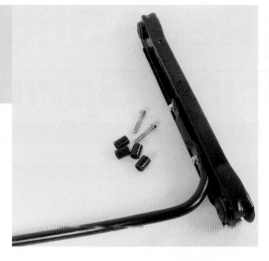

pattern of the sway bar to each control arm. Now, you are ready to drill.

The sway bar mounting kit comes complete with hardware and spacers for non-boxed control arms. The bolts supplied are 3/8 inch–16 (thread count), so make your holes accordingly. If at all possible, use a drill press to punch out the control arms. Your holes will come out clean and straight every time. If not, use a hefty power drill and be careful. When

drilling larger diameter holes, always use a center punch and a smaller pilot drill bit before reaming the final size. This will keep the larger drill bit from "walking" out of position on the surface and throwing off your placement.

Now, we are ready for the install. With the lower control arms bolted back in place, lift the sway bar to meet its newfound mounting holes. Just to be safe, install the bolts and washers through the sway bar first. If anything crazy ever happened and the bolt fell out, this would keep it from getting caught in the rear wheel. The spacers that come in the mounting kit actually belong inside the lower control arm (see top photo) to prevent excess load or stress on the sidewall of the arm while tightening the nuts and bolts.

While holding the nut in place on the back side with a wrench, crank the socket down on the bolt head to securely tighten.

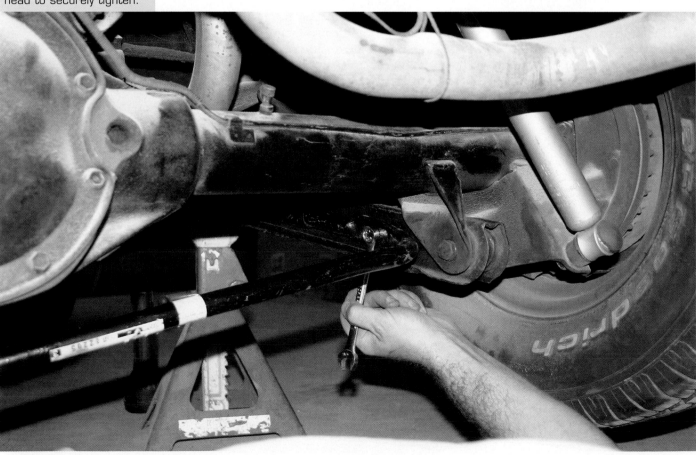

Installing Rear Shocks And Lowering Springs

Colin Date

YOU'LL NEED:

- Standard socket set
- Standard wrenches
- Floor jack
- Jack stands
- One pair of rear lowering springs
- One pair of matching shock absorbers

TIME
2 hours

SKILL LEVEL
★★☆☆

COST
$200–$250

APPLICABLE MODELS/YEARS
All

PERFORMANCE GAINS
A more positive, responsive rear suspension with improved handling and a smoother ride

The rear suspension design on any older car with coil springs is about as basic as it can get. It consists of two upper and two lower control arms, a pair of coil springs, and a couple of shock absorbers. The rear springs are located between brackets on the axle tube and the spring seats in the frame. Sitting in a saucer-type seat, the springs are held in place merely by the weight of the car. The rear shocks, which also aid in spring retention, are mounted at a slight angle between the spring seat (top) and the axle housing (bottom). Depending on the year of the vehicle, the shock absorbers are either both mounted behind the axle housing (pre-1968) or in a staggered configuration (1968 and newer). The staggered configuration cuts down on excess wheel hop and further improves the car's rear-end traction.

If you own and actually drive one of these cars on a regular basis, you know full well what a 35-year-old stock suspension feels and handles like. Although the longevity and sheer toughness of this caveman design is impressive, it leaves a little to be desired. Years and years of speed bumps, potholes, and not-so-delicate cargo have taken a hammering toll on your rear springs and shocks absorbers.

In any high-performance car, whether for the street or the strip, the suspension plays a prominent role in determining its physical capabilities. For example, a rear drag-car suspension is set up to take the initial and sudden weight transfer from the front, plant the rear end and the tires, and steer the car down the track in a rigid, straight line. A canyon-carving street car is designed to do the exact opposite. It relies heavily on tuned suspension systems for extreme side-to-side cornering, braking, and acceleration. No matter what your drive, it's important to lay down a solid foundation.

With the car securely supported on jack stands, remove the lower shock absorber nut and mounting stud.

As you can see, the old springs and shocks were long overdue for replacement. The Gabriel Hi-Jackers (the rear shock of choice throughout the 1970s) were completely collapsed and offered zero support in dampening the rear-end travel. We decided on a pair of KYB GR-2 gas shocks to fix the problem.

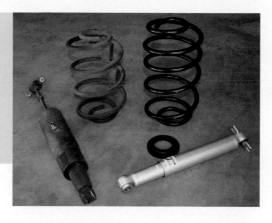

Left: By removing the shock absorber and allowing the axle tube to drop, you should have plenty of room to place the new spring into position by hand. (Note the rubber insulator at the top of the spring.)

Right: When reinstalling the shocks, start at the top and loosely secure the nuts to allow for any angle adjustment on the bottom.

We'll start by swapping out the old, dilapidated springs and now-useless shocks and replacing them with a new set of lowering springs and gas shocks. Get the rear of the car up in the air and secured on a pair of jack stands. Place the floor jack underneath the axle for support and disconnect the shock absorber (lower first, then upper). With the shock removed, slowly lower the jack and allow the axle to drop. By releasing the load, the rear springs should be free of all tension. Carefully pry the lower end of the spring over the retainer and remove. If the springs are still loaded after lowering the axle, a spring compressor should be used to safely remove them from their seats.

When installing new springs—either stock or lowered—don't be fooled by the height of the new springs compared to your old ones. The true difference lies in the spring rate. It's impossible to tell how the car will sit with any pair of coil springs simply by looking at them. If they truly appear suspect, call the man-

ufacturer and double-check the part number before scuffing them up and installing them.

Most cars came equipped from the factory with rear spring insulation pads. These small rubber pads are installed between the top of the spring and its upper retainer to avoid rubbing or excess noise. The new springs may take a little extra muscle to place, but they should basically go in the same way the old ones came out. Make sure the entire diameter of the bottom coil is fully seated in its groove.

The new shocks are now ready to be installed. Starting at the top mounting location, secure (hand tighten) the upper end of the absorber to the spring seat (two bolts). Again utilizing the floor jack, support and raise the axle to meet the lower mounting stud of the shock absorber and loosely install the nut. Return to the top and tighten; then tighten the lower.

With the car back on the ground, forcefully bounce the rear end and check for any signs of leakage or geometry problems. New springs need time to settle in place and find their home in the seats. So hit the road, and enjoy the ride.

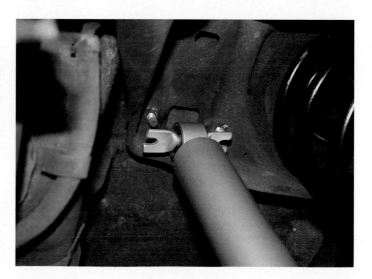

Chapter 4

ENGINE
UPGRADES

This chapter covers all those bolt-on additions and maintenance tasks that can help make more power or increase your engine's reliability. Everything from your carburetor selection and maintenance, to exhaust upgrades, to nitrous kit installation, is covered here. You'll also discover solutions for your ignition, cooling and fuel delivery systems.

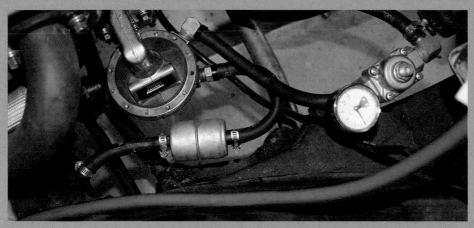

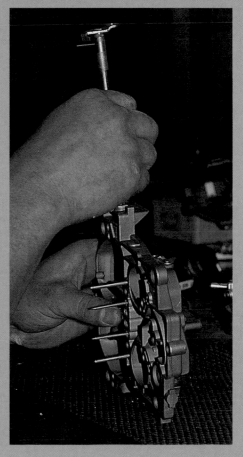

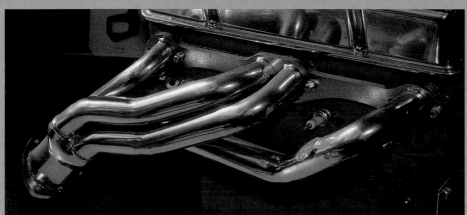

Installing A New Intake Manifold

Colin Date

YOU'LL NEED:
- Standard socket set
- Standard wrenches
- Flat-blade and/or Phillips screwdriver
- Putty knife or scraper
- Torque wrench
- Aftermarket aluminum intake manifold
- High-performance intake gaskets
- Gasket sealer

TIME
3 hours

SKILL LEVEL
★★☆☆

COST
$100–$300

APPLICABLE MODELS/YEARS
All

PERFORMANCE GAIN
A cooler, higher-flowing intake charge; aluminum manifolds typically drop 25 pounds off the weight of your engine

Swapping in an aftermarket aluminum intake manifold is one of the most popular engine upgrades of all time. It's easy, it's cheap, and the bottom line is it works. Not only does aluminum dissipate heat faster and more efficiently than cast iron, it will also save you about 25 pounds of dead weight. The new aftermarket manifolds have an improved plenum design and will far outflow a factory cast-iron piece. In fact, most are dyno-tested and proven to yield power and torque increases throughout the entire powerband.

With any manifold swap, the first order of business is to remove all the attaching components—the carburetor, distributor, and thermostat housing. Note: Be sure to fully drain the cooling system before disconnecting the upper radiator hose. The proper procedures for removal of these items can be found elsewhere in this book.

Working in a zigzag fashion, loosen and remove all the bolts securing the manifold to the engine block. The number of bolts varies depending on the size and make of your engine. Using a long

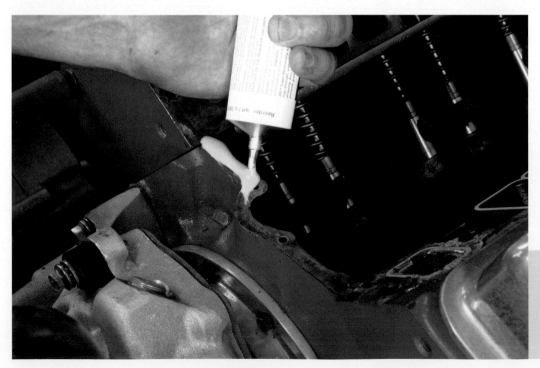

To bridge the gap between each intake gasket, lay down a thick, even bead of sealer across the block. Caution: If too much is applied, the excess may fall down inside the lifter valley when compressed.

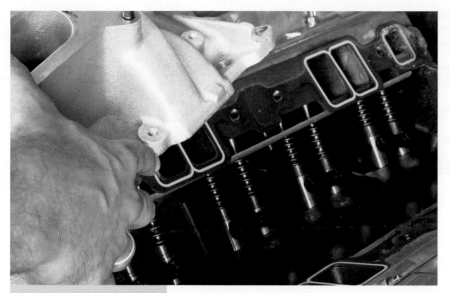

With the intake gaskets lightly tacked in place, carefully lower the manifold into position.

screwdriver or pry bar, gently lift up on the edges of the manifold. A little leverage should break the bond between the two pieces. You may need to unbolt the valve covers for adequate clearance and to keep from damaging them when prying up the manifold.

Before removing the old gaskets and silicon, lay a clean towel in the lifter valley to prevent any debris or contaminants from entering the engine. Use rags to plug the intake ports in the cylinder heads as well. With a small putty knife or scraper, remove the old gasket material from the mating surfaces of the head and the block. Follow up by thoroughly wiping down the areas with an industrial stripper or cleaner. This is a crucial step in ensuring a lasting, leak-free seal. All

bolt holes should be inspected and properly cleaned out with a tap if needed.

When installing, first apply a thin coat of gasket sealer to the back sides of the manifold gaskets and place them on the cylinder heads. This will keep them from walking around and sliding out of position when dropping the manifold into place. Using quality oil-resistant silicon, apply a thick bead of sealer across the front and back of the engine block. (Most intake manifold gasket kits include formed-rubber end seals for this purpose. However, they are terrible in sealing the manifold and should be discarded.) Be careful not to use too much silicon in any one area. When the manifold is installed and tightened down, the excess sealer can fall down inside the lifter valley and harden, leading to serious blockage and interference problems in the engine block.

With the gaskets and sealer in place, carefully lower the manifold into position. Apply a fair amount of thread sealer to the intake bolts and snug them down by hand. Depending on manifold selection, it may be necessary to purchase a longer set of mounting bolts. I recommend using ARP's line of stainless-steel bolts and hardware for just about any job. They are strong, durable, and provide the perfect finishing touch for any fresh engine rebuild.

Last but definitely not least is the final tightening of the manifold bolts. Using a standard foot-pound torque wrench, start at the center of the intake and work your way to each end in a cross pattern. To prevent warping or cracking the manifold, work in gradual steps with the torque wrench. For example, if your final torque specification is 20 ft-lb, torque all of the bolts first to 10 ft-lb, then 15 ft-lb, and finally 20 ft-lb. It's a good idea to check them once more after running the car and allowing the manifold to heat up.

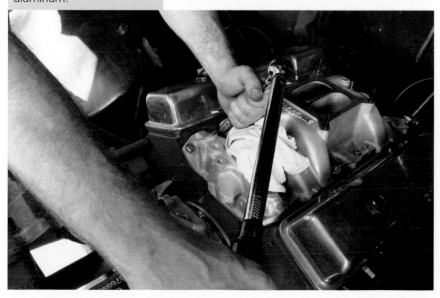

Torque the manifold down to manufacturer's specs, which will change depending on the material used—cast iron versus aluminum.

Throttle Body Cleaning

Richard Newton

COMPLEMENTARY MODIFICATION:
Replace the air filter when you're done with the cleaning.

TIME
30 minutes to several hours

SKILL LEVEL
★★☆☆

COST
$40

APPLICABLE MODELS/YEARS
Corvettes 1985-1996

PERFORMANCE GAIN
You should notice an improvement in the idle quality

YOU'LL NEED:
- Screwdrivers
- Metric sockets
- Metric open-end wrenches
- Throttle body to plenum – 18 foot-pounds

We never really think about the throttle body much. We can't even see a problem about to happen unless we start taking things off the car. We just assume all the air gets to the combustion chamber. We know it has to get through the air filter, but we never think too much about the throttle body. Still, this throttle body gets just as dirty as the old carbs used to get. The throttle body on your Corvette can really benefit from a good annual cleaning.

One thing you need to remember about the throttle body is that it's a system for controlling dry air. Keep in mind where your fuel injectors are located. Until the air reaches the fuel injectors you simply have a dry air passage. Those of us raised with carburetors have a tendency to forget that very simple fact.

The other thing to keep in mind is that these throttle bodies have been around since the 1985 Corvette. That means some of them are simply worn out. It also means that some of them are incredibly dirty. This filth can cause a variety of problems, the most common being a fairly high or erratic idle speed. This happens because the vacuum can't completely close the throttle plates. The throttle plates are normally drawn shut with engine vacuum. If the plates remain slightly open, you'll have a higher idle speed.

We're going to deal with several types of cleaning here. The best way is to simply keep everything clean on a regular basis. The process is so easy you could probably do it on a bi-monthly basis. It's just a matter of removing the air intake assembly and spraying some air intake cleaner on the throttle plates.

A lot of us bought our cars on the used market. The only thing we could afford was a high-mileage Corvette with an unknown maintenance history. These

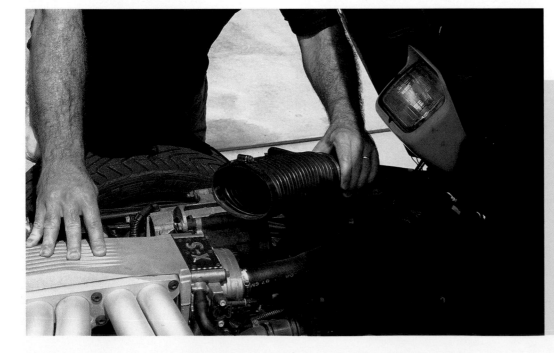

The first step is to remove the intake hose that runs between the Mass Airflow sensor, or MAF, and the throttle body. Now you can get a good look at the amount of dirt in your throttle body. If there's very little dirt, a simple cleaning with an air intake cleaner will get the job done. Remember, though, that most of the buildup will be behind the throttle plates. You have to open the throttle plates to see what the back side looks like to make a true determination on the condition of your throttle body.

If your throttle body hasn't been cleaned in the last decade, it's a good idea to remove the entire assembly from the car. When you do this, you can get the rear half of the intake areas really clean. The first step is to remove the throttle linkage from the throttle body. This linkage is held together by a couple of small clips. You don't have to worry about anything special at this point.

Don't expect the throttle body to simply fall off easily. You might have to tap it with a small rubber mallet. Resist any temptation you might have to pry it off with a screwdriver. Any gouges in the surface will cause a major air leak when you put things back together. Remember, aluminum is a very soft material.

TIP:

A new 52mm throttle body is an option if you've made any other improvements to the intake system. If you have a stock intake system, it's best to stay with a stock throttle body.

Corvettes are usually candidates for a major throttle body service. This means taking the throttle body completely off the car. It also means cleaning the Idle Air Control, or IAC.

Removing the throttle body from the car will also require that you drain some coolant from the radiator since you're going to have to remove the coolant hoses at the lower part of the throttle body. If you live in Florida or California, you might just plug them or buy the little kit that was designed for this purpose. If you live in Minnesota or Michigan, you better hook them back up when you

place the throttle body back on the plenum. This heated water really is important in a cold climate.

If you own a late model C4 Corvette, you can probably skip the removal step. If you aren't experiencing any problems, just clean the throttle plates from the outside with some air intake cleaner. Don't get too carried away with the cleaner since most of it will puddle on the floor of your plenum. It won't harm anything, but it won't do any good either. If a simple spray doesn't clean the throttle plates, try using a toothbrush on the plates.

Here we can see how black the rear part of the throttle body has become. There are times when the buildup is so bad that the entire unit has to be submerged in solvent for a day or so. These cases are unusual, but possible – especially if your old Corvette has not been properly maintained.

The best way to clean the unit is to spray it down with the Wynn's Air Intake Cleaner and then use a toothbrush to scrub the area. Don't use anything stiffer than a toothbrush for this job because you don't want to scratch any of the aluminum. A couple of scratches here, and you could find yourself looking at a new throttle body. If the residue won't come off with solvent and a toothbrush, let it sit overnight.

Carburetors: High Aspirations

Jim Richardson

Probably the most poorly understood aspect of engine tuning is the carburetor. Many novice street rodders think that the bigger their carburetor is, the better their engine will perform. Not true. In fact, the most common reason for customer unhappiness with high-performance carbs can be traced to overcarburetion.

People often buy a big 850-cfm carb when 600–750 cfm is ideal for their engine. Then when they install it and put their foot in it, their engine stumbles and sags before finally coming to life. They return the carb thinking it's faulty, when in fact it is their thinking that is faulty. The problem is that the big carb gets a

weak signal because of the lack of air velocity—it doesn't come on when it needs to for good midrange acceleration.

You see, a carburetor's job is to vaporize gasoline and mix it with air. Bigger carbs can mix more fuel into more air, but that is only useful if you have a bigger engine. Actually, for routine driving with a stock Chevy small block up to about 3,500 rpm, a stock two-barrel works fine.

It's only when you jump on the gas and take the rpm up past where most people routinely drive that two more throats will do you some good. In fact, if your carburetor is too big, your engine will not get enough fuel at low rpm

Think three carbs are better than one? Not necessarily. The linkage is more complex, and a properly sized four-barrel will work better for most street applications.

starve for air. Coming up with a good compromise between low-end oomph and high-end horsepower is the key to a great street rod engine, and it's actually harder to accomplish than setting up a constant throttle racer. So how do you determine which carburetor your small block needs? It's simple. We'll get to that in a minute, but first, let's look at how a carburetor works:

A tunnel-ram manifold looks dramatic and smooths airflow while maintaining velocity, but it's definitely not for the street because of its limited power range.

because of inadequate air velocity. When you install a jug the size of a hot tub on your small block, air can take its time getting to where it is going, so the drop in pressure from piston suction isn't enough to pull much fuel into the slow air stream of a too-large carb.

In fact, a small carb gives great performance until the engine gets up into the higher-rev ranges, where it will then

Deep Breathing

Did you ever fool around with your mother's old-fashioned squeeze-bulb perfume sprayers when you were a kid? Well, they are nothing more than a primitive type of carburetor. Perfume sprayers and carburetors both take advantage of the Bernoulli effect. Daniel Bernoulli was an eighteenth-century Swiss mathematician who was probably goofing around

HOW MUCH IS ENOUGH?

Use this formula to determine what size carburetor your small block needs:

Engine size in cubic inches x maximum rpm/3456=cfm

This formula assumes 100 percent volumetric efficiency. Most street rod engines will be running around 85–90 percent volumetric efficiency, so the formula provides a more than adequate size of carburetor.

with his own mother's spray bottles when he came up with his principle. What he found out was this: As the velocity of a liquid or gas increases, its pressure decreases.

That's why air sucked at high speed past a fuel tube inserted into the side of an air horn will draw the fuel out into the rushing air. And this effect can be increased dramatically by narrowing the air inlet just at the point where the fuel tube enters it.

That's called the Venturi effect and it's named after an Italian physicist who first figured out this little trick a couple hundred years ago. When you narrow the tube, the incoming air must speed up to get through the narrow spot, where it loses more pressure, thus creating an even greater pull on the fuel tube.

Of course, there is a lot more to a modern carburetor than just the Venturi effect, but it almost all works on the same principle. For instance, there is an accelerator pump that shoots extra fuel into the carb when you tromp on the gas suddenly, and there is a choke to increase the air vacuum and draw out a rich fuel mixture for cold starts, and then there are jets that determine how much fuel is released into the air through the carb.

In addition, there are float bowls (that operate much like toilet tanks) that provide your carb with an adequate fuel supply at all times. And there is a needle valve that shuts the fuel off when the float bowl is full. Each of these systems is simple enough in itself, but when you put them all together, the result is several hundred small parts that add up to a fairly complex device.

If you decide you want to rebuild or custom-tailor your own carburetor, even though you'll find some of the basics in this chapter, I strongly recommend that you pick up a book on your particular brand and model of carb and study it before you start tinkering.

And if you can afford it and want the ultimate in performance, I recommend sending even a new carb to a place like the Carb Shop in Ontario, California, to have them adapt it and jet it to your engine's needs. They build carbs for winning race cars and will put your carb on a Dyno to make sure it will do what it is supposed to do before they send it back to you. It is important that you provide them with all pertinent information such as engine size, cam duration, and header type, plus what kind of car the engine will be going into, and what kind of racing you might want to try.

Holley

Rochester Quadra-Jets, Carter AFBs, and Holley four-barrel carburetors will all give good performance, but the easiest carbs to set up are Holleys. And you can buy them in just about any cubic-foot-per-minute (cfm) rating, so you can

On most Holley four-barrels you can check the float level through the sight glass without removing the float bowl cover.

If you need to change the float level, you can adjust it right on top of the carb.

Idle mixture screws are conveniently located so you can get at them without contorting yourself.

have exactly what you need for your application. They are inexpensive when compared with the new knock-offs of the old Quadra-Jets and Carters being sold under other names and will provide equal or better performance. And Holley sells literally everything you might need or want to tune your carb yourself.

Because Holleys are modular and because they have been designed to be easily custom tuned, they are certainly the best choice for the novice street rodder. You can determine the float level in a

Holley just by using the sight glass in the side of the float bowl, and you can make any necessary adjustments without even removing the float bowl cover. You can also easily get at the jets and the accelerator pump(s). Every new Holley also comes with the springs and other items you need to fine-tune it.

If you want great out-of-the box street performance with no fuss, I recommend a four-barrel Holley matched to your engine (according to the formula on page 136), and a Holley Weiand dual-plane intake manifold to go under it. The Holley company has been around for as long as the automobile, and has been making racing carbs longer than anyone, so you can take advantage of their millions of dollars and thousands of hours of research. And you can rely on their quality because each carb is tested and tuned before the company sends it out the door.

Rochester Quadra-Jet

The old Rochester Quadra-Jet was superbly engineered and is one of the best small-block carbs ever. They flow 750–800 cfm in stock form and can be set up for just about any street or strip application. The only problem is that they don't make them anymore. And yes, new Quadra-Jet knock-offs are available, but they are expensive. You can have the same thing for less by buying a reworked Rochester

Everything you need to install and tailor a Holley comes with the carb.

or, if you already have a Q-Jet on your engine, you can send it out and have it rebuilt and super-tuned to your needs.

Q-Jets will provide race-winning performance with a little tweaking and tuning. Of course, the least expensive way to go with a Q-Jet is to rebuild and rejet it yourself if you have the experience and skill to do it. If you don't, send it to a shop where it can be custom tailored and rebuilt by experts. The accompanying photos in this chapter show some of what the Carb Shop does with each Q-Jet they rework.

Carter AFB

These are great carbs, too, and can be made to run with the best of them. There are modern knock-offs of the old Carters available, too, but once again, you can save money by having your old one rebuilt and tested. Carters aren't as easy to work on as Holleys, but one point in their favor is you can change the metering rods in them without removing the float bowl lid. If you have a good Carter already, don't toss it out. Rebuild it and run it. They're hard to beat.

REBUILDING YOUR ROCHESTER

Continued on page 140

Otis Bretzing is the Carb Shop's Rochester expert and he believes Q-Jets are the best all-around carb there is. He can go through one in half the time most people can.

To disconnect the accelerator pump, Otis taps out the pivot pin rather than disassembling the lever mechanism.

Unscrew the top of the carb to get to its inner workings. Keep everything in order as you take things apart.

Remove the idle mixture needle next. Clean and inspect it. If it is damaged or pitted, replace it.

Continued on page 142

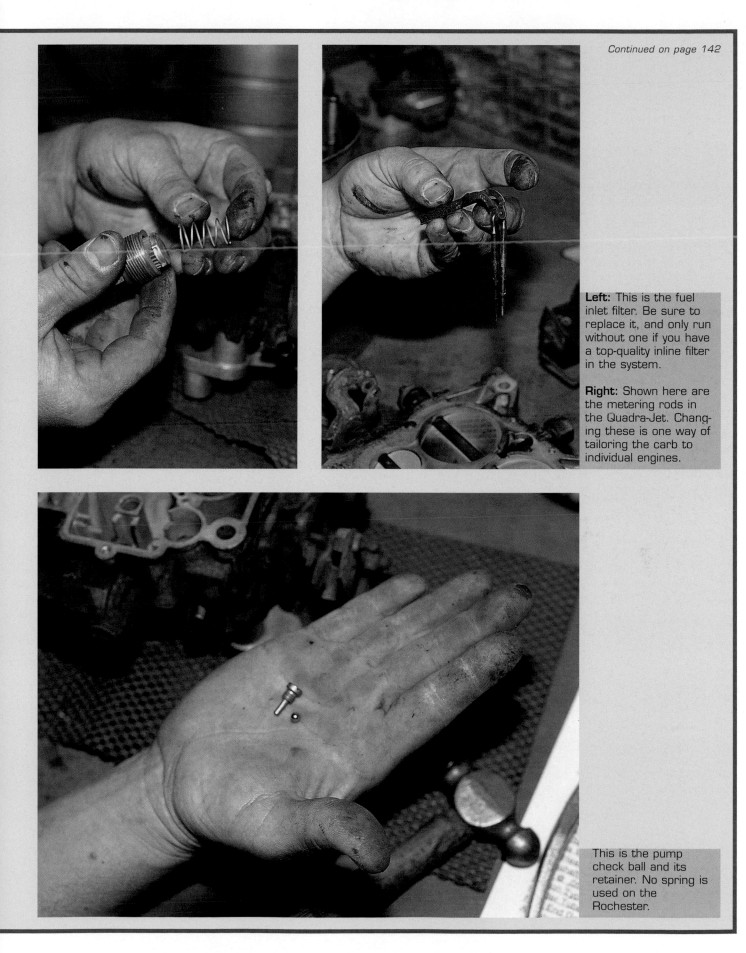

Left: This is the fuel inlet filter. Be sure to replace it, and only run without one if you have a top-quality inline filter in the system.

Right: Shown here are the metering rods in the Quadra-Jet. Changing these is one way of tailoring the carb to individual engines.

This is the pump check ball and its retainer. No spring is used on the Rochester.

Right: Fuel chamber plugs are driven in and surrounding metal is peened over them. Remove the metal, pull out the plugs, and when replacing them, use epoxy to hold them in place.

Above: Otis at the Carb Shop can put everything in a pile because he knows these carbs inside and out, but most of us have to lay everything out in order to do the job right.

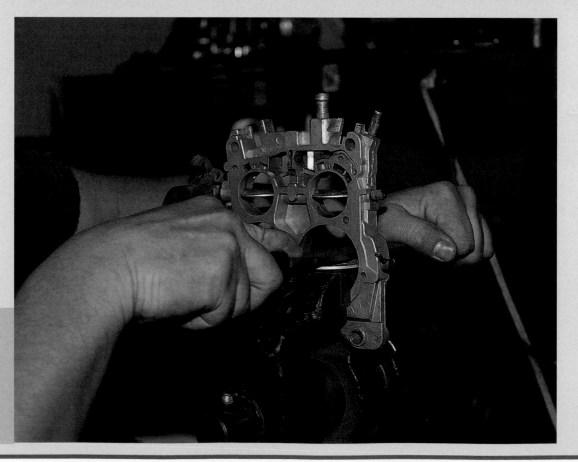

Throttle butterfly screws are swaged in place and must be filed flush before they will unscrew. Use new screws and swage them in place when rebuilding the carb so they can't come loose.

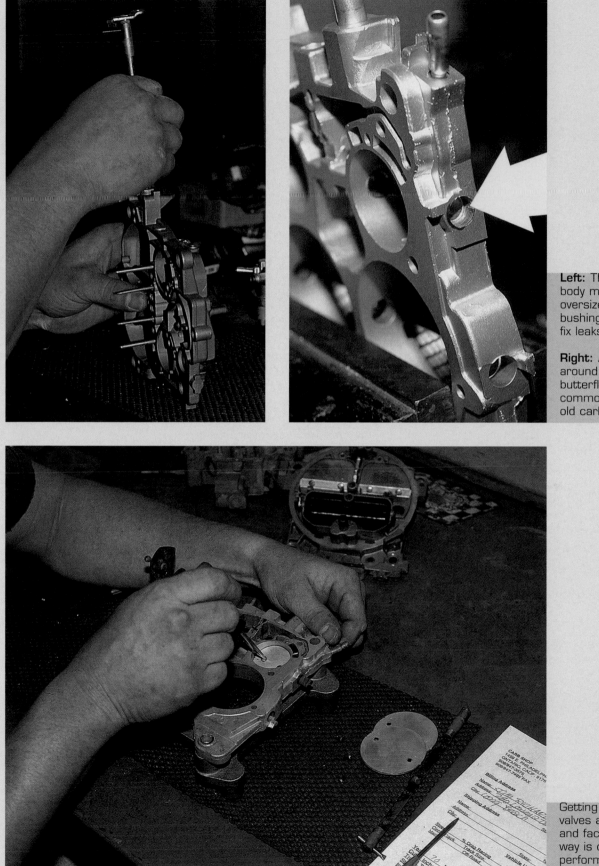

Left: The throttle body must be drilled oversize with brass bushings installed to fix leaks.

Right: Air leaks around the throttle butterfly shaft are a common problem on old carbs.

Getting butterfly valves aligned properly and facing the right way is critical to good performance.

Manifold Destiny

There are three common types of intake manifolds. The most popular one used for the street on Chevy small blocks is the dual-plane type. It helps provide better low- and midrange power, but sacrifices a little at the top end of your engine's rpm range.

The second common type of intake manifold is the single-plane configuration. Inline six- and four-cylinder engines generally have single-plane manifolds because they are simple and efficient, but V-8 engines suffer to a degree when using single-plane manifolds under certain circumstances because of the fact that adjacent cylinders (5 and 7) can have open valves at the same time, allowing the fuel mixture to become diluted at low rpm.

Also, because fuel/air velocity is low at low rpm in an open-plenum single-plane manifold, fuel can actually condense and puddle out on the manifold floor, especially in cold weather. On the plus side, single-plane manifolds have shorter, straighter port runners, so at high rpm they really come into their own. They have an edge over dual-plane manifolds up around 7,500 rpm and beyond. So what it comes down to is this: If you want maximum top-end horsepower and don't mind going from rather sedate acceleration at lower rpm to sudden, tire-smoking torque as the engine comes up on its cam, go for a single-plane manifold.

But if you want neck-snapping launches from idle when you hit the gas, and steady power up through to the power peak on your street engine, go with a dual-plane manifold. Single-plane-manifold-equipped cars are harder to drive, though they have an edge in straight-line acceleration at peak power. Most street rodders prefer a good dual-plane manifold because they make their car more user-friendly. Cornering can be a real problem if the power comes on abruptly in midcorner, as it can do with a single-plane manifold.

On single-plane manifolds, all of the barrels of the carb dump into a large, common plenum that feeds short, straight runners. The loss of gas velocity at low rpm because of the open plenum is the single-plane manifold's biggest

shortcoming, but its straight port runners are its virtue. As we said in the chapter on head porting, air doesn't like to turn corners, especially when it's moving fast.

Dual-plane manifolds are set up so that each side of the carb feeds one side of the engine, and it does so through different-length, rather curvy runners. These are marginally less efficient than straight runners, but they do keep the gas velocity higher at low rpm, giving the carb much clearer signals. The chances of bogging down at low rpm are diminished, unless you have installed a carb that is too large for the engine.

A single-plane intake manifold gives great performance in the higher-rpm ranges, but can be a little soggy on the bottom end.

This is a Performance Products dual-plane manifold. It outperforms many name brands.

When it comes to air filters, bigger is better. Taller is also good. This one from TD Performance Products will do a great job if the element is changed periodically.

The ultimate air filter is a K&N. They're washable and actually increase performance over what can be had by running with no filter at all!

scoop that blocks your vision to the right of you. The other problem with tunnel ram manifolds is that they only provide an advantage in a limited, high-rpm range. They look impressive, but they aren't very practical for street use.

Air Filters

This is one situation where bigger is always better. The more filter area you have, the less restrictive the filter will be. Air filters can be especially restrictive if their tops are too close to the carb. The top of the filter should be at least 3 inches above the carb, and 4 to 6 inches are better. The diameter of the filter should be as big as your wallet can accommodate. It has always seemed crazy to me to see street machines with top-quality, Holley double-pumper carbs topped with tiny air filters.

If you can afford it, a K&N filter is the way to go. Standard paper filters work well and offer very little restriction if they are kept refreshed. But K&N filters offer virtually no restriction and are designed to be washed out and reused. In fact, engines often run more efficiently with a K&N filter on them than they do with no filtration at all! The reason is, without some kind of filter, turbulence can develop at the carb throat that will cause less efficient breathing. K&N air filters cost more, but you only have to pay for them once, and they are the least restrictive filters available.

Paper filters work because they have millions of tiny holes in them that are too small for dust particles to pass through. However, the dust gets drawn in to all those tiny holes and slowly clogs them. K&N air filters somehow trap the dirt without clogging. Of course, in dusty situations, they will eventually start restricting air, but it takes a much longer time for that to happen. Dirt-track and off-road racers favor K&N reusable filters overwhelmingly just for this reason. Baja 1000 drivers have even been known to breathe through them.

The third type of manifold you sometimes see is the tunnel ram. Some of these use a plenum chamber on top to even out the vacuum pulses, and others use individual port runners right from the carb. Either way, the point of a tunnel ram manifold is to iron out those abrupt turns the air/fuel mixture has to make when it leaves the carburetor and enters the intake manifold. The long port runners help maintain gas velocity into the engine, and that helps fill the combustion chambers to the max.

There are a couple of big disadvantages to tunnel ram manifolds for street use. The first is hood clearance. The usual solution to hood clearance is a big

Carburetor: Dual-Feed Conversion

Colin Date

YOU'LL NEED:

- Socket set
- Flat-blade screwdriver
- Small putty knife or scraper
- Adjustable wrenches (optional)
- Rubber mallet
- Center-hung float fuel bowls (if needed)
- Metering block and hardware (sold as kit)
- Metering jets
- Replacement gaskets
- Dual-inlet fuel line

TIME
45 minutes

SKILL LEVEL
★★☆☆

COST
$100–$300

APPLICABLE MODELS/YEARS
All

PERFORMANCE GAINS
Increased fuel delivery and tuning accuracy

Whether you're working with an old factory Holley or a fresh, out-of-the-box unit, making the switch to a dual guzzler can significantly boost your carburetor's performance. To avoid confusion, I am not talking about double-pumpers. Although they may reign supreme at the track, some of us simply must work with what we have in our pockets or what has been reluctantly handed down over the years.

For most mild street applications, just about any standard Holley 600- or 650-cfm carburetor (model 4150 or 4160) should do the trick with minimal adjustment. These carburetors are engineered and built mainly for everyday economy and reliability with a little added performance on the side—not a bad route to go for the family truckster, but if you're serious about maximizing your engine's potential, a change or upgrade must be made.

First and foremost, let's take a look at the float bowl. Most of the smaller 4160 models share the same ill design of a side-pivot float. Mounted to one inside wall of the fuel bowl, these floats fail to control the proper level and flow that is needed under hard cornering. Think about it—if centrifugal forces push the fuel inside the bowl away from the float, the leverage to close the inlet valve is naturally decreased. In turn, this allows more fuel to enter the bowl than is really needed. The same goes for a turn in the opposite direction. This time, with an increase in leverage, the float is tricked into believing there is ample fuel present in the bowl, causing the inlet valve to close prematurely. Either way, it makes for pretty lousy performance.

In addition to the float flaw, 4150s and 4160s are equipped with somewhat problematic and restrictive fuel transfer tubes. This small 1/4-inch tube carries the fuel from the primary bowl, down the side of the carburetor, and into the secondary bowl. On each end of the tube is an O-ring seal. Non-reusable and stubborn to properly reseat, these gaskets can make something as simple as a jet change a true test of patience. This is about the last

Start by removing the existing secondary fuel bowl (four bolts). Be careful not to tear the small circular gaskets behind the bolt heads, as these are prone to leakage if damaged.

2

I recommend Holley's reusable, non-stick foam gaskets over the stock paper ones. Without the hassle of cleanup, projects like this are much easier. Notice the secondary jets have already been placed in the block.

With everything back in its proper place, we now add the new dual-inlet fuel line. Braided stainless steel might be a little overkill for the low pressures this system will see, but it's nice just knowing it's there, and it looks great to boot.

3

TIP:

Transfer the carburetor from the engine to a clean, open workbench. If you don't have a carburetor stand, simply slide four bolts of your choice through the mounting holes in the bottom plate and "nut" them up at the top. All you need is enough clearance for the levers and protruding linkage.

thing any of us care to deal with at the track, or anywhere for that matter. Luckily, there are plenty of upgrade kits available from Holley for just about anything you might be running. The swaps are fast and relatively straightforward.

With that said, let's get busy. We selected a stock 750-cfm vacuum secondary Holley (model 3310) for the project. Factory equipped with dual center-hung float fuel bowls, we were only in need of a secondary metering block and hardware (Holley p/n 3413) to complete the conversion. The smaller models mentioned earlier would require the additional purchase of Holley p/n 34-2, a pair of dual-inlet fuel bowls and their respective gaskets.

In our case, we start by removing the rear fuel bowl (see photo 1) to access the metering plate. The bowl is held in place by four small bolts and a gasket. Loosen the bolts and lightly tap the bowl with a mallet to break the seal. If your carburetor still has gas in the bowl, grab a rag or a small "catch cap" to keep from spilling. Once the bowl is off, carefully unscrew the metering plate from the carburetor's main body. There will most likely be some leftover gasket material stuck on the mounting surface. If so, remove it with a small blade or scraping knife.

Replace the bowl seals with Holley's non-stick, reusable gaskets. They require no sealant or glue and install in seconds. The metering block and its jets follow suit and pop right into place (see photo 2). Similar to the front primary system, the addition of the metering block gives you total control of secondary delivery and allows you to tailor it to your application and needs.

Using the supplied longer bolts, simply snug the fuel bowl back onto the housing. Be cautious not to over-tighten the bolts, which could tear or damage the seals. Tip: To keep track of your jet sizes, either front or back, use a washable marker to write the numbers on your fuel bowl for quick reference.

Now, all that's left is slapping on the new fuel line (see photo 3). Regardless of the brand or style, all aftermarket fuel lines are similar in function and are made to easily adapt and fit your specific carburetor. If your local parts store does not carry what you need, try Summit Racing, Jegs, or any other major high-performance parts supplier.

Carburetor: Installing A New Accelerator Pump Cam, Discharge Nozzle, And Power Valve

Colin Date

YOU'LL NEED:
- Flat-blade screwdriver
- Phillips screwdriver
- Adjustable wrench
- Pump cams
- Discharge nozzles
- Power valves
- Replacement gaskets

TIME
1½ hours (then test time at the drag strip)

SKILL LEVEL
★★☆☆

COST
Pump cam kits: under $20; discharge nozzles: about $11 each; power valves: about $7–$13

APPLICABLE MODELS/YEARS
All

PERFORMANCE GAIN
Better throttle response right across the rpm range (if done right!)

Now that you've got your metering jets dialed in properly, let's move ahead with some more basic carburetor tuning projects. This one is really three separate deals, but they're all fairly minor and can do wonders to help your street/strip performance.

First, we'll tackle the accelerator pump cam. Working on our 750-cc Holley, we have a nice choice of cams right out of the box. Actuating the accelerator pump with a plastic cam (instead of the typical lever and rod) affords a number of tuning opportunities. By changing the curve of the cam and the cam's position as it relates to the throttle lever, you can alter both your pump timing and the discharge volume. All of Holley's small plastic cams are color-coded and have a number embossed on them. Don't get too excited with visions of drastically increasing your off-the-line grunt here. Changing out a pump cam is easy to do and the results are not huge. It is essentially one of the small steps that, done properly with other modifications, will add up to quicker track times. Switching the cam out to a more radical profile changes the accelerator pump fuel-delivery timing as it corresponds to the throttle-opening cycle, which causes minor changes in the volume of fuel when it

comes out of the pump nozzle. Let's give it a shot.

As shown in photo 1, use a flat-blade screwdriver and unscrew the small bolt that retains the plastic cam. Once again, we can go mild or wild (well, maybe not too wild). Most street-driven cars should have a cam lift that is relatively slow. You want just enough fuel to be discharged

This is a selection of available cams from Holley. There are lots of choices to fit your application and desired result.

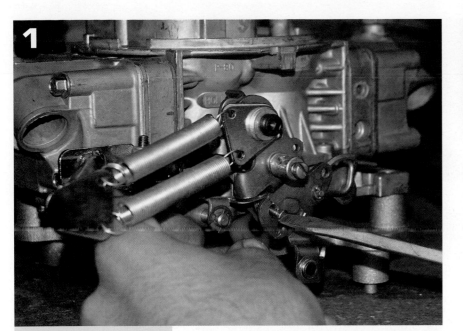

Remove the one screw that retains the accelerator pump cam and remove the cam.

Left: Remove the brass fitting with the Phillips screwdriver. The fitting retains the accelerator pump discharge nozzle. *Colin Date*

Right: The discharge nozzle can be replaced with many different sizes. It's the perfect combination of these sizes and the accelerator pump cam that makes the difference.

TIP:
Think of these as three mini projects to experiment with. Try them one at a time, and keep a log of your results.

early in the throttle-opening sequence to avoid an off-idle failure. But there also has to be enough lift to achieve good part-throttle-to-full-throttle acceleration. At the other end of the spectrum, drag racers are after good fuel delivery later in the throttle cycle. Once they're off the line and the cam has done its job, drag engines no longer need the assistance of a pump cam. As you can see, you've got a few choices to make here. As a good starting point, use Holley's white plastic cam (stamped number 218). It's a good middle-ground cam and is probably Holley's most popular piece. Move up from there, experimenting with different cams, until you get the desired effect. As we said, baby steps! The cam is held in place by a single bolt. Removal and installation is the same.

Now, we move on to the discharge nozzles. Officially, these are called accelerator pump discharge nozzles, sometimes referred to as squirters or shooters. Like all the other variables on a Holley carburetor (most carburetor manufacturers make their units infinitely tunable), the discharge nozzles are available in different sizes. The nozzles are individually stamped with a number indicating the orifice size. Here's how they work: The size of the nozzle and the pump-cam shape work in unison to achieve a measured pump "shot." They time the fuel-delivery volume during various stages of throttle lever movement. The shot can be adjusted to be long or short and early or late (whatever works best for your application) in the throttle cycle.

Check out photo 2. Here, we're using the Phillips screwdriver to remove the brass fitting that retains the nozzle. Photo 3 shows the nozzle removed, ready for replacement. Depending on your carburetor model, you may have two discharge nozzles. Vacuum-actuated versions only have one nozzle. Double-pumper units will have two. You can experiment with many combinations of nozzle sizes and pump cams. It's easy to get confused. Just make sure you keep an accurate log

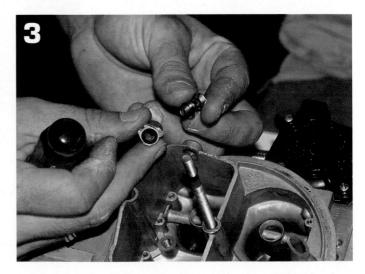

Left: Remove the primary fuel bowl. Take care to place a cap or rag under the bolt holes to catch the fuel still in the system.

Right: Remove the metering block, taking extra care to pry it off gently. Remove the metering block at the same point as in the photo to avoid damaging the block.

Remove the power valve gently, with a counterclockwise turn. Now it's experimentation time.

of where you started (your benchmark) and where you're going. Again, make sure you're comparing apples to apples. Try to run your car at the same track and during similar conditions each time you try out the different combos.

Much has been written on the subject of power valves. By name alone, a lot of folks figure that by swapping a power valve out for a larger volume unit, they'll immediately shave a 1/2 second off their 1/4-mile times. Remember—baby steps. Swapping out a stock 6.5-inch for an 8.5-inch valve will bring an engine to maximum richness more rapidly, but that's about it. There are a lot of variables within the confines of a carburetor. Depending on how everything else is set up, upgrading your power valve could result in a noticeable improvement right out of the gate or offer no improvement whatsoever. In fact, you could start hurting gas mileage without the perk of extra power. Again, it's best to experiment. If you have everything else dialed in properly, installing a larger power valve should bring about an immediate out-of-the-gate acceleration improvement (for a second or two), but that's where it'll end. Once the valve is fully open, the amount of enrichment is the same regardless of the manifold vacuum figure at which the power valve operates. A word of caution: If you're after performance, stay away from two-stage power valves. Originally designed for greater fuel economy, they restrict overall fuel flow.

Pull off the primary fuel bowl (photo 4). After removing the fuel bowl, use a flat-blade screwdriver to gently pry off

the metering block (photo 5). Make sure you do this the way the photo shows (in the middle of the block), as you can damage the block if you try prying it off from the side. Once the metering block has been freed, you can access the power valve (photo 6). Use an adjustable wrench (to suit any application) and turn the valve out counterclockwise. Reinstall the new power valve and hit the track. You can experiment by changing out the valve in conjunction with the jets and pump cams. Remember, with a carburetor, it's all about trying different combinations until you get what works best for you.

Converting To An HEI Distributor

Colin Date

TIME

2 hours

SKILL LEVEL

★★☆☆

COST

Varies by manufacturer ($175–$400)

APPLICABLE MODELS/YEARS

All

PERFORMANCE GAIN

Increased coil saturation, higher spark output, more reliable performance

YOU'LL NEED:

- Standard wrench set
- Flat-blade and/or Phillips screwdriver
- Wire strippers/crimpers
- HEI distributor (new, rebuilt, or used)
- HEI ignition lead connector
- HEI style plug wires

The majority of cars produced during the 1960s and early 1970s were factory-equipped with a point-type ignition. Although not likely to be considered the greatest manager of spark, there was no other option at the time. It was not until the 1974 model year that GM offered the new HEI ignition system as an alternative. One year later, it became standard equipment for all and with good reason.

The GM HEI, which stands for High-Energy Ignition, is a breakerless, transistor-controlled, inductive discharge system. It operates much like the conventional point-type ignition, but relies solely on a series of electronic signals to turn on and off the primary current rather than the mechanical opening and closing of points. This task is routinely carried out by the switching transistor, located inside the ignition module. In fact, the ignition module, the ignition coil, the pickup coil, the magnetic pickup assembly, and the mechanical and vacuum advance units are all nestled tightly under the HEI distributor cap.

It is my assumption that anyone owning or driving one of these vehicles, at one time or another, has run into problems with the stock ignition system. Let's face it—points are not our friends. No matter what you drive in what application, points always seem to be in a constant state of tune, looking for that elusive, if not imaginary, sweet spot.

I finally found it—and it's called electronic ignition! Seriously, with so many other performance improvements that can be made to a car, who wants to spend their time adjusting the dwell angle of all things? Electronic ignitions such as the HEI are typically a little more expensive than the rebuilt "el cheapo" special at your local parts store. However, in the long run, the time and headaches you spare fiddling with your ignition will more than make up for the initial deficit.

By simply switching over to an electronic distributor, not only do you eliminate the aforementioned hassles of points, but you will also notice a significant increase in your car's overall performance. From crisper, off-idle throttle

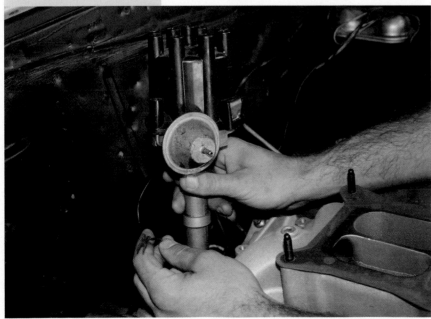

After removing the ignition coil, leads, and plug wires, the distributor is ready to come out.

TIP:

Label or mark the location of your spark plug wires on the distributor cap for fast, easy reference.

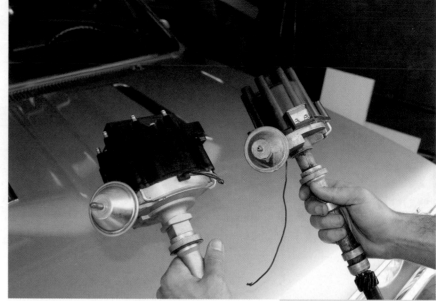

What a night-and-day difference between the two! The HEI distributor actually houses the ignition coil underneath that massive cap.

response to extra top-end pulling power, the gains from merely removing and replacing your stock distributor with a high-performance HEI are downright impressive.

And so this brings us to the garage. Anytime you pull the distributor out of an engine, it's important to note a couple of key elements beforehand. First, detach the spark plug wires and the coil wire, and then remove the cap. Before loosening the distributor clamp and allowing the housing to rotate, mark the position of the housing as well as the vacuum advance unit and the rotor, all in relation to the engine block. Loosen the clamp and lightly lift up on the housing (see photo on page 151).

If the engine is undisturbed while the distributor is out, installing the HEI is simply a matter of reversal at this point. Realign your markings and let it fall back in place. Do not force it. The teeth of the gears must properly mesh together in order to fully reseat. Once in position, hand-tighten the single bolt and clamp to allow for slight adjustments when restarting the engine.

If the engine has been moved, you will need to locate its TDC (top dead center). One easy way to do this without removing the valve covers is to pull the No. 1 spark plug. Place a finger over the hole and rotate the engine by hand until you feel the compression. When the timing mark on the crankshaft pulley matches up with the "0" on the timing tab, you have reached TDC. Now install the distributor with the rotor pointing at the No. 1 terminal on the cap.

With the ignition coil neatly tucked inside the HEI, the electrical hookup is a cinch. Splice the HEI connector (see photo 3) into the existing "hot" ignition lead. The connector then plugs into the cap at the "BATT" terminal. If you run an aftermarket tachometer, a second connector will be needed. It plugs in

adjacent to the ignition lead at the "TACH" terminal. Points-type spark plug wires are not interchangeable with an HEI cap and vice versa (see photo above). You will need to purchase a new set to match your distributor. Reattach the individual plug wires to their proper posts. Take your time and make sure you have them right.

With everything back together, reconnect the negative battery cable and fire the engine. Proceed to set the timing and secure the hold-down clamp. Check the timing once more to ensure the housing did not move while tightening.

When reconnecting the new unit, you will need to purchase and splice in a single HEI terminal connector. This is your "hot" ignition wire coming from the engine harness.

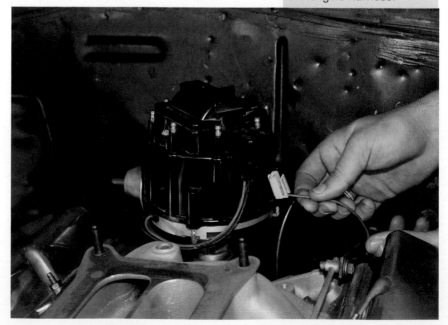

Opti-Spark Solutions

Richard Newton

TIME
2 hours

SKILL LEVEL
★★★☆

COST
$500-$1,000

APPLICABLE MODELS/YEARS
Corvettes 1992-1996

PERFORMANCE GAIN
Reliable ignition

YOU'LL NEED:
- A credit card with a large credit line.

These dreaded holes create the infamous Opti-Spark problem. If you kill the unit, you must be prepared to spend some very serious money to fix your mistake. I would search out one of the upgraded units – don't even consider another original equipment part.

COMPLEMENTARY MODIFICATION:

This would be a very good time to install new spark plug wires. Spark plug wires on the LT1 are a major effort. It usually takes around four hours to install them. I would install the new Opti-Spark, and once I'm sure the engine runs properly, I would get started on the spark plugs and the spark plug wires.

This new Opti-Spark distributor was supposed to be the greatest thing since GM did away with ignition points. Instead they had an internal mistake, and the Opti-Spark caused Corvette owners a tremendous amount of aggravation.

One of the goals of the distributor was to control spark scatter during transient maneuvers, such as acceleration. GM also wanted to eliminate the large timing errors that occur during starting. This was a well-known problem with magnetic reluctance timing sensors.

The Opti-Spark is a distributor with a two-track optical position sensor, a keyed driveshaft, an ECM, a single ignition coil and driver, and conventional secondary wires and spark plugs. Contrary to what many people believe, most spark errors actually occur at low speeds, especially starting, rather than at high rpm. Spark errors also occur during transient movements such as acceleration, deceleration, and transmission shifts.

A key element in this Opti-Spark system was the increased overall diameter of the distributor. This allowed for greater separation between the secondary terminals within the cap. This reduced cap and rotor wear by reducing the ozone formed when the spark is jumping large rotor-to-cap gaps.

The Problem

Despite all of the Opti-Spark's innovations, one major problem occurred in the transition to actual production. The casing of the Opti-Spark, which was mounted to the front of the engine, just behind the water pump, was designed with a small hole at the base. This would allow any condensation formed within the distributor to drain out. The design engineering team was very precise about the size of this hole.

After the design was completed, the unit was passed on to a group called validation engineering. This group changed the size of the hole without communicating this change to anyone else. The validation team felt the hole was simply too large and would allow water to enter into the distributor. Unfortunately, this new drain hole was simply too small to allow condensation to flow out of the distributor.

To make matters just a little worse, the validation team changed the composition of the internal components, making them less corrosion resistant. That was

TIP:

Don't ever let any water get in the area of the Opti-Spark when you detail your engine compartment.

all that was needed to make this one of the most failure-prone components in Corvette history. Eventually a recall campaign led to all (or most) of the units being replaced.

Today there are several units on the market that incorporate some design changes that make the distributor very reliable. This is important since there are no alternatives on the market for the Opti-Spark. It's not as if you can simply install a different type of distributor.

One Type of Retrofit

At one time, Borg Warner offered an Opti-Spark repair kit called C400. It was listed for the 1992 to 1996 Corvettes. This kit worked fine on 1995s or 1996s, but it needed a little help to fit the earlier units. You might want to look around and see if it's still available.

At $153, the kit isn't cheap so be careful with the installation. The kit gives you a vented cap and rotor, and the inside cover is different than the stock unit. The ECM plug is on the new part, but the old unit had the plug already molded and attached to the base. It goes in a notch in the old cover.

It is tempting to use the old inside cover, but, keep in mind, it may have carbon tracks due to its close proximity to the rotor and may not work when you are done. Using a Dremel tool or a small hobby saw, carefully cut the plug snout off of the new cover flush with the outside diameter. Saw a notch in the new cover working a little at a time until you are satisfied with the fit. Leave a little room for some epoxy or JB weld.

You'll notice the flange in the center will not clear the photo receptor on the base. Remove a small section of the flange until it just barely clears. Now clean everything as well as possible and put the

unit together. Put a very small amount of Vaseline on just the portion of the cap seal directly above the ECM plug so the epoxy won't stick to it. Leave the screws a little loose until the epoxy sets and then tighten them to compress the seal.

Corvette Clinic in Sanford, Florida, is the only firm that sells the Opti-Spark with all the upgrades. They actually use a flow-through ventilation system that circulates air through the distributor cap. I've never heard of anyone having a problem with one of their units.

Before you do any detailing, you should take a towel or shop rag and cover the hole in the Opti-Spark casing. I use a shop rag and then duct tape it so no moisture can possibly destroy the unit. You simply can't take chances. You have to be very careful when you do any engine detailing with the LT1. A lot of folks have gotten a little carried away cleaning their engine compartments and killed the Opti-Spark in the process. That's a very expensive mistake.

Installing Underdrive Pulleys

Huw Evans

TIME

3 hours

SKILL LEVEL

★★★☆

COST

$200

APPLICABLE MODELS/YEARS

Mustangs 1979–1995

PERFORMANCE GAIN

Improved power

YOU'LL NEED:

- Screwdriver
- Adjustable torque wrench
- Sockets
- Underdrive pulley kit
- Replacement belt

COMPLEMENTARY PROJECT:

Cooling system upgrade, timing advance

All 5-liter Mustangs use a single serpentine belt drive for the accessories—so named because it snakes between the drive pulleys (shown is a 1992 Mustang GT with the stock clutch fan driven off the water pump). Driving the accessories robs the engine of quite a bit of power, so installing underdrive pulleys is a popular and effective performance modification.

Underdrive pulleys reduce parasitic loss of power and torque by slowing down the turning speed of the accessory drive. They often come in two- or three-piece sets—crank and water pump or alternator, crank, and water pump. If you tend to drive your car on the street, be careful, because the slower turning speed of the underdrive pulleys can affect cooling (1979–1993 cars) and can reduce voltage output from the alternator, resulting in a poor charge at idle speed.

The best solution for a regularly street-driven Mustang is to use the large underdrive crank pulley and a 1993 Cobra water pump pulley (for 1979–1993 cars, available from Ford Racing Performance Parts). The Cobra pulley is of

smaller diameter than the aftermarket underdrive water pump pulley, which means it rotates more quickly. Therefore, you gain a power increase without having to compromise the effectiveness of your stock cooling system.

Unplug the negative battery cable before turning your attention to the factory radiator shroud. Before you begin unfastening it, check the condition of your factory clutch fan (if it's still in place). The 1979 5-liters use a flex-blade fan, and 1982–1993 models use a rigid plastic clutch type fan. (The 1994–1995 cars use a far more efficient electric fan, so you don't have to worry about fan removal to access the water pump and crank pulley.)

The rigid plastic clutch fan is prone to cracking where the blades meet the hub, and over time the clutch mechanism can start to slip. Try to move the fan forward and backward, to see if the blades wobble. If so, you'll need to replace the fan and clutch assembly. Also try spinning the fan with the car at rest. If it doesn't turn at all, or freewheels, again the clutch assembly is worn and will need replacing.

Unbolt the fan and clutch assembly by undoing the bolts that secure it to the water pump pulley. Then unbolt the shroud (it attaches to the radiator at the header panel with two bolts) and lift the shroud and fan out of the engine compartment. If your clutch is worn but the fan is okay, you can remove the former by undoing the bolts that attach it to the plastic fan. When replacing the clutch, it's a good idea to upgrade to the Special

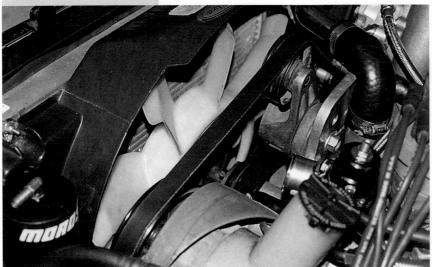

Left: Probably the best-known aftermarket supplier of replacement pulleys for domestic performance vehicles is March Performance, which offers both two- and three-piece underdrive pulley sets for 5-liter Mustangs.

Right: For most street cars, consider going with two-piece pulleys like these, which have a replacement crank pulley (the larger one) and water pump pulley (the smaller one). Three-piece sets add an alternator pulley, but the slower turning speed can cause voltage problems and hard starting.

Service Package/OPEC-style clutch with revised release points, which will improve power and cooling. Performance Parts, Inc. (703-742-6207) is a good source for these.

Next, remove the drive belt. All 5-liter Mustangs use a single serpentine belt of a V-ribbed design to drive the accessories. The accessory drive incorporates self-adjusting automatic belt tensioners and a wear indicator. If the belt has been on the Mustang awhile, check the indicator and also look at the belt's overall condition. If it's fraying or cracked, replace it—installing underdrive pulleys often puts a strain on the cooling system, because the fan will be turning more slowly, and a worn belt exaggerates the problem.

It's worth checking the belt routing. If your Mustang hasn't been repainted under the hood, chances are the emis-sions and belt routing stickers will still be in place. Two types of belt routing are employed on 5-liter Mustangs—one with air conditioning, one without. Note which yours has before removing and replacing the belt, so you can route it correctly (this may seem obvious, but you'd be surprised how easy it is to overlook).

If you own a 1979–1984 5-liter Mustang, pull the tensioner away from the belt and hold it to remove the belt. On 1985 and later Mustangs, use a breaker bar and socket to rotate the tensioner and slip the belt off. Then you can unbolt your crank and water pump (and alternator if you're doing three-piece) pulleys and install the new ones.

With the pulleys on, grab your new belt and make sure it's free from dirt and debris. Make sure the tensioner is held back while you install the belt. Once it's on, release the tensioner, and you're all set. Now you can reinstall your clutch fan and radiator shroud.

TIP:

Use a Cobra water pump pulley on your Fox 5-liter.

Left: With the stock crank pulley off, bolt the replacement on the end of the crank balancer, using the stock holes for the bolts, as seen here.

Right: This 302 engine already has the two-piece crank and water pump pulleys installed and is shown removed from the car for illustration. Above the water pump pulley is the factory tensioner for the serpentine belt system.

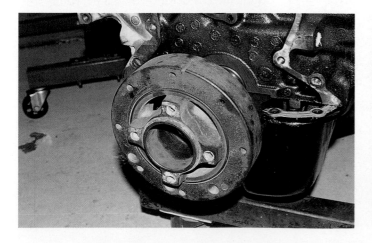

Installing A Mechanical Fuel Pump And Fuel Pressure Regulator

Colin Date

TIME

2 hours

SKILL LEVEL

★★☆☆

COST

$100–$150

APPLICABLE MODELS/YEARS

All

PERFORMANCE GAINS

Superior fuel flow over stock pumps (80–130 gallons per hour), and the pressure adjustability to ensure the right mix

YOU'LL NEED:

- Standard socket set
- Adjustable wrench
- Flat-blade screwdriver
- Allen wrench set
- Fuel pump and mounting gasket (supplied)
- Fuel pressure regulator and gauge
- 3/8-inch fuel hose and clamps
- NPT pipe fittings

When reinstalling the pump, use a small screwdriver to carefully hold the pushrod up and out of the way.

When it comes to cars and our beloved combustion engines, fuel and plenty of it is the name of the game. Regardless of size or design, all engines rely solely on fuel being pumped in from an outside source, such as the tank. And for this we look no further than the workhorse we know as the fuel pump.

Fuel pumps come in a variety of forms and can be mounted in several locations. Today, most late-model vehicles utilize an electric pump, which is typically installed inside the tank. However, the older, and by far the most common, design is the mechanical fuel pump. Mounted on the side of the engine block, these pumps use the age-old method of a single pushrod to get things flowing. The fuel pump pushrod is driven by the camshaft to actuate the pump's rocker arm, much like the valvetrain in the cylinder heads.

Supplying the fuel to the pump is an automatic process. Basically, there is a main line, either 5/16 or 3/8 inch, running front to back (the length of the car) between the fuel tank and the pump. This is the suction line. The spring-loaded rocker arm is actuated up and down by the rotation of the cam, creating a vacuum in the system and drawing fuel in from the tank. On the outlet side of the pump is the pressure line, which then feeds the fuel into the carburetor's bowl(s). Install a quality fuel filter between the tank and the inlet of the pump to keep the debris in the tank from entering your fuel pump and, more importantly, your engine.

Although it's not uncommon to see a 35-year-old car still running and retaining its factory fuel pump, these components will eventually wear down and fail. Even at their best, the factory units of yesteryear pale in comparison to the high-performance standards of today. Therefore, a little preventative "remove and replace" is a good idea.

Starting with the disassembly, first remove the lines from the inlet and outlet ports of the fuel pump. Place a container underneath the pump to recover any spilled fuel, and then plug or clamp off the lines if needed. The pump, held on by two bolts, should now be free and ready for removal.

To be on the safe side, I recommend using new pipefittings on projects such as this one. If your new pump did not include them, you can buy them at any hardware store on the cheap. Keep in mind you will need fittings for the regulator as well. Install the proper fittings in the pump and regulator prior to mounting the new pump. This gives you a little more room to ensure everything is tight and ready to go.

After cleaning the mounting surface of old gasket material, apply a small dab of sealer to the new gasket and reinstall the fuel pump. Getting the pump into place and making sure the pushrod is properly seated on the rocker can be a little tricky. The pushrod has a tendency to slide down past the point of actuation inside the block. If clearance allows, use a small screwdriver to retain the rod while backing the pump in (see photo on page 157). An alternative is to pull the

(see photo on page 157)

TIP:

When rerouting new lines, closely measure all of your lengths beforehand to avoid last minute miscalculations.

pushrod all the way out, "pack" it with some heavy engine grease, and lodge it back in. However, this will only work with a cold motor. With the pump in place, you can reattach the fuel lines and secure them with hose clamps. If you choose to run AN lines (recommended), clamps are not needed.

With any temperamental high-performance engine, the more tuning flexibility you have the easier it is to consistently control. Adding a fuel pressure regulator guarantees consistent fuel pressure is delivered to the carburetor without fail. To install, merely route the pump outlet line to the regulator inlet port. The line coming out of the regulator will then serve as the carburetor inlet feed (see photo above). Adjusting the reg is as simple as turning a wrench, literally. And the small, but clear pressure gauge lets you dial it in just where you need it for maximum performance.

With everything back in place, the only thing left to do is securely mount the regulator to its bracket and attach it to any rigid surface. In this case, we will most likely use the inner fenderwell.

Installing A Nitrous Kit

Huw Evans

TIME
4 hours

SKILL LEVEL
★★★☆

COST
$80–$200

APPLICABLE MODELS/YEARS
Mustangs 1986–1995

PERFORMANCE GAIN
Improved exhaust flow, horsepower, torque, throttle response

YOU'LL NEED:
- Wrench
- Adjustable torque wrench
- Sockets
- Screwdrivers
- Drill
- Portable MIG welder
- Nitrous bottle
- Nitrous management unit
- Brackets
- Screws
- Braided lines
- Jets and fittings (complete kit)

Besides installing a supercharger, bolting on a nitrous oxide kit is one of the most talked-about topics when it comes to 5-liter Mustangs. This special chemical compound, N2O, gives you an extra shot of oats on demand, without having to build a complete hot rod engine or install a supercharger. You can plumb in your nitrous kit, turn on the bottle, and hit the switch at the track, then turn it off to drive home and back and forth to work.

Nitrous is attractive because it costs a lot less than installing a supercharger or building your motor up and doesn't give up any power, drivability, or fuel economy. However, nitrous has its downsides, too. Most systems can't be operated on the street, because of state or provincial requirements. Also, in many cases, installing a nitrous system has caused the engine to blow up or the car to catch fire. If you've gone to the drags and watched Mustangs race, you've probably seen something like this at least once. Therefore, when considering a nitrous

install, tread with extreme care and select the kit that's right for you.

How It Works

Oxygen represents about 21 percent air but about 36 percent of a nitrous oxide molecule. Nitrous oxide is stored under pressure, to keep it liquid. This liquid rapidly expands into a gas upon release—usually upstream of the carburetor or throttle body—and absorbs a large amount of heat, providing a dense, cool charge of oxygen. This dense, cool air rushing into the engine allows it to burn more fuel and produce more power.

Wet Versus Dry

This is a hot topic in the world of nitrous systems. The wet setup uses two solenoids—one for the nitrous and one for the fuel, both of which are sprayed into the engine's intake assembly at the same time. A dry system, designed for sequential fuel injected engines only, uses a single solenoid for the nitrous. A second line connects the nitrous bottle and the fuel pressure regulator. Pressure from the bottle boosts fuel-line pressure, which richens the air/fuel mixture to boost power and ward off detonation.

What are pluses and minuses of wet versus dry systems? The latter are emissions certified by the California Air

Nitrous kits come in many forms, but for 5-liter Mustang enthusiasts on a budget, one of the best choices is the one from ZEX. Traditional nitrous kits are usually fiddly to install, because of all the separate solenoids and wiring, but ZEX takes the pain out of this by incorporating most of the hardware in a single box, the nitrous management unit (NMU). *Evan Smith*

COMPLEMENTARY PROJECT:

Upgrade your ignition and, especially, use colder spark plugs.

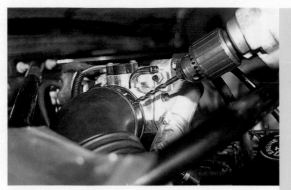

Resources Board (CARB) for 75 and 150 horsepower but cannot support more than that, because they use the stock fuel system. Wet systems can support far bigger horsepower numbers while still being emissions friendly, but if you install one on a sequential fuel injected Mustang, poor fuel atomization will cause puddling, backfires, and even more serious internal engine problems (some Mustangs have even burned). Therefore, on most street and injected 5-liters, consider going with a dry system, while on more street/strip and carbureted applications, a wet system is the way to go.

Nitrous Oxide Systems (NOS) and, more recently ZEX, are among the top vendors for dry systems. The latter is particularly good for 5-liter owners who regularly drive their cars and just want a little extra zoom at the track. It's also one of the easiest kits to install.

Installation

Because most 5-liter Mustangs are getting on in years, a few important aspects must be considered before performing a nitrous install. The first concerns the mileage and condition of the engine. The stock 5-liter HO, with its heavy-duty internals, will put up with a lot of abuse, thanks to small crank journals, a short stroke, and a stock roller camshaft (on 1985-and-up models). However, if the engine has never been apart and didn't receive regular maintenance, it's probably not a good idea to plumb in a nitrous system. Nitrous is an amplifier that boosts engine power and torque but will also increase the chance of serious engine damage.

The risk of damage increases with the amount of nitrous you're forcing into the engine. On a regularly driven Mustang with a stock 302, you shouldn't really consider more than a 100-horsepower shot. Anything more and you run the risk of blown head gaskets, detonation, bent valves and rods, and other serious problems. Some owners install 150-horse dry systems on their weary stock fuelie Mustangs, but in most cases, it isn't long before their engines give up the ghost. Some people will also try to use nitrous in conjunction with a blower or turbocharger on their street cars, though this isn't recommended for pure street 5-liters (go with a single power adder) unless you like uncontrollable driving characteristics and frequent engine rebuilds.

When it comes to nitrous oxide for 5-liter beginners, not only is the ZEX kit easy to install, but the activation switch, solenoid, and wiring are contained in a single box, called the nitrous management unit (NMU). This enables you to complete the installation in less than half the time of other systems. All you need to do is plumb into the throttle body, hook up a few wires, and install the nitrous bottle in the trunk.

Nitrous is often associated with blown engines because of a lean condition—too little fuel and too much oxygen. The ZEX system's NMU is great because, once you've armed the system via the toggle switch, it uses signals from the throttle position sensor to control the nitrous solenoid. The system can constantly adjust the ratio of nitrous to fuel, to maximize performance and minimize the risk of detonation. It does this by bleeding off a small amount of pressure to the NMU, so that the latter has an accurate reading of bottle pressure at all times. Therefore you'll always have the correct amount of fuel flowing through the system as it compensates for high or low pressure.

TIP:
Mount the bottle before delving under the hood.

To begin installation, pop the trunk and pull up the carpet, so you can install the bolts and attach the bottle brackets. (Always install the bottle on the right side of the trunk if you can, so that it aids weight distribution.) Once the bolts are installed, lay the carpet over them, but punch small holes, so you can bolt the brackets to them. When they're secure, you can install the nitrous bottle.

With the bottle in place, run the braided line supplied in the kit from the trunk to the engine compartment. A good way is to drill a hole in the floorpan just behind the rear seat. Secure the line on the right side of the passenger compartment, hiding it under the plastic trim. Then run it through the hole and up to the right inner fender.

A good place to put the NMU is on the right inner fender, behind the air box assembly. Here it can easily mate with the nitrous bottle supply line and is also in close proximity to the throttle body. Follow the instructions in the kit by drilling four small holes in the fender and fitting the NMU backing plate over them before installing the bolts.

Once everything is in place, drill and tap a hole for the nitrous jet at the top of the plastic intake sleeve, right before the throttle body. Screw in the nitrous spray nozzle, hook up the jet, and connect the nitrous line to the jet and NMU. Hook up the fuel jet and line between the NMU and fuel pressure regulator. Then connect the white wire that runs from the NMU to the voltage output wire that mates with

the factory throttle position sensor. Ground the black wire and install the arming switch for the nitrous system to the NMU and harness. Some people choose to install nitrous switches in the ashtray receptacle on their 1987–1993 Mustangs, but a better location is on the console, right in front of the center armrest.

Activate the system by flipping the arming switch and turning the ignition key on. Keep the throttle open for a few seconds. If all is well, the light on the NMU should change from green to red, indicating that it has learned the change in voltage from the factory throttle position sensor.

Before using the spray, two more steps are required. First, cycle the arming switch, after which the light on the NMU should turn green. Open the throttle again and listen for the solenoid. If you hear it clicking, all is well. Second, retard your engine's ignition timing (if it's been advanced), to avoid detonation. Use a timing gun and twist the distributor back to between 8 and 10 degrees before top dead center. If your spark plugs haven't been changed, now is a good time to do it. Switch to colder, shorter spark plugs.

You'll need to run high-octane fuel when using nitrous—try Sunoco Ultra 94 if you can get it, and don't use anything under 91. At the track, if you can get only the latter, add some octane booster as a further defense against detonation.

Nitrous can be great fun, but it also poses the risks of damage and fire mentioned. Be sure you read and understand all the manufacturer's documentation. Also buy a fire extinguisher and mount it in your car, where you have ready access to it. A good place is on the floor, just between the glove box and the front passenger seat.

Test your nitrous setup at the track, giving yourself plenty of room to accommodate the rush of power. If you're starting with a small shot—50 or 75 horsepower—and wish to increase it, you can do this by swapping the nitrous jet in front of the throttle body and the fuel jet that hooks up to the NMU. But remember, you shouldn't use more than a 100-horsepower shot consistently on a stock 5-liter engine if you don't want things to break.

Once the hole has been made, plumb in your nozzle and hook up the piping to your NMU. After installation, you can change the size of the jets to increase or decrease the amount of nitrous. *Evan Smith*

LT1 Coolant Change

Richard Newton

The introduction of the LT1 in 1992, with the new reverse cooling system, complicated the changing of the engine coolant a little bit. This reverse flow cooling was the key to the enhanced performance of the LT1, but it requires a little more care when flushing the cooling system.

Reverse flow cooling is superior to the cooling systems used in the L98 since it cools the cylinder heads first, preventing detonation. This in turn allows for a higher compression ratio and more spark advance on a given grade of gasoline. A fringe benefit is that cylinder bore temperatures are higher and more uniform, thus reducing piston ring friction. Because of the new cooling system, the LT1 could meet the ever-increasing emissions standards with significant gains in power, durability, and reliability.

The incoming coolant first encounters the thermostat, which now acts both on the inlet and outlet sides of the system. Depending on the engine coolant temperature, cold coolant from the radiator is carefully metered into the engine. This allows a more controlled amount of cold coolant to enter the engine. The cold coolant immediately mixes with the bypass coolant already flowing. This virtually eliminates the thermal shock that existed in the old system.

After entering through one side of the two-way thermostat, the cold coolant is routed directly to the cylinder heads where the combustion chambers, spark plugs, and exhaust ports are cooled. Then the heated coolant returns to the engine block and circulates around the cylinder barrels. The hot coolant from the block re-enters the water pump and hits the other side of the two-way thermostat. Depending on the temperature, it is either re-circulated back through the engine or directed to the radiator.

The main concept behind reverse flow cooling is to cool the heads first. This greatly reduces the tendency for detonation and is the primary reason that the LT1 can run 10.5 to 1 compression and

fairly significant ignition advance on modern lead-free gasoline. Reverse flow cooling is the key to the Generation II LT1s increased power, durability, and reliability over the earlier small-block engines.

Corvette LT1 applications use a pressurized coolant recovery reservoir instead of the nonpressurized overflow tank that was used with conventional cooling systems. All of the coolant flows continuously through the pressurized reservoir, which is an integral part of the cooling system. The pressurized reservoir in the LT1 is connected to the cooling system in three places. One inlet hose connects to the top of the right-hand radiator tank, a second inlet hose is attached through a "tee" connection on the heater inlet hose, and a third outlet hose is connected to a "tee" connection in the throttle body heater outlet.

The pressurized reservoir is mounted at the highest point in the system, and it provides a place where all air can be continuously scavenged from the coolant. Any steam and bubbles are allowed to rise to the surface, eliminating foam and providing pure liquid coolant back to the engine. Pure liquid coolant is returned to the system via the heater outlet hose connection. The pressure relief/vent cap in these systems is rated at 15psi and is located on the reservoir rather than the radiator.

Unless you know the little tricks, flushing the coolant can aggravate you.

TIME
1 hour

SKILL LEVEL
★☆☆☆

COST
$25

APPLICABLE MODELS/YEARS:
Corvettes 1992-1996

PERFORMANCE GAIN
None

YOU'LL NEED:
- Screwdrivers for hose clamps
- Pliers

This is the LT1 water pump. One of the reasons it seems twice as large as the traditional Chevy water pump is that the distributor is mounted directly behind the water pump. The other reason is that this water pump is gear driven. If you have to replace the Opti-Spark, you might want to consider a new water pump. You can't just remove the distributor. The water pump has to be removed in an effort to get to the distributor. Luckily, this water pump isn't much more expensive than the traditional Chevy water pump. Unfortunately, when it starts to leak, it often destroys the Opti-Spark, and fixing this will add more than $600 to your bill.

You'll need to open this bleed screw to release the air out of your cooling system. This bleed screw is mounted on the top of the thermostat housing, placing it at the highest point in the system. When you bleed the cooling system, remember to protect the Opti-Spark from any water.

The problem is getting all the air out of the system so that it's completely full. Often you'll think you have the radiator full, but after driving down the road, you'll start overheating and see a Low Coolant message appear on the dash.

The first problem to address is just getting all the old coolant out of the system. You need to take special care with the LT1 to keep any coolant off your Opti-Spark distributor, which is located in the front lower portion of the engine. This is especially important on 1993 and 1994 models, as they're not properly vented. Water will destroy your Opti-Spark.

This will also be an issue when filling your cooling system. Make sure that you bleed the cooling system by opening the air bleed valve on top of your engine. This will allow any air to escape. Once again, though, be careful as this valve is located directly above the Opti-Spark. It's a lot easier to get to this valve if you remove the air intake duct that connects the air filter to the throttle body.

If you remove the cap on the fill reservoir that's up on the passenger side and then open the air bleed valve, the water will come out faster. Also, don't completely remove the petcock from the right lower part of the radiator—it's designed to stay there.

In order to completely flush the cooling system, you'll have to remove both knock sensors out of the block. You'll find one

on each side, just above the oil pan. Remember, the engine block holds almost 60 percent of the coolant in the system. Removing these knock sensors will require a 23mm socket and ratchet or a 23mm offset box-end wrench. The knock sensors will come off fairly easy if they were tightened to the correct specification in the first place. Avoid rounding off the bolt on the sensor. Resort to the vice grips only as a last resort, grasping the round base of the sensor. If you damage a sensor, you can get a new one for about thirty-five dollars from your local Chevy dealer. Always stick with the genuine AC/Delco stuff and don't use the cheapies from places like Auto Zone or Pep Boys since they may be calibrated to different specs and can cause Trouble Code 43. When reinstalling the knock sensors, set your torque wrench to 11 to 15 foot-pounds.

Once you have the system completely flushed, you can close the petcock in the bottom of the radiator, replace the knock sensors, and start to slowly fill the radiator with new DEX-COOL mixed in a 50/50 ratio with distilled water. Use a funnel and pour very slowly so as not to slosh stuff on your engine or your car's paint job. If you crack open the pressure side-bleed screw on the thermostat housing while slowly refilling, you can displace most of the trapped air. Fill the system, retighten the bleed screw, and replace the radiator cap.

I've actually heard of people who jack the front of the car up so that the air bleed valve is above the level of the recovery tank in an effort to get all of the air out of the system. I've never found that necessary, but it's a thought worth considering. But, as far as I'm concerned, just getting everything up to temperature and then letting it cool down so that you can fill the recovery tank a second time seems to work very well.

After you think the cooling system is full, take the car for a five-mile ride and watch your coolant gauge very carefully. Get the car up to its normal operating temperature before you return home to the garage. If everything goes smoothly, park the car in your driveway and check the coolant level in the reservoir. Just remember that it's a lot easier to do all this now than to have a surprise problem on the road later.

TIP:

You should change the coolant on an annual basis with any C4 Corvette.

COMPLEMENTARY MODIFICATION:

This is also a good time to consider replacing your upper radiator hose. The hose is cheap enough that you can and should replace it every two or three years. It's also the first hose that will go bad on your vehicle. Usually the lower hose lasts twice as long.

Headers And Exhaust: Piped-In Power

Jim Richardson

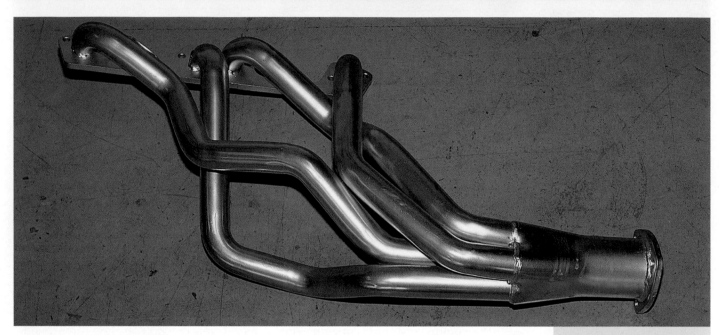

Long primary tubes such as this keep gas velocities high and produce lots of torque in the low- to mid-rpm range.

These graceful tri-Y, four-into-two-into-one headers with fairly short primaries would be great for fairly high-revving radical street machines.

When I was a young lad, I used to love shoving my Chevy into second gear and backing off the throttle, just to hear that sexy rumble as I blasted through a local tunnel. It was music to my ears. Unfortunately, not everybody shared my tastes in music. One set of 17-inch glass packs only lasted a week before the local constabulary wrote me up. But the craziest part of the whole thing was that my loud exhaust system probably actually hurt my Chevy's acceleration and top end.

As we have said several times in this book, knowing what you want your engine to do, then selecting the right mix of cam, heads, manifold, and carb, along with the right exhaust headers, are all keys to getting more usable horsepower and torque out of your Bow Tie small block. Putting together a winning combination requires thought and planning, but the results can be dramatic. On the other hand, carelessly mixing together even the best components could easily result in an engine that is less depend-able, less enjoyable, and less powerful than the stock one you started with.

Begin by asking yourself how often you will actually be driving around in the 6,000–8,000 rpm range. Are you building a racer that you only want to be able to coax to the strip and don't mind back-shifting constantly to get it there? Do you care that the car will not climb

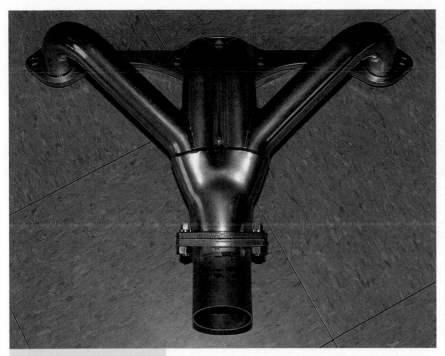

A nice step up from stock ram's-horn manifolds is this set of tight-clearance headers from Doug's.

These short, primary, four-into-one headers are for racing and produce maximum horsepower at 7,000–8,000 rpm.

behaved, or do you want a wild bronco? Unfortunately, you can't have both in one car.

A radical cam with lots of overlap needs one kind of exhaust headers and a street rod needs another. If you choose a cam designed to produce midrange grunt, you will want an exhaust system designed to complement it. The same is true for a cam designed to produce awesome high-end horsepower.

At a casual glance, you might think an engine would develop maximum power if it had large diameter short stacks right off the heads. They certainly looked cool on the old slingshot dragsters. But they don't work so well because the diameter of the header pipes determines the velocity of the exhaust gasses and the intensity of the resulting negative pressure wave. If the primary pipes are too short, no beneficial scavenging effect takes place, or if it does, it is at a very high and very limited rpm range.

It all has to do with taking maximum advantage of that "fifth cycle"—the overlap between intake and exhaust valve opening and closing—and how much overlap your engine can tolerate. Timing the overlap and exhaust pulses correctly can actually suck the last of the exhaust gasses out of a cylinder and can even help pull in the fresh fuel/air mixture.

hills worth beans and will have a big flat spot in its acceleration just at the rpm range you are used to driving in around town?

Or are you building a hot machine intended for the street that you would like to run through the traps occasionally just to see what it will do, but will be driving back and forth to work occasionally? In short, do you prefer a car that has impressive performance but is well

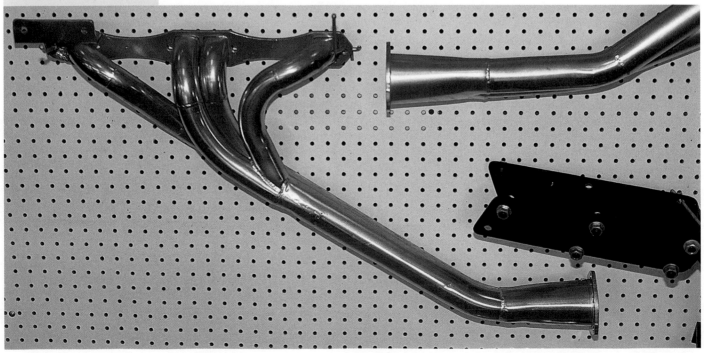

Sticking With Stock

The stock exhaust systems on classic Chevy engines were developed to be completely adequate for normal driving, and they were designed to be quiet and durable. They were also designed to fit in crowded engine compartments. In fact, lots of two-barrel–equipped, standard-performance, V-8–powered Chevys only come with one exhaust pipe and muffler, which is all they really need.

Such systems are quieter, less expensive, and they don't rust out as quickly as dual systems. Of course, high-performance, four-barrel–equipped Chevys came with twin exhaust systems with one pipe for each bank of cylinders. This setup is generally adequate for normal street use, except in rev ranges near the redline of the engine.

Your Bow Tie mouse motor probably came with cast-iron log manifolds. These are very restrictive in performance situations. The next step up in efficiency would be to find a set of original Corvette ram's-horn, cast-iron manifolds with the center exhaust dump going straight down, or canted slightly to the rear of the car. They are less restrictive than log manifolds, less expensive than headers, and will still fit nicely in most engine compartments.

The big problem with stock systems at high rpms is that your engine starts developing what is called back pressure. The exhaust gasses being pushed out of the system by the pistons are under so much pressure that they can actually back up into the incoming fuel/air mixture of adjacent cylinders and dilute it, especially when all the exhaust ports dump into a log manifold instead of being separated. The effect is used intentionally to some degree in later, smog-controlled engines to develop a leaner, cleaner-burning mixture, but it cuts performance dramatically in the process.

Stock ram's horns can actually be opened and port-matched to produce almost as much power as cheap headers. If you use the exhaust gasket you will be running in your engine as a template and open and smooth the cast headers as far up into them as you can go with your die grinder and abrasive rolls, you can actually develop about 65 percent of the performance improvement that a set of

A set of old-style ram's horns can be made to work well at lower rpms, and are the best choice among the stock manifolds.

conventional headers will make. All it will cost is a little labor, and your exhaust system will be quiet and long-lived.

Stock, ram's-horn cast-manifold dual exhaust systems don't develop harmful back pressure in normal service, but they aren't very good for pedal-to-the-metal performance either because they don't do anything to help the engine perform better. That takes tuning. And by tuning, we mean using the high- and low-pressure waves through the exhaust system to increase performance dramatically.

With tuned, tubular headers, when the exhaust valve opens, a burst of high-pressure hot gasses moves down its individual primary tube at very high velocity. This creates a high-pressure wave that sends a low-pressure wave back up the exhaust system. The gas particles don't actually change direction. It works sort of like when you throw a stone into still water. Behind the high-pressure waves are low-pressure troughs pulling the next wave along, though the water keeps moving in the same direction.

These low-pressure counter-waves can help create more torque at certain rpm ranges, depending on primary pipe length, pipe diameter, and valve overlap. Incidentally, there used to be a lot of fuss about having equal-length primary tubes, but this has not turned out to be as important as once thought, even for constant-throttle racing motors. That's because equal-length pipes, though they might theoretically produce the ultimate torque, can only do it at a very spiky, narrow rpm range. With primary pipes that vary in length by as much as a foot, the benefits are spread over a range of 3,000 to 4,000 rpm.

Doug's makes tri-Ys for tight spots too. These will give you great performance and still not get in the way.

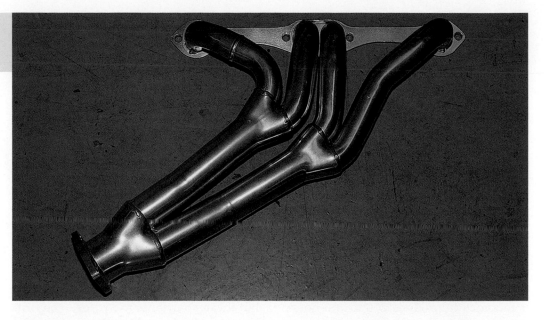

Why Tri-Y?

For street use, tri-Y, or four-into-two-into-one headers are superior to four-into-one headers that just dump straight into a collector, or secondary tube. By pairing two primary tubes before having them go into the collectors, you get much more usable, midrange torque, and your engine will pull well over a broader range.

These headers don't look quite as cool as the four-into-one headers so popular today, but they don't give you a large flat spot at lower rpm ranges like the four-into-one headers do either. Four-into-one headers are great for racing, but they're not so great for street use. Tri-Y, two-into-one headers help time the negative pressure waves much better by having that extra step, which makes them work well at more street-usable rpm ranges.

These four-into-one headers will produce prodigious amounts of power, but do so within a narrower rpm range than tri-Ys.

Pipe Diameter Matters

As a rule of thumb, a Chevy small-block primary pipe inside diameter should be about 1.16 times the exhaust valve open area. If you go bigger, you will slow down the exhaust gasses and hurt bottom-end performance. If you go too small, the pipes will be restrictive and you will lose velocity due to friction loss. Also, you will make the system susceptible to back pressure.

So how does that translate into usable numbers? Well, a Chevy small block that is intended to produce 200 to 400 horsepower will work well with industry standard 1⅝-inch inside diameter primary pipes. From 400–600 horsepower, 1.75-inch I.D. pipes are what you want. On a Chevy small block, anything above 1.75-inch I.D. won't fit without an adapter anyway.

For secondary, or collector tubes, 2.5 inches to 3 inches is about right. Slightly larger collectors may be required for very-high-performance street engines. Short collector lengths of 18–24 inches are right for a 7,500-rpm, radical-cam racing engine, but longer collectors will get you launched quicker and are better for street use. The same is true for primary pipes. Longer primaries in the range of 24 inches to 36 inches help bottom-end power.

Making Choices

Choose your headers carefully because not every manufacturer makes headers for every application, and quality isn't always consistent. I like Doug's Headers because the quality is consistently high, and Doug Thorley has been developing and manufacturing winning headers for many years. Check any headers you buy for flatness at the mounting flange and for good clean welds at the joints.

When you order a set of headers, make sure to tell the vendor the make and model of your vehicle, the year, and which transmission and accessories your car has. You will also want to specify whether you want plain pipe, chrome, stainless, or a special coating such as Jet

Thick, ⅜-inch plates are important to prevent warping due to high heat at the mating surfaces with the heads. Don't settle for thinner brackets.

Hot. Plain pipe must be kept painted to prevent rust. I like black barbecue paint for this job.

Chrome looks oh-so-nice until it blues, but it can contribute to hydrogen embrittlement, which weakens the pipe. Jet Hot coatings coat the pipes inside and out to prevent corrosion, and are very durable. Stainless (if available) is quite durable, but it does expand and contract more than mild steel, so it is more prone to leaks and loosening.

Installation

Installing headers isn't as easy as it might seem on a fully assembled car. Some must come in from the top; others must be installed from the bottom. Talk to the manufacturer, get a guarantee that they will fit your application, and read and follow the instructions that come with the headers. You may have to remove certain accessories to get the things in, and you may have to dimple

On some later cars with lots of accessories, it is necessary to custom build headers to clear everything.

the headers in a few cases to get them to clear everything.

Finally, you will want to install a cross-over pipe or X pipes to help even out the exhaust pulses and quiet the system. A cross-over tube will also cut vibration noticeably, and with headers, ringing and vibration can get irritating. To figure out where to place the cross-over tube, shoot a little cheap aerosol paint down the sides of exhaust pipes, run the engine for about 20 minutes, then determine just where the paint stopped burning off. That's where to put the cross-over, if possible.

Muffler Mythology

Many old-timers still think that a straight-through glass pack is less restrictive than a reverse flow. Not true. Unless the straight-through muffler has a very large inside diameter (which will be much too noisy), it will actually restrict flow through it. Those cheap glass packs on my aforementioned Chevy of years ago sounded cool, but slowed me down

considerably. And some of the new reverse-flow mufflers offer no more restriction than open pipes!

Place your mufflers as far from the engine as possible, and run the exhaust pipes all the way to the rear of the car. Shorter exhaust pipes don't help performance, and you run the risk of dangerous fumes getting into your car. Also, running the pipes to the rear helps cut noise in the cockpit. Longer pipes behind the muffler don't make any difference to performance, so there is no advantage to cutting them short.

Final Thoughts

If you install a set of headers on an engine that has been performing well, it will probably run a bit lean afterward. In that case, you may have to rejet the carb. Retune and retime your engine to make maximum use of your new exhaust system. If you've gone a bit radical, watch those back shifts through tunnels. The local cops may not like your taste in music, either.

These vintage megaphone headers look good and sound outrageous, but they don't produce the torque or horsepower of later, tuned headers.

Installing Aftermarket Headers

Colin Date

YOU'LL NEED:

- Standard socket set
- Standard wrenches
- Gasket scraper
- Set of application-correct headers
- Header and collector gaskets

TIME
3 hours

SKILL LEVEL
★★★☆

COST
$100–$600

APPLICABLE MODELS/YEARS
All

PERFORMANCE GAIN
Up to 30-plus increase in horsepower

Everyone is familiar with headers. They have been around since the beginning and for good reason—the realistic horsepower gains from aftermarket headers can make a big difference in your vehicle's performance. When paired with a high-flow exhaust system, aftermarket headers will yield significant improvements in throttle response, acceleration, and fuel economy. They will cause other performance components such as intakes, carburetors, camshafts, and ignitions to reach their fullest potential as well.

Think of your engine as an oversized air pump. Naturally, the faster the air is able to flow through the pump, the more power it creates. Headers offer an improved and more efficient way to scavenge the exhaust gasses and draw clean, fresh air into the cylinders. Headers are also designed to balance the pressures found between the intake and exhaust systems.

Unfortunately, just about every muscle car of the era rolled off the assembly line with a highly restrictive "pea-shooter" exhaust system. Stock cast-iron manifolds, small-diameter pipes, and a single outlet was the norm, even on some high-performance models. Therefore, installing aftermarket headers and a free-flow exhaust system is one of the most popular external engine upgrades.

When it comes to selecting headers and your new exhaust, think practical. Primarily, you will be switching from a single pipe and exit system to a dual. Along with a cross-over tube or balance pipe, this will literally open up a world of difference in your engine's characteristics. Choose the headers that will closest meet your driving and performance needs, not the biggest and loudest pipes you can stuff into your engine bay. A well-tuned, complete package is the key. Do not hesitate to call manufacturers' technical support lines and ask for advice. They are product specialists and can definitely steer you in the right direction.

Although many exhaust manufacturers now offer all-inclusive kits with pipes, clamps, and mufflers, your local muffler shop can handle the minor fabrication of the pipes and collectors. Be sure to request the use of aluminized tubing. Its corrosion resistance and longevity are far superior to the factory steel pieces. Mufflers are basically a matter of preference. From loud and crazy to sweet and low, there are seemingly endless options on the market today. Simply select the one that delivers your desired tone and flow.

Installing a pair of headers is never fun. With so many variables on each year, make, and model, the installation process fails to provide any regularity. In other words, be prepared to make adjustments. You will need the car in the air, on either a lift or a sturdy pair of jack stands. You may need to remove the hood for additional clearance. In some extreme cases, you may need to remove the engine from the chassis to fit the headers into position. You can install them from the top or the bottom of the car, wherever clearance allows.

First, loosen and remove the spark plugs and the exhaust manifold bolts from the cylinder heads. Disengage the bottom of the manifold from the collector pipe. Unbolt the muffler and its hanger from the rear of the vehicle and remove the exhaust pipe. Thoroughly clean the gasket-mating surface of the cylinder head before installing the new header gaskets. Paper header gaskets are often included with the headers but lack rigidity and are prone to breaking and leakage. Spend the extra money and purchase a set of quality, steel-reinforced gaskets. They will far outlast the paper gaskets and can be reused. Install the headers as necessary and torque them to manufacturer's specs. Some headers will require slight modifications to the primary tubes in order to clear suspension control arms, accessory brackets, and the frame of the vehicle. There are a number of ways to create the correct dimple in the headers without damaging them or compromising their structural integrity. First, test-fit the header, and mark the location of the needed dimple. Secure the header in a press or a bench-mounted vise, and carefully apply heat from a

> **TIP:**
> After the installation, you may need to change your spark plug wires to accommodate the new headers. Although 90-degree boots are by far the most common, 135-degree or straight boots are sometimes necessary.

small propane torch. Squeeze the tube until the desired dimple is formed. This may also be accomplished with a steel bar and a hammer. Heat the tube and use the bar and hammer to create the extra clearance.

At the bottom end of each header is a collector-mounting flange that will mate the header to the collector and the exhaust pipes. The collector and the pipes, along with the mufflers, should be welded by a professional. After running the car, retighten the bolts periodically to guarantee a tight seal.

With the engine slightly hoisted, we first unbolt and remove the right side header from the top of the vehicle to allow extra clearance to maneuver the left header up and around the clutch linkage.

How To Hot Rod Your Carbureted Small-Block Chevy

Jeff Hartman

Hear that little cough two blocks back under acceleration? Sounds a little lean somewhere—the kind of annoying little thing that's a nightmare to get rid of when you're shaking out a new carb, cam, and intake manifold.

Fortunately, this '55 Chevy does not have a carb. Instead of pulling the car over to the side and attacking the carb with a screwdriver, we reposition the cursor on the laptop PC resting on the bench seat of the 400-horsepower '55 Chevy, put that little arrow on the bar graph representing the exact rpm range and engine loading conditions, and hit a few function keys. As always, the computer is highlighting the current rpm range exactly when the engine coughed, so we know which graph to diddle. The laptop is connected by a thin black wire to the programmable electronic control unit driving the EFI-conversion 350 Chevy small-block V-8. Under the hood, four Weber look-alike throttle bodies with stacks sit hissing atop the Chevy mouse V-8. Exhaust rumbles out the back with just enough lope so you know this car has a good cam even though it works through a ratchet-shifter turbo 350 automatic. We lengthen the bar graph, hit the enter key, and immediately data is stored in electrically erasable programmable read-only memory in the Haltech ECU—and punch the gas pedal hard. The instant the hammer goes down, the eight Bosch injectors spritzing fuel directly at the intake valves will change their opening time by a tiny fraction of a millisecond and fatten up the mixture at the right rpm under the right load as measured by manifold absolute pressure.

Left: Just a red '55 Chevy "Shoebox," still popular among older hot rodders, equipped with the original small-block Chevy V-8, of which the General would eventually manufacture and install about 60 million in trucks and cars into the 21st century with power ratings from about 100 SAE horsepower to 405 in the high-water mark early-1990s ZR1 'Vette. Its age made this car perfect street-legal hot rodding material that would forever be exempt from modern emissions requirements—and yet cleaner than it had ever run when carbureted.

EFI in 1955

In the 1990s, Ivan Tull concentrated on building integrated fuel injection and EFI turbo systems for hot rod Chevys. A critical success factor was understanding that when people spend a lot of money on their car, the results had better look great. Tull injection systems display the exotic look of multicarb Weber induction systems, with great attention to detail. This kind of high-buck add-on engine system can't just look great. It has to perform noticeably better after than before.

Tull likes to call turbo-EFI conversions the last best speed secret for hot rod vintage muscle cars and trucks—the difference between a cylinder or two filled almost right with fuel and air, and every cylinder filled perfectly with exactly the right amount of fuel as the air enters the combustion chamber. That difference spells horsepower—sometimes a lot of horsepower!

Tull induction systems use multiple throttle bodies and port fuel injection—from the simplest naturally aspirated powerplant utilizing double cross-ram throttle body pairs to a maxed-out full-bore motor with eight throttle bodies, sixteen injectors, twin turbos, and over a thousand horsepower. Tull designed one such configuration for use on a Donovan aluminum small-block Chevy V-8 in a custom-designed laminar-flow airframe built to take on P-51 Mustangs at the Reno Air Races—where the competition was hot rod World War II war birds running supercharged mega-cubic-inch Rolls Royce Merlin V-12 motors. The Tull Systems' sixteen-injector motors idled nicely on eight injectors sized reasonably for a smooth slow idle—while the other eight injectors were designed to kick in only for high-end power.

The great thing about programmable EFI is that when Tull was done messing around with a normally aspirated cross-ram Chevy V-8 with Haltech EMS, he simply plugged his IBM laptop computer into the Haltech ECU, fired up the graphical display of injection pulse width for various engine rpm and loading, and modified the bar graphs for loads beyond zero vacuum as reported by the two-bar MAP sensor.

A 5.7-liter custom cross-ram EFI system with programmable aftermarket injection and twin turbos seemed like a much better idea than the original V-8.

Building a beautiful and complex add-on turbo system to jack up the power to extreme levels was no trivial thing. The project involved installing new cast-iron exhaust manifolds designed to bolt directly to twin Garret TO4 turbos. It required plumbing in high-pressure oil lines to lube the turbos and the larger low-pressure oil drain lines to return oil directly to the oil pan. It involved plumbing cooling water from the water pump to the center sections of the turbos to keep them running cool in south Texas' scorching summers. And it required building air boxes around the outboard side of the fuel injection throttle bodies and plumbing in the big 2-inch lines feeding boost air from the turbo compressors.

But once all that was accomplished, recalibrating the Haltech involved creating a superset of the existing calibration. The Haltech behaved exactly the same at lower loading, until you jumped on the throttle and the big turbos whistled up to speed, blowing in 7 or 8 psi more air than that Chevy 350 mouse motor could otherwise gulp down. At this point, the Haltech would obey the high-load graphs for air pressure higher than atmospheric, keeping the engine rich and happy. The engine would fire right up and idle perfectly. Later, he'd review the calibration under actual road-test conditions, or possibly on a dyno to get the mixture exactly where he wanted it. All this would be absolutely legal on a '55 Chevy, because America had no emissions laws for cars this old.

A customer looking for an EFI conversion could just bolt on junkyard TPI parts to a small-block Chevy V-8, but if he wanted an exotic-looking system with multiple TWM DCOE Weber-type throttle bodies on a cross-ram Weber-bolt-pattern manifold, this type of system is hard to beat. This system—available with either downdraft or side-draft throttle bodies—offered exotic looks and tremendous flow capacity but would not be cheap. Throttle bodies of 45 millimeters and above will flow plenty of air for any small-block-Chevy motor, while eight individual runners flow a massive 1,800 cfm with quad 45-millimeter TWM throttle bodies with two butterflies per throttle body.

The '55 Chevy pictured here uses a medium-compression 350 Chevy small block. Tull modified the fuel tank's sending unit to accept a fuel return and installed a fuel return line. A high-pressure fuel pump replaced the old mechanical fuel pump, and a block-off plate sealed up the block where it had been. TWM Weber DCOE bolt-pattern throttle bodies bolted to the cross-ram manifold without modifications, and Tull constructed a two-piece fuel rail from D-section aluminum, ready to accept O-ringed injectors. The pressure regulator connected to the outlet end of one side of the rail, the pressurized inlet fuel line to

the other, with a cross-over hose connecting the two rails.

After calibrating the fuel curve for the first normally aspirated iteration of the hot rod, recalibration for turbocharging basically meant changing the flat segment of the loading bars at higher than atmospheric pressure to the correct pulse widths for fueling the higher turbocharged volumetric efficiency. Tull would remove the K&N air cleaners from the throttle bodies and fabricate plenums from intercooler end-tanks to pressurize the throttle bodies. The turbos were a simple bolt-on to the cast Chevy small-block turbocharger exhaust manifolds. That's the great thing about small-block Chevys—whatever you want, somebody makes it! The rest was muffler shop-type stuff, piecing together constant radius tubing to feed air from the two compressors to the throttle body plenums.

The great thing about such a car is that it is radical but very streetable, no hangar queen but rather a daily driver. And a legal one at that.

The "Last, Best Speed Secret"—high-compression V-8 power, programmable EFI, and turbocharging—turned this old dog into a raging power freak that could idle smoothly.

1970 Dodge Challenger B-Block

Jeff Hartman

What did it take to change a 1970 Dodge Challenger B-block from a dinosaur into a creature of the new millennium? Perhaps good modern tires and wheels, some suspension gimmicks, hardened valve seats in the heads, things like that. And an upgrade to electronic fuel injection.

The application of electronic fuel injection to American V-8s and turbocharged fours and sixes in the late 1970s and 1980s spawned a performance renaissance that could not otherwise have happened. Fuel injection directly led to greatly improved emissions and economy, while maintaining or improving the power output of modern V-8s and smaller turbo engines. Injection improved drivability by increasing and broadening engines' torque curves with tuned dry manifolds and improved fuel distribution and more accurate air/fuel mixtures.

Electronic fuel injection improved efficiency by allowing higher compression ratios on modern pump gas, and improved power by eliminating the need for certain emissions-control strategies such as retarded ignition timing and low compression. Since electronic fuel injection requires a computer for calculating injection pulse width, the existence of an onboard computer on an injected vehicle made it not only feasible to compute and time sequential injection pulses, but to apply computer control to spark advance and to dynamically coordinate injection control with ignition and emissions-control devices such as EGR, making all these systems work together on a millisecond-to-millisecond basis—yielding clean power with good economy. A win-win situation. This is what you get when you buy a modern performance car like a millennium-vintage V-8 muscle car like a Mustang, Camaro, or Corvette.

Although the Mopar V-8s of the 1960s and early 1970s are famous for high-performance, high-output Mopar V-8 cars departed the scene in the mid-1970s along with big-block Mopar V-8s in anything but trucks. However, it is very possible to retrofit electronic fuel injection and computer-controlled spark advance—even emissions controls—to older carbureted Mopars. I had a 1970 Dodge Challenger with the big-block 383 V-8, and electronic fuel injection seemed like a great idea.

1970 Dodge Challenger B-block 383 four-barrel with sidepipes: the retro look.

Phase 1. Throttle-Body Injection

Holley's original TBI Pro-Jection system was designed as an affordable self-contained injection system that is simple to understand, install, and tune. It was designed to replace the four-barrel carb on older V-8s, and it is still selling for this purpose nearly 15 years after its introduction (though the control unit now uses a digital microprocessor instead of analog circuitry and logic). And you still tune the TBI Pro-Jection by adjusting five pots on the side of the control unit with a screwdriver. Holley started with a single-point-injection throttle body with two injectors that essentially had been developed as an OEM replacement part for certain late-model vehicles and made it part of a kit that also included an MSD-designed and manufactured control unit, wiring, a sensor or two, and some miscellaneous mounting adapters. The Pro-Jection was simple and cheap.

Naturally, there were trade-offs.

An installer paying the half a grand or so for a Pro-Jection 2 system (now superseded by Holley's 670 CFM Two-Barrel Pro-Jection Digital system) could expect the following advantages compared to a carb:

- There is no float bowl, so hard acceleration and cornering or harsh terrain cannot degrade the operation of the fuel system as it can with a carb.

- Fuel delivery is precise and infinitely variable because the Pro-Jection provides fuel in multiple bursts or pulses that can be timed in increments of less than a thousandth of a second. Since the Pro-Jection system does not use separate and overlapping fluid/air systems as a carb does for idle, midrange, top-end, transient enrichment (accelerator pump) and cold-start operations, a properly tuned system has the potential to conform more perfectly to an ideal air/fuel curve, yielding more power and economy compared to a carb.

- The Pro-Jection allows adjustable enrichment for cold starting and includes a fast idle solenoid.

- The Pro-Jection system can be tuned with a set of screwdriver-adjustable dashpots while the vehicle moves down the street or rolls on a dyno—obviously an advantage compared to the repeated disassembly that may be required when making jet changes on a carb.

- The Pro-Jection, being a pulsed fuel injection system, is not subject to mixture problems resulting from reversion pulses flowing backward through a carb particularly in a wild cammed engine with a single-plane manifold—resulting in the carb over-richening the mixture by adding fuel to the air twice as it reverses direction.

- Since the Pro-Jection instantly cuts fuel delivery when you turn off the key, dieseling cannot occur as it might with a carb.

- Vapor lock is much less likely under the 12–20 psi Pro-Jection fuel pressure, compared to the reduced pressure of a mechanical vacuum pump sucking fuel forward to the engine.

- Hot air percolation, in which gasoline boils and overflows the float bowl(s) in a carb in hot weather—additionally pressurized by the action of vapor pressure in fuel lines—is not possible with the Pro-Jection.

On the other hand:

- One of the trade-offs of the simple and affordable Pro-Jection is that fuel is injected from only two injectors at one place—at the two-barrel throttle body. Compared to supplying fuel from individual injectors at every intake port, throttle-body injection's ability to deliver equal fuel and air to every cylinder is subject to the same limitations and design flaws of any intake manifold that must handle a wet mixture. Gasoline tends to fall out of suspension in the air of the intake manifold during cold starting or sudden throttle openings that rapidly change manifold pressure—and then tear off the surface of the manifold unpredictably in sheets of liquid in a way that can interfere with equal distribution to individual cylinders. There is simply no way to guarantee equal distribution with single-point fueling. In addition, high air velocity is required to keep fuel suspended in the air at low rpm, which means that the Pro-Jection cannot use the radical dry manifolds of port fuel injection that provide great high-end breathing while relying on port injection to put fuel directly into the swirling dry air at the intake valve at low speed for equal distribution and consequent good idle.

- The Pro-Jection 2 did not control ignition spark advance or other emissions-control devices.

- The Pro-Jection estimates air mass entering the engine based on throttle position and rpm, with no provision for measuring actual mass airflow (MAF) or manifold absolute pressure (MAP), which means it was not able to compensate for VE changes to air entering the engine at equal rpm and throttle position based on, say, the action of a blow-through turbocharger. There is also no provision to raise fuel pressure (a relatively low 15 psi) to compensate for air pressure changes.

- Obviously, the Pro-Jection cannot time fuel injection for individual cylinders as in sequential fuel injection (a tactic used to improve emissions and fuel economy).

When I first began to work on this '70 Challenger, it was running an ancient Carter AFB carb on a single-plane Edelbrock Streetmaster 383 aluminum intake manifold. The engine was still running the stock compression ratio (9:1) but now ran a fairly hot auto transmission Competition Cams camshaft. The L code on the car told me that the vehicle had originally been built as a 290-horsepower two-barrel 383. The engine was now equipped with a new Carter AFB four-barrel carburetor.

With fresh paint and interior on the Challenger plus a freshly rebuilt engine, new air conditioning compressor and a host of other details like a new wiper switch and door handles, I later set about

This car started out life as a 290-horse 383-ci two-barrel big block. With four-barrel Carter AFB carburetion and some other mild hot rod parts (Edelbrock "Streetmaster 383" single-plane manifold, better cam, headers, and so on), we guessed the "Commando" V-8 was up to the standard of the factory 335-horse "Magnum" four-barrel. Everything worked, including the air conditioning.

to install the Pro-Jection. Although the Pro-Jection 2 is a two-barrel throttle body, it will not fit on a stock two-barrel manifold. The Pro-Jection bolted to an adapter plate made to bolt on a four-barrel manifold and is workable on most small- and medium-displacement American V-8s, flowing up to 650 cfm.

It is very easy to install this type of Holley EFI system. You begin by designing a way to return fuel to the gas tank. Like virtually all injection systems, the Holley system must provide constant pressure to the injectors, regardless of the engine fuel requirements. This is done by providing a fuel loop that pumps pressurized gasoline from the tank to a pressure regulator in the engine compartment and then back to the tank. The regulator, integral to the throttle body in the Pro-Jection, pinches off return flow to the degree required to maintain a preset pressure in the fuel supply line. The amount of excess fuel returning to the tank varies depending on engine fuel consumption. A lot of fuel is returning at idle, very little if the engine fuel consumption approaches the capacity of the fuel pump under high-rpm heavy loading.

I removed the fuel filler neck pipe, cleaned it carefully, and welded on a fitting to attach the returning fuel line. An alternative return might also have been possible by removing the sending unit for attachment of a return fitting. Obviously, you can't simply drill a hole in the tank. If it were necessary to remove the tank for drilling or welding, you should have the work done by a fuel tank specialist. An empty fuel tank, inevitably loaded with fuel vapor, is incredibly explosive!

Mount the fuel pump in a safe low spot near the fuel tank, preferably where it will be primed by gravity rather than the reverse. Holley suggests mounting the fuel pump no higher than the top of the tank, and suggests locating the pump at the bottom of a loop of fuel line so the pump will always have liquid fuel to pump when it first starts. When you turn on the key, the computer will momentarily activate the pump to pressurize the injectors. If fuel is not immediately available to the pump, the engine may be very hard to start. Naturally, on an old dog like a '70 Challenger, you'll want to remove the mechanical fuel pump from the engine, and blank off the hole in the block with a plate (available at most speed shops).

I next removed the old carb, and mounted the Holley adapter plate and throttle body, connecting the fuel supply line and a return line I installed and connected to the return fitting on the filler neck. Chrysler automatic transmission cars, using a mechanical kick-down linkage, may require an adapter to attach the linkage to the Pro-Jection. Holley builds a Mopar adapter, but doesn't include it in the standard kit. I got one at a local speed shop. The linkage on the Challenger, having already been doctored in the conversion to the Carter AFB four-barrel, required some fudging to get it perfect.

Aftermarket fuel injection computers, other than incredibly expensive mil-spec

racing units like EFI Technology's Competition unit, tend to work better in a friendly environment, away from lots of heat and electrical interference, which means inside the car or in the trunk. I mounted the Pro-Jection computer on the console ahead of the shifter, and fed the wiring harness through an existing hole in the firewall to connect to the Pro-Jection throttle body, the new EFI water temperature sending unit (which I'd mounted in a 1/8-inch fitting in the water pump), and the fuel pump. That left several wires that needed to be connected to constant positive 12-volt, switched +12 voltage, and negative 12-volt coil or tach-drive voltage.

Start-up time.

Since an EFI fuel pump usually only runs a second or two on initial energizing before start, it's a good idea to jumper the fuel pump to +12 voltage on the battery in order to fill the fuel system with gas, and then to listen carefully when you turn on the key to make sure that it is operating full time (if you wire it wrong, some ignition switch connections specifically do not provide voltage while cranking).

With the fuel pump working, I verified that the dashpots on the computer were at the correct position specified by Holley for initial start-up, then cranked and watched the injectors with the air cleaner removed from the throttle body. It is easy to see the big throttle-body injectors spraying fuel, and in a few seconds the engine came to life. I immediately went to work on the idle mixture dashpot, hunting for the position that would give the smoothest idle. Disconcertingly, this was as lean as it would go.

Consulting the manual, I decided that perhaps the throttle position switch (TPS)—a linear potentiometer mounted on the throttle shaft on the side of the throttle body—might not be calibrated correctly. Since the computer determines engine loading directly from throttle position and rpm, it is essential that the switch read the right voltage. Using a digital resistance meter and some jumpers, I was able to watch the resistance of the switch change as I opened the throttle. Bingo. The switch was reading too high with the throttle closed. Loosening the TPS, I was able to rotate it

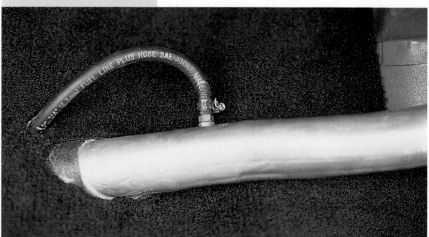

You're going to need a fuel return line. We did it the easy way, adding a hose barb to the fuel filler neck so unneeded fuel that bleeds from the fuel rail can return into the fuel tank. We also installed a coolant temp sensor, 15-psi electric fuel pump, fuel return line, and a few other tricks.

until the meter showed the correct voltage for a closed throttle. Starting the engine, the idle mixture dashpot now yielded the best mixture farther up the scale as it should.

Holley's installation manual lists procedures for tuning the midrange and high-end power, which basically involves tuning for best mixture at 3,000 rpm unloaded in neutral, then using a stopwatch to time acceleration runs at wide-open throttle (WOT) until the Pro-Jection is set up for best power as indicated by the stopwatch. Pro-Jection 4 units have one extra pot for tuning high-end power. Of course, the best procedure is to attach a wideband air/fuel-ratio meter and tune for 12.5–13.5:1 mixtures.

Out on the highway, I noticed an interesting thing: Although the car felt—seat of the pants—as if it had better low-end torque, what was missing was the sudden burst of power under hard acceleration you get with a four-barrel as the secondaries open up under WOT.

The Pro-Jection system was a vast improvement over the carburetor on the Challenger. It started quickly in all weather, provided fast idle when cold, and was free of the hot weather starting problems encountered by the AFB in the heat of a south Texas summer. Throttle response was good under all conditions. The system had no way of compensating for the air conditioning compressor coming on line, but had it really mattered, I might have rigged a relay to trigger the cold-start solenoid.

Phase 2. Port Fuel Injection

In the meantime, I got access to a Haltech ECU capable of controlling multiple port injectors on a V-8. I decided to convert to the Haltech. It turned out this was extremely easy, given that I had already made the conversions for the Holley TBI. I already had a fuel return line. I already had a mounting port for a coolant-temperature sensor. It turned out to be possible to use the Holley throttle body to meter air. The throttle position switch on the Holley throttle body is compatible with the Haltech. The injector/regulator/fuel fittings assembly is a one-piece unit that bolts to the main section of the Holley throttle body with three Allen screws. I removed it and fabricated an aluminum plate to cover the hole.

The single-plane Edelbrock manifold on the Challenger uses runners that are perfectly in line with each other. I milled holes for injector bosses in the roofs of the runners working through the runners from the underside of the manifold, and welded the injector bosses in place from the bottom, grinding the excess boss material away so as not to interfere with airflow. I installed O-ringed Lucas disc fuel injectors in the bosses that were fitted for hoses on the fuel input side, constructing a D-section fuel rail with hose barbs to supply fuel.

The biggest problem had to do with the fact that 1970 Chryslers used a mechanical kick-down linkage that had originally connected to the carb linkage. Later, with adaptations, I had attached it to the Holley throttle body. Unfortunately, the injector assembly and fuel rail were now exactly where a linkage support had bolted to the intake manifold. Fortunately, I discovered it was possible to move the kick-down linkage outboard of the left bank of injectors by cutting the linkage support in two pieces and welding it back together with the addition of some mild steel bracketing. I cut the linkage itself and inserted a 3/4-inch inward offset so it could properly connect to the Holley throttle body.

It was an easy matter to connect the fuel lines to the new fuel rail (using 900-psi hose at $0.33 an inch!). I used a 39-psi pressure-referenced regulator from an L-Jetronic injection system, and I robbed the Bosch fuel pump I'd used in the original XKE turbo-EFI system featured in another chapter of this book, installing it inline in the return side of the Challenger's fuel rail. The fuel pump was necessary since the Pro-Jection pump is not designed to provide the high pressure required to provide stable fuel pressure to eight batch-fire port injectors.

Wiring the Haltech ECU was simple, and programming is discussed in other sections of this book. Haltech provided a start-up map designed for a modified V-8 that provides a nice rich set of base fuel maps as a good starting point for a car like the Challenger. Although this big-block Mopar 383 engine is not particularly radical, given the hotter-than-stock

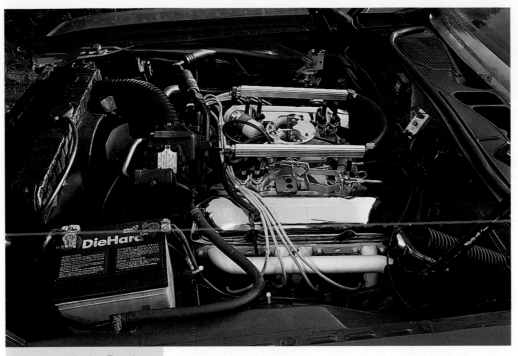

Starting with the Pro-Jection TBI system made the port-injection conversion a little easier. We removed the two big injectors from the throttle body, drilled and welded-in injector bosses, constructed a fuel supply rail, and installed a high-pressure inline fuel pump. The Haltech EMS generic harness plugged into the injectors and sensors straightforwardly. We plugged in a laptop, fired up the car with a library calibration, and tuned the car for drivability with the Haltech mixture trim module as best we could on some Texas back roads. Later on we found some free power with a Horiba wideband AFR meter.

cam, the headers, and the large-port intake manifold, the modified V-8 map seemed like a good place to start, since it is always preferable to begin rich and work lean when calibrating an engine.

I installed an air temperature sensor for the Haltech ECU in the air cleaner inlet. This is much better than milling a port hole in an intake manifold runner, which is much more likely to heat-soak the sensor and lean out the mixture as the ECU tries to correct for unrealistically hot intake air.

Finally, I had to build a connector to adapt the Holley TPS connector to the foreign Haltech wiring harness. I located the Haltech ECU inside the car on the side of the transmission hump near where the Pro-Jection system had been. I removed the Holley wiring harness and equipment and set it aside. It would be easy enough in the future to replace the Holley throttle body with something else and use the whole Holley system on some other project.

There is a wonderful crispness to multi-port injection that is properly set up, given that the injectors are spraying fuel at high pressure directly at intake valves only an inch or two away on a setup like that of the Challenger. The Haltech ECU offered excellent resolution, basically providing a 512 element matrix of speed-load breakpoints that

define the engine fuel map. Obviously, this provides greater flexibility that the Pro-Jection system that defines the base fuel map with three control knobs.

Is multi-port injection worth the additional expense over a programmable throttle body system? The point about the Holley system is that it was easy, affordable, and had clear advantages over the AFB four-barrel carb it replaced. A properly tuned Pro-Jection system will always outperform a poorly tuned software-programmable port-injected system, and a system like the Pro-Jection is much easier to tune. Gasoline-fueled engines can be reasonably forgiving about mixture, with a fairly wide margin in air/fuel ratio separating lean best torque and rich best torque.

The fairest thing to say about whether it's worth it depends on what you are asking the simpler Pro-Jection system to do. How good is the manifold you're using for wet mixtures? How smooth and consistent is the volumetric efficiency of the engine as power and airflow increase? How peaky is the engine in its torque curve; how much does torque vary from a truly flat curve? How high is the compression? How important is fuel consumption? Do you have the equipment and patience required to really take advantage of the programmable port EFI system's flexibility? It you have a radical manifold on a peaky engine with a lot of compression, it is very important to have the flexibility to build an oddly shaped fuel curve to match torque, and then you'd clearly want a programmable multi-port engine management system.

But on many engines, considering only peak power at wide-open throttle, the Pro-Jection is right up there with the best of them. Of course, it will clearly not have the wonderful low- to midrange broad torque range of a tuned multi-port injection system with long runners. But that's a different story. And when you've got 383 cubic inches under the hood, you've always got torque.

Chapter 5

Cosmetics

Everyone wants a good-looking car, and these three projects will help you spiff up your car's interior and exterior. Start by refurbishing your leather seats. Then replace your worn-out, smelly old carpet. Finish up with a complete restoration of your bumpers.

Leather Care

Richard Newton

YOU'LL NEED:
- Clean towels
- Rags

COMPLEMENTARY MODIFICATION:

The huge Corvette C4 dash needs regular treatment with something that contains an ultraviolet blocker. You really can't treat the upper dash panels too often. Sun is the major enemy of the Corvette interior.

TIME
1 hour

SKILL LEVEL
★★★☆

COST
$25

APPLICABLE MODELS/YEARS
Cars with leather interiors

PERFORMANCE GAIN
When the seats look nice, you'll feel faster

Leather is a natural product and has microscopic holes that allow moisture to pass through very tiny pores. These pores also absorb human perspiration. When the water evaporates, the salts remain to absorb the essential oils in the leather. This accumulation of salts and other grunge should be cleaned from the leather about twice a year. The loss of oils within the leather is really the first step in the leather's process of hardening, cracking, and shrinking.

You can clean your leather seats with a mild soap and water or, better yet, with a specifically designed leather cleaner. Of all the products I've tried, I still like Lexol pH Cleaner. It's both pH balanced and gentle. Any of the cleaners on the market, though, will rehydrate the leftover salts and grime and wash them from the leather fibers.

Make sure that you only use leather products on leather; don't use vinyl cleaners on your leather seats. These vinyl cleaners tend to be much harsher and can actually damage your leather.

Any cleaner should be rinsed thoroughly from the leather. I've tried spraying it off with a hose. Unfortunately, this just seemed to fill the car with soapy water. I went back to using a damp cloth towel, repeatedly wiping down the leather. Once the leather is clean, a conditioner should be added to restore the lost oils.

You need to think of leather as a sponge. When the leather is new, the sponge is full of oil, and it's soft and pliable. Body salts, UV, heat, and other factors drive the oil from the sponge, allowing the leather to shrink and become brittle. A quality leather conditioner will help maintain the oil in the leather.

There are several conditioners on the market. My favorite is Lexol Leather Conditioner. I've tried other products over the years, but I always go back to the Lexol. It seems to be the product that is most easily absorbed into the leather fibers and tends to leave a relatively less greasy finish than any of the other products I have tried. It still leaves an oily surface, though, and you'll need to buff it before you sit in your seats.

Another good product is Connolly Hide Food. This is the product that Rolls Royce owners are known to use. It's made from rendered animal parts and will turn rancid in about two years. This, and the distinctive cow smell it possesses, removes it from the top of my list. Nevertheless, it's really a great product. Can several generations of Rolls Royce owners be totally wrong?

One Grand Leather Conditioner is a petroleum-based conditioner that seems to work great on Corvette leather. Again, don't use a vinyl product as a conditioner on your leather and avoid any products that contain raw silicone oils. Silicone oil dissolves the leather's natural oils and makes the leather sticky.

Silicone oil also has a very high electrostatic attraction and will invite practically every dust particle within five miles to set up camp in your interior. There's nothing worse than having a fully detailed interior and then having it covered in dust several hours later.

The application process is the same for all of the products you might use. Simply apply the conditioner to a soft cloth and work it into the leather. Then allow it to sit for a few hours, or a day, so the product can be absorbed into the leather. After a sufficient amount of time, you can buff off the excess material.

You can condition the leather as often as you wish. As a rule, however, condition your leather three to four times a year. The leather will tell you if you apply too much or apply it too often. The leather fibers just won't absorb the excess. If you apply the conditioner and it immediately soaks into the interior, you should consider treating it a little more often. On the other hand, if it doesn't seem to sink into the leather very quickly, you can go a little longer between treatments.

If your leather has hardened or needs some intensive softening, there's a product called Surflex Leather Softener. This product is made from natural and synthetic oils that restore the natural softness to neglected leather. Clean the leather and then apply a liberal coat of the product. Then cover the treated area with plastic. Allow the Surflex to pene-

TIP:

This should be done on a regular basis. Exactly how often you do it depends on your local climate and how often you leave the car out in the sun.

trate the leather for at least 72 hours. Wipe off the excess. If it needs an additional application, repeat the above. For really bad areas, cover with plastic and allow to sit for a few days. Once the leather is sufficiently softened, allow to cure for another 24 hours and buff off any excess.

The real secret to leather care is that it needs to be done on a regular basis. Once the leather in the seats has hardened, you have a major task on your hands. The good part is that the seat leather in the C4 Corvette is very high quality and very tough. When it comes to seats, we really have far better seats than the folks who purchased C5s do. Take care of these seats, and they'll last forever.

The first step is to clean the leather with a good-quality cleaner. Follow up with a leather conditioner. These conditioners contain oils that will keep your leather soft.

Carpet Installation

Richard Newton

COMPLEMENTARY MODIFICATION:
This is a good time to replace any broken plastic parts in the interior. You may want to wait to place your order, however, since you may break some additional parts while installing the carpeting.

TIME
6 hours-2 days

SKILL LEVEL
★★★☆

COST
$500-$700

APPLICABLE MODELS/YEARS
Corvettes 1984-1996

PERFORMANCE GAIN
None

YOU'LL NEED:
- Screwdrivers
- Carpet cement

The later doorsills are a lot easier to work with than the early ones. The 1984 to 1987 cars have one huge piece of plastic that's almost impossible to remove. I suspect the assembly plant had the same sort of problems because in 1988 it went to a two-piece unit that lasted until the end of the C4.

The first step to replacing the carpet is to decide how much carpeting you're going to replace. The 1984 to 1996 carpeting really consists of three different sections. You have the driver's side area, the passenger area, and the rear cargo area. If you really feel energetic and have a decent balance on your credit card, you can do all three sections at the same time. A more realistic approach is to simply do one area as the spirit moves you. If you're a typical person, you probably tend to lose interest about halfway through a project. Keep in mind that taking everything apart is easy. Putting things back together is where the frustration exists. However, you already knew that, didn't you?

A lot of people purchase the entire carpet set at one time because they want everything to match perfectly. Carpeting today is dyed in huge quantities, and the quality control is far better than it used to be. A few months, or even a year, between purchases won't make a great deal of difference in the carpet color. However, as we all know, these projects tend to drag on far longer than we ever intended. This means it could be years between carpet purchases. And this means you could end up with carpet in different shades of the same color. More likely, though, the problem will come from having the first part of the project start to fade as you get around to finishing things up.

You should purchase carpet that matches the original perfectly. Corvettes that have been repainted will always lose some value, but if you install a different type, or even color, of carpeting in your Corvette, be prepared to take a serious financial hit upon resale. The $200 you save by purchasing something that is almost correct, instead of something that is perfect, won't be a wise decision.

The two carpet areas that take the greatest abuse are located in the rear area and on the driver's side. The rear area really fades quickly. If you want to see how much your carpet has faded, simply pull up the edge of the center section and look at the carpet that's been hidden from the sunlight. The good news is that the rear area is also the easiest section to work on.

The first job is to remove the front seats. This task takes a lot less time if you take off the roof—unless, of course, you own a convertible where you can simply lower the top for seat removal. Look at the chapter on swapping the seats around to remind yourself how to remove the four bolts that hold each of the seats in place. Also, be careful with all the electrical connections that have to be undone.

Left: You can always tell when a car has been repainted. This car was originally a black car. The body shop left the little adhesive pads for the sill plate in place during the painting process. This picture shows where you can expect to find the adhesive pads. Run your hair dryer in these areas to soften up the adhesive. Then carefully remove the huge plastic sill.

Right: The center console is a difficult area. Make sure the carpeting tucks under the panels with no wrinkles.

With the seats out of the way, you can progress to the most difficult part of the project—removing the sill covers without breaking them. The early sill covers come out easily in two pieces. The only problem is that's the wrong way to do it. If you break one, the replacements are over $100 for the early cars. This is a task for two people working slowly and carefully.

The technique is to remove all the screws and then slowly move the sill cover around. They're really glued firmly down onto the doorsill. Chevrolet used some black putty between the plastic cover and the sill to prevent squeaks. There are three different areas under the sill where this putty was applied.

Over the years, the putty has hardened and will fight all reasonable attempts to remove the sill. One good technique is to use a heat gun to warm the sill cover so the putty will soften. While this makes the removal a little easier, it's still not the

TIP:
You might want to do one section at a time.

greatest job in the world. Just take your time here, and the cover will eventually pull off the doorsill.

Removing the carpeting from the floor is pretty simple. The only other area of difficulty is where the carpeting tucks up under the center console. It helps if you remove the screws that hold the center console plate in place. You'll have to do this to get the new carpeting tucked up into place so you may as well do it to remove the old carpeting now.

Don't try to remove backing that goes over the transmission. Although it's easy to remove, it is a nightmare to replace.

The factory laid this insulation down over the tunnel and then placed everything over the top of the backing. If you try to replace this backing, you're going to have to remove all of the center console, not to mention the panels that go up the center of the dash on the early cars.

Be very careful with all the backing material since it isn't readily available. Before you start your project, check to see if this situation has changed.

When you remove the under padding, it might not be a bad idea to install some sort of sound deadener on flat panels in the rear. I used some cork that I found at Home Depot to do this. You can find better material at a local stereo store but plan on spending over $100 for it. You can also install a heat barrier kit in the front area of the car. The kit uses a ceramic cloth that's only 1/8 inch thick. Considering how hot the C4 Corvette gets, this may be a wise investment.

Repairing The Front Fascia and Rear Bumper

Huw Evans

YOU'LL NEED:

- Adjustable torque wrench
- Sockets
- Jig
- TPO plastic repair kit
- Instant glue
- Adhesion activator
- Sander
- Sandpaper (different grits)
- Flashlight
- Reputable paint shop

TIME
15 hours (prep work)

SKILL LEVEL
★★★★

COST
$1,200

APPLICABLE MODELS/YEARS
Mustangs 1979–1993 (1994–1995 similar)

PERFORMANCE GAIN
Showroom-quality bumpers without fit problems

Parking lot scrapes, road debris, and the weather all conspire to turn the exterior of your once pristine Mustang into something fit for the local speedway. One of the most common areas of bodywork to suffer from these blues is the front and rear fascias, or bumper covers.

Like most Detroit vehicles with their origins in the late 1970s, the 5-liter Mustang has big 5-mph steel bumpers mounted on massive rams, to withstand low-speed shunts. Over the bumpers were mounted a urethane front and rear cap that blended with the body contours. If the Mustang was hit at speeds below 5 mph, not only would the steel bumpers return to their original position, but the flexible urethane plastic would also return to its original shape. However, Fox Mustangs in particular are not getting any younger, and over time the urethane loses it flexibility and becomes brittle and prone to cracking.

Another problem is that the factory-applied paint—especially pre-1990 models, which didn't use clear coat—starts to fade, and with the plastic beneath it changing structure, tends to flake and peel off. The front and rear fascias bear the brunt of kicked-up road debris and the actions of careless motorists—scrapes, scuffs, gouges, and even cracks are common, especially on regularly driven 5-liters. So if your car is starting to look a little unsightly at the front and back or at the rocker panels (on

1987–1993 GTs), here's what you can do to remedy the situation.

On 1987 and newer cars, depending on the level of damage, you can strip the bumper cover down to its bare urethane surface and repaint it, or you can install brand-new covers and prep and paint them. On 1987–1993 GTs, the rocker panel extensions are secured by small pieces of steel that you need to carefully remove to pull off the extensions. If you're doing the rocker panels, check the condition of the steel retainers—some of them will probably be bent or rusted and should be replaced.

If you own a 1979–1986 Mustang, things are a little more difficult. After-market replacement bumper covers for 1979–1982 models are nonexistent. You'll need to source a NOS (new old stock)

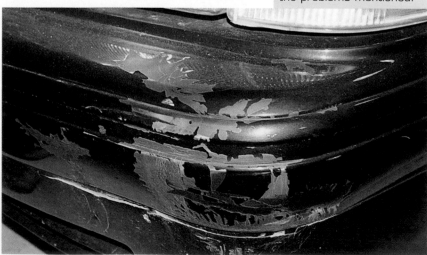

Plastic flexible bumpers often bear the brunt of road debris. Scrapes, scratches, and even cracks are all too common on 5-liter Mustangs. If the plastic bumper covers have been repainted without using specially formulated paint, the finish will peel and crack too. This one is suffering a combination of all four of the problems mentioned.

Left: For fixing cracks or blemishes in flexible plastic bumpers, use a special repair kit, such as 3M Automix, shown here.

Right: With the bumper cover removed, the repair process can begin. One of the first jobs is using a strong adhesive to fix any cracks.

TIP:
Take your time doing the prep work, and make sure you get a good body shop to paint the parts.

piece or a quality used one. Usually the only way to find one is via a swap meet or a Mustang salvage yard. If you have a 1983–1984 GT or 1983–1986 LX, you can obtain a new front cover but not a rear one. If you have a 1985–1986 GT, much as with 1979–1982, you'll have to go the swap-meet and salvage-yard route.

If the surface of your cover contains minor cracks, crazing, flaking paint, and scrapes, it's probably cheaper to strip it down and repaint it than fork out for a new one. You'll be surprised at the results you can get from what appears to be a cover fit for the trash. Repairing and bringing your bumper covers back to showroom condition takes time and a lot of preparation. Although the paint application is best left to a professional, there's no reason you can't do the preparation work on the bumper cover yourself.

The first thing to do is find a place to work—a garage, or better still, a friend's body shop. Don't try this outside, even if you live in southern California or someplace else where it's sunny and 75 degrees every day of the year. Also find someone experienced in plastic body repairs for questions or supervision, especially if you have limited bodywork experience.

If you're doing the rear bumper, bring the car in and support the rear on axle stands. If you're doing the front one, jack up the front of the car. Use a torque wrench and deep socket to remove the bolts that secure the bumper cover. The rear has three on each side: two at the bottom near the tailpipes and the third

in the trunk floor by the taillights (you'll probably need a flashlight to locate this one). On 1987–1993 GTs, 11 stud fasteners and four clips fasten the lower part of the rear bumper valance to the support brackets and need to be removed before the cover can be pulled off.

For the front cover, unfasten the nuts at the back on each side that secure the cover to the fenders. Undo the rivets that hold it to the front bulkhead at the top and the bolts that fasten it to the bottom. On 1979–1986 cars, you'll find four rivets at the top and four bolts at the bottom. On 1987–1993 models, 17 small rivets attach the cover to the radiator support at the top and bottom of the headlight pockets, along with a couple of push nuts on each side that fasten the cover to the lower fender. Once you've done this, you can pull the cover off.

Now the real work begins. If you're using your existing bumper cover and it has any cracks, put it in a jig and line them up properly, so you can repair and fill them. Use a strong adhesive, like Instabond, to weld the cracks and restore the cover's integrity. Let the cover set for at least an hour.

Once the glue is set, you can start sanding. Use 80 grit to remove the weld imperfections, until the surface is smooth. Turn the cover over and do the inside as well.

Spray on an adhesive activator once you're done, to strengthen the welds. Let this set for a good 15–20 minutes before adding the epoxy adhesive. This is necessary to cover cracks and prevent them from reappearing. A good adhesive is DuPont's Flexible Parts Repair Squeeze kit. It comes in two tubes, one black, and one white. You mix both substances together until you get a consistent medium-gray color. When you do, paste the adhesive onto both sides of the damaged

COMPLEMENTARY PROJECT:

This would be a good time to repaint the rest of the Mustang.

When it comes to actual painting, unless you're in the trade yourself, it's best to farm out the work to a good, reputable paint shop for quality, long-lasting results.

area of your cover, using a spatula. Once the affected area has been covered, let the paste set for at least an hour.

When the repair area is dry, reinstall the bumper cover on the car, so it doesn't flex and damage the repair. If you're doing the front fascia on a 1984–1993 GT Mustang, remove the foglights and mask around the housing. Using 80 grit, begin dry sanding the repair area, then do the rest of the cover to remove any paint and major blemishes. Follow it with another round of 80 grit, then 120, then 180, to get rid of the stress cracks, and finally 320, to get in really tight areas (including the trim indentations) and remove the smallest blemishes. You'll be glad you did this once the bumper enters the painting stage.

Your fixed bumper is now ready for paint application. When getting bumper covers done (and the rest of the car, for that matter) use a reputable body repair shop—don't go with the cheapest. A number of special substances are required to paint plastic body parts properly and prevent the paint from peeling and crazing. Although you won't often be doing this part of the project yourself, it's worth noting what's required to produce a quality, long-lasting result.

Before anything, the shop should carefully mask off the area around the bumper (you don't want primer or paint getting anywhere it shouldn't). They should also use an adhesion promoter, which is sprayed on the bumper cover to help the primer and paint stick to the plastic surface and prevent it from peeling off. One of the best is Dupont's 2330S Plas-Stick. It should be sprayed over the entire cover and allowed to set for at least 40 minutes.

Once the adhesion promoter has set, the primer can be applied. A good-quality primer should be mixed with an activator, primer converter, and drying accelerator. For best results, apply at least three or four coats of this mix to the cover. Dry

sand the cover between each coat with 600 grain. Before sanding the last couple of coats, get a trained body person to look for any small indentations and fill them. A painted bumper with lots of little dimples is unsightly and frustrating.

Now it's time for painting. Paint has come a long way since the old days of lacquer finishes. For plastic parts, especially if the Mustang is going to be driven, consider an acrylic urethane or similar paint that's hard, durable stuff and flexible enough to withstand stone chips and other maladies. The brand of paint is largely a personal preference, though DuPont is a popular and good choice among those in the trade. Once the paint shop has finished your bumper—for good results, at least a day in the paint shop is required—you'll be really glad you did all that prep work, and nobody at the cruise night or show field will ever know there's a 15-to-20-year-old bumper cover beneath that glossy paint.

You'll be amazed at what's possible. The once tatty, cracked front fascia on your 1987 GT can emerge as good as new.

Index